The Symphony: Structure and Style

Shorter Edition: Revised

BY

ROLAND NADEAU

Professor of Music
Northeastern University

CRESCENDO PUBLISHING CO.

BOSTON

For

RAYMOND KNAPP

Library of Congress Catalog Card Number: 74-75700

ISBN 0-87597-089-3

Printed in the United States of America

Contents

Preface

This book represents my third in the field of symphony. The first, <u>Notes On The Symphony</u> (1966) was used in our Music Department course, <u>The Symphony</u> for three years. During that period I gathered ideas on how to improve the text both from music faculty and students. In 1969 I started to revise <u>Notes On The Symphony</u>, but as I progressed I saw that I really was writing a new text. Accordingly, I redesigned its format and gave my second effort a new title: <u>The Symphony: Structure and Style</u>. In class, this text worked fairly well, but there were indications from students that the material was too advanced for those without previous musical background. Because of the great increase of students electing the Symphony course the first printing of <u>The Symphony: Structure and Style</u> was quickly depleted, requiring a second printing in the spring of 1972.

As early as 1971 I had decided to revise it thoroughly. My aim was to simplify by deleting many musical examples, but also to add more text on the historical aspects of symphonic style. In the process I added many more listening guides on symphonies from the classical through the contemporary period. I also added biographical material on major symphonists, and a selected bibliography and discography.

Since this text is intended for non-music majors at the first music course level I now have a further ambition. I hope some day to expand the 1970 version to become a comprehensive book on the Symphony for music majors. It will be longer, more detailed and more technical, and include material on little-known composers of the symphony. I will take a close look at the development of the contemporary symphony in general and in particular of the symphony USA.

Roland Nadeau

ACKNOWLEDGMENTS

Thanks and appreciation are given:

  --to Vice President Kenneth G. Ryder for making this book possible

  --to Dean Alan A. Mackey for seeing it through

  --to Dr. Herbert Silverman and Professor Helen Keaney for their comments and
    suggestions

  --to Victoria G. Peterson for careful typing and handling of the manuscript

  --to Robert Buckholt who copied the music

  --to Bruce Thrasher who did the art work in Part 3

A special note of appreciation is given to Mr. Paul Jastrem of the music faculty.
He did the chronologies in Chapters 3, 4, and 5, as well as the bibliography and discography.

The drawings were done by Clinton Arrowood and first appeared in <u>Music for the
Listener</u>, written by William Tesson and Roland Nadeau and published by Allyn and Bacon
in 1968.

Introduction

Music speaks for itself. No amount of verbal explanation, analysis, or interpretation can give music more meaning or take its place. Though this book will point you toward an understanding of music, and in particular the symphony, this understanding can only happen through your direct experience of the music itself.

All that really counts is your personal relationship with the composer through his music. The re-creative artist, performing at the keyboard or on the podium, is only the medium. He is a practiced listener and technician whose job it is to convey as closely as he can what the composer expresses. If he is good, the re-creative artist will have special insights into the composer's musical thought, but his interpretation of the composer's expression need not necessarily be more valid than your own. His ultimate test and success depend on whether or not this insight brings the composer's true expression to you.

Music needs nothing outside of itself except someone to perform it and someone to hear it. But we need music. It accompanies us through our life: at the cradle, in love and war, at the time of death. We seek it out at rock and folk festivals, at jazz concerts, at the opera and in the concert hall, in the church and synagogue, with our phonographs, radios, and tape recorders.

Why? Because music challenges us while it assures us. By entering into the composer's inner world and feeling intensely with him, we are assured that we really do have an inner world that can be expressed. Sigmund Freud put it this way, "The artist or poet forces us to become aware of our inner selves in which the same impulses are still extant even though they are suppressed."

These impulses are not exactly the same as the composer's or the poet's. But they are impulses, common to all of us, that prod us to express whatever there is in our inner selves to be expressed.

The inner creative urge, activated by our experiencing a work of art, challenges us to express what is unique to us alone. Such expression is as varied, many-sided, and unlimited as the human personality. Expressive creativity appears in art, science, technology, business, social relationship -- in any area of human work and interest.

The composer of the symphony creates an inner world of unique sound. Reverberating within that inner-world are harmonies tuned to everything that he feels and knows. Shaping his materials -- tone, rhythm, harmony -- he then expresses his inner world.

As you learn about the symphony, through reading, listening, and feeling, you will come to know that its expressions are as rich as they are manifold. Some will carry a program; others will be abstract. Expressions will vary from composer to composer, land to land, and from period to period.

The symphony since Beethoven has become an extensive form, long enough and diversified enough to project the composer's deepest musical ideas and most important symbolic expressions. It is one of man's great achievements, representing his urge to speak of what is most beautiful, most enduring and most important to his world.

PART I
Form, Style and Medium

Chapter I

FORM AND STYLE I N THE SYMPHONY

A symphony is sound: a kaleidoscope of multi-hued tonal colors. In our day this sound is meant to be realized by a group of massed performers in large halls for massed audiences. Full sound and variety of musical color is basic.

The players in the different orchestral choirs and sections play <u>collectively</u> as a body; whether that body is a 50-man string section or only doubled flutes. The instrumentalists <u>play together</u>. In that respect the symphony is an impersonal medium. The psychology of the soloist is foreign to it. To be sure, solos are often heard in the standard symphony orchestra, but they are incidental. The occasion-al soloist, whether he be the concert-master, principal oboist, harpist, or whoever, never intrudes his personality to the extent that the ensemble suffers or the total musical impact is destroyed. In his <u>Treatise of Instrumentation and Orchestration</u> (1843), Berlioz states: "Even in a [string] quartet, it is seldom that the individual feeling of the players can be left entirely free to follow its own dictates. In a symphony, that of the conductor must rule. The art of comprehending it, and fulfilling it with unanimity, constitutes the perfection of execution; and individual wills--which can never agree one with another--should never be permitted to manifest themselves. . . ."

Occasionally a symphony is written which features a major part for one or more soloists. <u>Harold in Italy</u> by Berlioz features a viola soloist; the <u>Symphony on a French Mountain Air</u> by D'Indy spotlights a piano soloist. However, collectivity is still primary; the basic objectivity of ensemble still holds. Works such as these are not concertos. A symphony differs from a concerto precisely in the sense given above: It is performed collectively by grouped players. The solo concerto is built <u>around</u> and <u>for</u> one or more soloists whose subjectivity is pitted against or blended with the massed collective of the orchestra.

STRUCTURE

A symphony is a mass of varied sound, collectively realized by the players and subjectively projected by the conductor. A symphony is also structure. If communication is to happen, the composer's musical thoughts must be clearly defined and mesh with one another in meaningful patterns. For this to happen, two basic conditions of good formal organization must be present. These are <u>unity</u> and <u>variety</u>. No successful symphony, nor, for that matter, any other serious musical composition, succeeds without them.

UNITY AND VARIETY

Unity is arrived at by well-timed repetitions of rhythmic, harmonic, and melodic elements. What this means is that themes and rhythmic patterns recur within the movements of a symphony (occasionally throughout all movements) periodically. Sometimes the repetition is immediate; sometimes it occurs after contrasting materials have taken the attention of the listener.

Unity also means that one musical idea flows naturally into another. It is also created through repetition of orchestral texture and key. In relation to this, it will be seen that most symphonies begin and end in the same basic key. Beyond this and more important, strong, long-established formal structures, such as sonata-allegro, rondo, theme and variations, and ternary dance forms, provide overall unity within the movements.

The ability to achieve great variety despite the constant need for repetition is the hallmark of the greatest masters. Repetition is meaningless without contrast, change of pace, and fresh occurrences of theme, key, rhythmic pattern and timbre.

Variety is arrived at chiefly by variation. The master composer takes care to decorate, transform, and alter his repeated melodies, harmonies, motives, and rhythmic patterns often. He knows that the ear wants to recognize previously heard musical elements, but that it wants to hear them fresh. Thus Beethoven repeats the famous opening theme of the Symphony No. 5 as expected in the recapitulation of the first movement. It is reviewed in the same key as at first, and with similar instrumentation. But there is a new occurrence: A single oboe interrupts the motion with a short, poignant cadenza before the music plunges on. Thus the return is varied.

Variety is also attained through juxtaposition of highly contrasted elements. The second theme of a movement often stands in strong contrast to the first (example 1).

EXAMPLE I-1 Sibelius, Symphony No. 2, Op. 43, first movement

4

Theme 1 (staccato) is both simple in melodic contour and in rhythmic pattern. It resembles a folk song or folk dance. By contrast, theme 2, (legato) shows more sophistication of melody and rhythm.

OVERALL STRUCTURE

You will now examine the overall structure of the symphony as well as various patterns used within each of its individual members. Since the symphony did not evolve into definitive form until the late 18th century with Haydn and Mozart descriptions and examples of its form are taken from that time and later. In Chapter III, you will see the structure of earlier symphonies and of pre-symphony forms of the Baroque period.

The specific overall formal structure of a symphony is either multiple-movement sonata or its modification. The usual number of movements is four, but occasionally this varies: Berlioz, in his Fantastique, wrote five movements; Stravinsky wrote a Symphony in Three Movements (1945).

Movements in the symphony are ordinarily separate, individual in mood and character, with full harmonic closes and a stop at the end of each. In performance, the movements are separated by a time lapse of several seconds, sometimes much longer. If a movement is meant to be separate but to follow without pause, the composer writes in the score, attacca.

Toward the beginning of the 19th century composers began to connect certain movements by the use of bridge passages. This, in effect, reduced two movements to one larger one, though the joined parts retained their musical individuality. One of the early examples of this unifying technique is found in Beethoven's Symphony No. 5, where the third movement bridges directly into the fourth.

A further example of this is heard in Beethoven's Symphony No. 6, the Pastorale. Here the last three movements are not separated by pauses of any kind; they in fact form one large, scenic movement.

TEMPO

Because of the symphony's length there is a strong necessity to achieve variety and change of pace from movement to movement. The chief way in which the composer accomplishes this is by writing successive movements in contrasted tempos. The first, third, and fourth movements are fast in different degree, while the second movement is usually slow. If the first movement is preceded by an introduction, this added section will be slow. If the third movement is a minuet--as in many early symphonies--the tempo will be moderately fast. Thus the tempo scheme of the standard symphony is:

First movement--fast (with possible slow introduction)
Second movement--slow
Third movement--either moderately fast if it is a minuet, or very fast if it is a scherzo
Fourth movement--fast

Sometimes this tempo plan is varied. Beethoven reverses the tempo order of the second and third movements in his Symphony No. 9. The scherzo comes second; the adagio movement, third. Tchaikovsky ends his Symphony No. 6 with an adagio. Haydn in his Symphony No. 100 (the Military) and Beethoven in his Symphony No. 8 do not include a true slow movement.

Following are the tempo plans for five symphonies analysed in Parts 2 and 3 of this book.

Haydn, Symphony No. 88
  First movement--Largo--allegro
  Second movement--Largo
  Third movement--Allegretto
  Fourth movement--Allegro con spirito

Mozart, Symphony No. 40
  First movement--Molto allegro
  Second movement--Andante
  Third movement--Allegretto
  Fourth movement--Allegro assai

Beethoven, Symphony No. 3, "Eroica"
  First movement--Allegro con brio
  Second movement--Adagio assai
  Third movement--Allegro vivace
  Fourth movement--Allegro molto

Berlioz, Symphonie Fantastique
  First movement--Largo--Allegro agitato e appassionato assai
  Second movement--Allegro non troppo
  Third movement--Adagio
  Fourth movement--Allegretto non troppo
  Fifth movement--Larghetto--allegro assai

Beethoven, Symphony No. 6, "Pastorale"
  First movement--Allegro non troppo
  Second movement--Andante molto moto
  Third movement--Allegro
  Fourth movement--Allegro
  Fifth movement--Allegretto

The tempos for the Haydn, Mozart, and Beethoven works are typical for the period. Further, if the second movement, "Valse," of the Fantastique and the fourth movement, "Thunderstorm," of the Pastorale were deleted, the remaining four movements in each symphony would show a completely normal tempo scheme.

Within the typical movement a basic tempo holds to the end, even though there may be some rubato. In other words, though there may be moments when the established tempo pushes ahead or slackens, it normally remains consistent. However, there are movements, especially in Romantic and Post-Romantic symphonies, in which distinct changes of tempo occur beyond any momentary application of rubato. The score of the fourth movement from Tchaikovsky's Symphony No. 5 shows no less than eight tempo indications:

Andante maestoso, Allegro vivace, Poco piu animato, Poco meno mosso, Molto vivace, Moderato assai e molto maestoso, Presto, Molto meno mosso

KEY

Symphonies written within the traditional system of tonality--and that means symphonies up to and into the beginning of the 20th century--are said to be in a key: Beethoven, Symphony No. 1 in C Major; Brahms, Symphony No. 4 in E minor; Haydn, Symphony No. 88 in G Major. This simply means that one basic key, one basic scale will predominate

6

throughout most of the work. The piece will generally start and end in one basic tonal area. As mentioned before, this is also true of individual movements: They usually begin and end in the same tonal center. Of course, there are changes of tonality within the movements themselves; the music would pale very quickly if modulation (change of key) did not appear fairly frequently.

KEY STRUCTURE WITHIN THE MOVEMENT

For example, in the first movement of Beethoven's Symphony No. 1, the key scheme is as follows:

The Movement begins in C Major (the key of both that movement and the total symphony).

EXAMPLE I-2 Beethoven, Symphony No. 1, Op. 20, first movement

It soon changes key center as it progresses to G Major. As will be shown later in the

EXAMPLE I-3

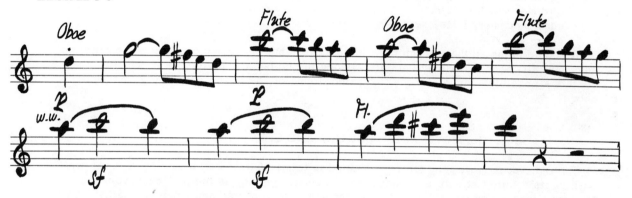

chapter, this shift of key from tonic to dominant early in the first movement (or in any sonata-allegro form) is a most significant harmonic event.

Shortly after, it touches on the key of G minor.

At the beginning of the development section, Beethoven modulates frequently and touches briefly upon the keys of D minor, G minor, C minor, E-flat minor, F minor, and A minor.

At a later, very dramatic moment, the music drops back to the primary key of C Major and stays in that general area until the final chord.

A measure count shows that 175 measures are in C Major, while 122 measures are devoted to all other keys combined.

7

KEY RELATIONSHIPS BETWEEN MOVEMENTS

Just as different keys are heard within movements, so certain movements contrast in basic key to the rest. Usually the contrasted movement is the second. Though the basic key of Beethoven's Symphony No. 1 is C Major, and C Major predominates in movements 1, 3, and 4, the second movement is in F Major. This key is closely related to the basic key of the symphony--only one flat separates F Major from C Major--and it provides sufficient contrast to avoid tonal monotony.

Sometimes a symphony contains greater contrast of key between movements. Following are the key schemes of three well-known symphonies:

Brahms, Symphony No. 2 in D Major
  First movement D Major (basic tonality)
  Second movement B Major
  Third movement G Major
  Fourth movement D Major

Berlioz, Symphonie Fantastique
  First movement C minor/C Major (basic tonality)
  Second movement A Major
  Third movement F Major
  Fourth movement G minor
  Fifth movement C Major

Tchaikovsky, Symphony No. 5 in E minor
  First movement E minor (basic tonality)
  Second movement D Major
  Third movement A Major
  Fourth movement E Major

It should be noted that though the middle movements of these symphonies use different keys, the first and last movements are wedded in one basic tonality. This remains true despite a possible change of mode from minor to major, as in the Tchaikovsky example above.

THE MOVEMENT: FUNCTION AND STRUCTURE

The individual movement can be examined in terms of its position and function as well as from its internal structure. What is meant by its function is the particular contribution that it makes toward the whole. For example, the scherzo and minuet, originating as they did in the dance, function as a diversion, a kind of intermezzo between the reflective second movement and the brilliant finale.

A movement's structure refers to the organizing principle within: the way in which the materials are logically presented and effectively balanced. Structure and function are of course related. The usual pattern used for the third movement minuet (ternary, ABA) is admirably suited to the simplicity of this dance. Theme and variations, which offers the possibility of extensive, dramatic, and varied structure is ideal for a finale. This is also true of the sonata-allegro and rondo forms.

THE INTRODUCTION

Function. The introduction is formal and serious. It sets the stage for important

8

things to come. Often an allegro in a major key will be preceeded by an introduction in the minor. If the allegro is not only major but sunny and humorous as well, its severe, dignified introduction can serve as an effective foil. Slow, majestic introductions preface many Classical symphonies: Beethoven's symphonies No. 1, 2, and 4; Haydn's symphonies No. 88 and 94; and many others.

Structure. Though the function of the introduction is well established, its internal organization is quite arbitrary. In a sense, it is a free fantasia. In length it ranges from a short prefatory section, such as that at the head of Beethoven's Symphony No. 1, to the extensive ones beginning his second and seventh symphonies.

As a rule, thematic material from the introduction is abandoned once the allegro begins. But there are important exceptions to this, especially in the Romantic period. Slow introductions preface the best-known symphonies of Tchaikovsky (Nos. 4, 5, 6). Each of these presents thematic material to be used later on. The fourth and fifth symphonies are each cyclic works, the leading ideas of which are introduced in the frame of an imposing and dignified introduction. At later points the cyclic theme reenters with striking effect. This theme is a kind of master theme, whose rule it is to be injected into the form at strategic points throughout the symphony.

A different situation exists in Tchaikovsky's Symphony No. 6. Here the thematic connection exists only between the motive of the introduction and the first theme of the following allegro (example 4). There is no suggestion of overall cyclic structure.

EXAMPLE I-4 Tchaikovsky, Symphony No. 6, Op. 74, Pathetique, first movement

THE FIRST MOVEMENT

Function. The first movement proper (whether or not an introduction precedes it) has great weight. Though it is true that the first movement need not be dramatic or heavy--indeed it often is quite humorous--the composer lavishes his finest ideas on it. It is here that he sets the mood for the symphony and fixes the direction of the piece as a whole. The first movement must be solid and lead convincingly to the other movements.

The most exciting part of this allegro is in the middle section, where development occurs. This development is sometimes dramatic, even in humorous works.

First movements need not be lyric. The opening movement of Beethoven's Symphony No. 5 is almost entirely nonlyric, yet it is hugely successful. The reason for this of course is that the ideas are clearly important and beautifully worked out by the composer. This last aspect is of utmost importance. Musical logic is important to all symphonic writing but never more so than in the opening movement. The success of the whole depends on the solid structure of the beginning.

Structure. First movements usually follow the formal plan called sonata-allegro. The important thing about this form is that development is present and primary. Melodic materials presented in the opening section will be expanded, explored, "treated," so that they are evolving, meaningful agents of musical motion.

That portion of the form in which thematic materials are systematically presented is called the exposition. The number and character of the themes given is up to the discretion of the composer, but a representative, "working" figure for analysis might be three. Often separating these themes there are transitions of a figurative character.

Looked at schematically, the typical sonata-allegro pattern is as follows:

Exposition--Themes presented (arbitrary in number). Transition between first and second theme is the vehicle for modulation from tonic to dominant (or mediant) key.
Development--Selected thematic materials from the exposition "treated" by various compositional techniques. Modulation prominent. Dominant harmony emphasized at close.
Recapitulation--Themes from exposition return usually in same order with all themes usually in tonic. Transition from first to second theme often different from that in the exposition.

AN EXAMPLE OF SONATA-ALLEGRO FORM

The opening movement of Mozart's Symphony No. 25 in G minor, K. 183, is typical of 18th-century usage of the sonata-allegro form.

Exposition. There is no slow introduction. Plunging immediately into the action is a rugged, syncopated theme in the tonic key (example 5). Examined closely, it shows a

EXAMPLE I-5 Mozart, Symphony No. 5 in G minor, K. 183, first movement - Th I

structure based on two motives. Once motive a has been repeated, extended, and then punctuated by a gentle, trill-like figure on the dominant, a strong transitional idea, featuring imitation enters.

A blithe and jaunty new theme in B-flat major begins, p, in the first violins over a syncopated tonic in the second violins, and over a staccato "walking" bass (example 6). After a repetition of this theme, the exposition closes with an energetic thematic idea

EXAMPLE I-6 - Th 2

beginning with rising scales. Repeat marks indicate that the whole of this exposition is repeated with no changes.

Stated in outline form, the exposition of the above work is as follows:

Meas. 1-28--Theme 1, G minor
       Character: dramatic, energetic
Meas. 29-58--Transition, B-flat Major
       Character: unsettled, leading, modulatory
Meas. 59-73--Theme 2, B-flat Major
       Character: rhythmic, light
Meas. 74-82--Closing theme, B-flat Major
       Character: formal, final

Note three important, salient points: the strong contrast between the first and second themes; the contrast established between the tonic key, of the beginning G minor, and the key of the mediant, B-flat Major, arrived at and corroborated by the transition; and the placement of the most important transition between the first and second themes. These structural features or very similar ones underly exposition sections in all Classical and Romantic sonata-allegro forms. In short, exposition sections present contrasted themes centered around two basic keys in an orderly, rational way.

Development. Once the materials of the exposition have been given out and the whole repeated, the development begins. Here there is no expected or traditional ordering of materials as in the exposition. Its essence is freedom, excitement, dynamism, the whole leading to a climactic section usually on the chord of the dominant of the tonic key.

The development section of Mozart's Symphony No. 25 is short but pithy. It begins with a figure (example 7) derived from the last two measures of the exposition's closing theme. This example illustrates an important procedure found in development technique: the

EXAMPLE I-7

fragmenting of themes into short, compact motives suitable for intensive reworking. After a quick modulation to C minor, the above motive is further fragmented (example 8). This motive is subjected to considerable sequencing and modulation, in imitation between

EXAMPLE I-8

soprano and bass. Ultimately the oboe twice gives out the four-note motive a from theme 1, before the strings, passing back and forth a tiny fragment in eighth notes, lead directly to a dominant chord in the winds, and then to the recapitulation.

Recapitulation. The recapitulation section functions as both goal for the development and review of the materials given out in the exposition. Its role as a culmination point for the development can best be seen in relation to the harmonic scheme for the whole movement. Though the opening of the sonata-allegro establishes the tonic key, it soon leaves this area and, beginning at or near the second theme, moves to a strongly contrasted but related key, that of the dominant. When the initial key is in the minor, as in Mozart, Symphony No. 25, the second theme is often in the mediant, relative major key. Once this new key has been established, it holds firm until the development begins. Here several arbitrarily chosen keys are used. At the height of the excitement of the development the dominant harmony is seized upon and it serves to funnel the musical action into the tonic of the recapitulation.

Once the tonic has been regained, the materials from the exposition, beginning with the first theme, return in the same order as before, but this time the tonic holds until the very end.

Looked at schematically, the essential key structure of the sonata-allegro is as follows:

Exposition--Tonic, then modulates to related key (usually dominant or mediant)
Development--Any of several related keys ending on the dominant
Recapitulation--Tonic, all the way to the end

Thus the tonic is left early and returns only in the recapitulation where it is present to the end, strongly insisting on its primacy.

The Coda. The coda is a section often seen appended to the close of the recapitulation. Like the introduction it is optional, and its structure is arbitrary. But whereas the introduction is in a mood and tempo contrasted to the main body of the form, the coda continues and punctuates the drama of the allegro itself. Occasionally this coda is written in faster tempo than the allegro in order to achieve heightened intensity and excitement. Typical is the first movement of Tchaikovsky, Symphony No. 4. Its introduction is marked andante sostenuto; the sonata-allegro proper, moderato con animo; and the coda, molto piu mosso. One may view this increase of tempo at the coda as the perfect balancing agent for the measured slowness of the introduction. The coda's role is to round out the whole movement. Its melodic materials are usually derived from theme 1; its harmonic emphasis is tonic.

SECOND MOVEMENT

Function. Lyricism is the basic ingredient of a slow movement; it is the most songlike of the four. If the opening movement is dramatic or tragic, the second is often reflective and introspective.

Stringed instruments were at a high state of development in the time of Mozart. For this and other reasons, many important melodies, especially the lyric ones in the slow movements, fell their way. In the later symphonies of the Romantics, because the winds had improved dramatically in tone quality and technical efficiency, many of their number were assigned lovely cantilena melodies. In these symphonies a highly personal, intensively subjective quality informs the lyricism.

Structure. Choice of a second-movement form is quite arbitrary. Almost any solid organizational structure suffices. Common are song form (ABA, ternary), theme and variations, development form (sonata-allegro), and rondo. The structures most appropriate are the simpler song forms. When the more ample and extensive patterns are used, strong contrast and dramatic conflict are often avoided.

THE THIRD MOVEMENT

Function. The third movement often gives the emotions respite by its elegance, vivacity, or good humor. This is the movement with the closest origins in a dance, the minuet. Of course it is not meant to be danced. Indeed its tempo--often allegro--is contrary to the spirit of the old courtly minuet, which was very stately. However, the essence of the minuet as a dance is always present, and its meter, 3/4 with an accent on the first beat, suggests the ballroom rather than the concert hall.

Sometimes, especially with Haydn, the trio section of this movement suggests the Ländler, an ancestor of the waltz. Later, true walzes were to be used as part of the symphonic structure: Tchaikovsky, Symphony No. 5; Dvorak, Symphony No. 8; Berlioz, Symphonie Fantastique.

Beginning with Beethoven, the third movement is often geared upward in tempo and becomes a scherzo. These are rollicking and humorous, and much of the time go very fast. The main interest is rhythmic, not melodic. Melodies often skip about and tend not to be particularly songlike. The third movement of Beethoven's Symphony No. 1 begins with a simple idea rising up 14 scale steps (example 9).

EXAMPLE I-9 Beethoven, Symphony No. 1, Op. 26, third movement

Structure. Whether the third movement is cast as an 18th-century minuet, a 19th-century scherzo or waltz, its form is almost always ternary: minuet with trio, or scherzo with trio. At first glance the form minuet with trio suggests a two-part structure; in fact, there are only two different sections. But because the minuet always returns once the trio is past, the actual plan is three-part: two contrasted parts followed by the return of the first. Returning to Mozart, Symphony No. 25, we can see a typical use of this simple design. The minuet proper begins with a dignified, somewhat solemn theme. This character is firmly held despite some passing poignant phrases (meas. 5-8, etc.). The trio enters in the tonic major with considerable lightness, carried entirely by a trio of winds: oboes, bassoons, and horns in pairs. The term <u>Menuetto D.C.</u> (da capo) tells the players to repeat the entire first section.

Examination of the above structure reveals a very simple design with effective contrast of timbre and style between the minuet and trio. The unsophisticated character of this "return" form is only underlined by the many repeats within the sections. Everything is stated simply, clearly, and at least twice. It has become traditional in performance not to take the inner repeats at the return of the minuet (meas. 12, meas. 36). More extensive minuets and scherzos are sometimes written with two different trios.

THE FINALE

<u>Function</u>. The finale poses a special problem for the composer. Here must be summary, climax, brilliance. The problem is caused by the first movement, which tends to be all-encompassing: In it the composer ordinarily has reached a certain intensity of meaning. The problem is to top himself. Put in another way, if the first movement possesses much weight, says important things, and seems to raise questions; the last movement must answer and actually go beyond it. This problem can clearly be seen if one considers the typical Romantic symphony with its tragic opening movement. Symphonies such as Beethoven's Nos. 5 and 9; Tchaikovsky's Nos. 4, 5, and 6; Brahm's Nos. 1 and 3; Mahler's Nos. 2, 3, 5, and 9; all contain this kind of questioning, profound opening. They require follow-through and musical catharsis. This must come in the finale.

Beethoven's <u>Symphony No. 9</u>, for instance, opens with a cosmos-shattering first movement theme (example 10). Beethoven is asking for all mankind and himself questions of utmost importance. The imagination reels under the impact of the possible meaning of

EXAMPLE I-10 Beethoven, <u>Symphony No. 9</u>, Op. 125, first movement

this work; the emotions are fully taxed; the nerves are exacerbated. This movement almost negates any possible music to follow. It especially challenges the last movement which, because of its culminating position in the work, must match the first, complete its thought, and indeed go beyond it. Beethoven solved this particular problem by introducing a chorus in the finale, writing music that, partly because of the text, partly because of its own massive power and strength, answers all of the questions posed in the first movement.

Generally speaking, then, from Beethoven on, the finale is often very dramatic, with a definite suggestion of triumph and climax. This is especially true if the first movement is itself dramatic.

<u>Structure</u>. The finale favors two plans: sonata-allegro and rondo. When rondo is used, it is not uncommon for the composer to substitute for the central episode an extensive development section. In this case, the form is hybrid, showing both the

charm of the circular rondo and the drama of the sonata-allegro. Occasionally, theme with variations is used.

Important to remember is that the above structural plans for individual movements are used commonly but not exclusively. For example, the third movement of Brahms' Symphony No. 1 is cast as a small rondo (ABACA). The finale of Berlioz' Fantastique almost defies traditional analysis. The finale of Brahms' No. 4 is a chaconne, originally a Baroque form.

Looking again at the inner structures of the movements in the symphony, one notices that two of the four are quite consistent in basic design, though not in detail. The first and third consistently use, respectively, sonata-allegro and ternary ABA form. The other two, the second and fourth movements, show wider variety. Dramatic development will probably occur in the opening and closing movements.

This is understandable for, as we have seen, the first movement establishes and challenges, while the finale gathers together and culminates.

This change of mood and pace indeed is one of the most charming aspects of the symphony just as it is of the dance suite of the song cycle.

CYCLIC FORM

But how was a composer to unify a work consisting of tremendously diverse movements which might require over an hour for its performance? How was the first movement to be related organically to a finale that might come 30 minutes later? One solution increasingly favored by composers of the Romantic symphony was to use cyclic form. Here a theme-- shared by two or more movements--acted as a kind of superstructure, binding the whole together no matter how individual the character of each movement.

The cyclic plan most favored was that in which one theme or motive, independent of the normal number and disposition of thematic elements within each movement, ran throughout the work. Because of the strategic placement of such a theme within the whole there is a tendency to identify it with an idea or notion germane to the whole conception of the symphony. For example, the essential character of the Fantastique by Berlioz lies in its depiction of the romantic artist's eternal quest for the ideal woman. The cyclic theme then is her theme, the idee fixe, which permeates and gives direction to the whole symphony.

Also typical of this is the Harold theme which appears in each of the four movements of the same composer's symphony, Harold in Italy. Suggested by Byron's "Childe Harold," this program symphony is quite long and consists of four vividly contrasted movements:

First movement--"Harold in the Mountains," scenes of melancholy, of happiness and joy
Second movement--"March of the Pilgrims," chanting their evening prayer
Third movement--"Serenade," a mountaineer of the Abruzzes singing to his mistress
Fourth movement--"Orgy of the Brigands," memories of past scenes

The idee fixe is not representative of the action suggested by each title, but hovers about other themes that are directly related to the scene. As Berlioz himself suggested, ". . . I put the viola in the midst of poetic recollections left by my wanderings in the Abruzzi, and make it a sort of melancholy dreamer after the manner of Byron's Childe Harold." The Harold theme is heard quite early in the introduction (example 11).

15

EXAMPLE I-11 Berlioz, <u>Harold in Italy</u>, Op. 16, introduction to first movement

CYCLIC THEME

Not only is the melody itself identified with the hero, but the solo viola represents him as well.

Because each movement represents a contrasted tableau, the Harold theme must adjust its "personality" to fit into each succeeding picture. The second movement, the somber March, is cast as an <u>allegretto</u> in duple meter. The pensive Harold theme is set in quite long notes against the measured tread of the march itself.

In the Serenade, movement III, a quiet picturesque tune setting the country mood leads to the love song proper, given out by the english horn. Shortly afterwards, this love theme is combined with the Harold theme, again heard in long note values (example 12).

EXAMPLE I-12

The finale, the "Orgy of the Brigands" is the agent through which the composer binds together the whole symphony. Here a muscular, syncopated theme starts the action, but is consistently interrupted by the solo viola presenting leading themes from all of the previous movements. The last "flashback" features the Harold theme itself this time varied considerably.

16

Summary:

The typical 18th symphony's overall structure consists of four separate movements, in the following sequence of tempos:

First movement--fast
Second movement--slow
Third movement--moderate pace (minuet)
Fourth movement--fast

A slow introduction often is linked to the quick-paced first movement.

These contrasted movements are held together primarily by a common key scheme, the first and fourth movements almost always in the tonic key. Cohesion among the several movements can also be provided by cyclic structure, and/or an extra-musical program as in Berlioz'z Fantastique Symphony.

STRUCTURE OF THE LATE 18th CENTURY SYMPHONY

Overall Form: Aggregate Sonata

Movement	Tempo	Key	Form	or	or	or
1*	Fast	Tonic	Sonata Allegro	———	———	———
2	Slow	Subdominant, dominant, or mediant	Ternary (ABA)	Development Form	Theme and Variations	Other
3	Moderate	Tonic	Ternary	———	———	———
4	Fast	Tonic	Rondo	Sonata Allegro	Theme and Variations	———

* When headed by an introduction this added section is in slow tempo, in the tonic, and in free form.

TYPICAL EXAMPLE

Joseph Haydn, Symphony No. 94, G major, (1791)
Genre: Absolute Symphony
Form: Aggregate Sonata in 4 movements

Movement	Tempo	Key	Form	Actual Pattern
1	Adagio contabile- vivace assai	G major	Sonata Allegro	Slow introduction – Exposition, Development, Recapitulation, Coda
2	Andante	C major	Theme and Variations	Theme, 4 variations, coda
3	Allegro	G major	Ternary, ABA	Menuetto, Trio, Min. D. C.
4	Allegro di molto	G major	Rondo	Refrain, Episode I, Ref., Ep. 2, Ref., Coda

18

SYMPHONIC STYLE

You have now seen what constitutes the essential inner workings of the symphony: its generic structure. By generic structure is meant the formal relationships that apply in general to all symphonies, from early Pre-Classic times to those of the late Romantic and even early Contemporary periods. Because this generic structure applies as well to other performance media, such as the string quartet, piano sonata, and concerto, consideration must be given to other factors inherent in the symphony: Those that constitute symphonic style. Each composer of symphony, because of his historical position, emotional make-up, and aesthetic outlook, brings to his work unique stylistic traits. There is then wide stylistic contrast from composer to composer. But beyond this, there are certain characteristic approaches to the symphony common enough to many composers to enable a few categories of style to emerge. There are program symphonies and there are absolute symphonies; either of these may be either dramatic or lyric. The Fantastique by Berlioz is a dramatic program symphony, while the Pastorale of Beethoven is a lyric program symphony. All four symphonies by Brahms are absolute. Symphonies No. 1, 3, and 4 are clearly dramatic, while No. 2 is lyric.

THE PROGRAM SYMPHONY

A work is said to have a program when it suggests things outside of its purely musical, or absolute, self. Indeed, all music that exists only for its primary beauty of design and sound is termed absolute.

A program symphony is usually double-titled. The generic title of Beethoven's sixth symphony is: Symphony No. 6 in F Major Op. 68. This indicates the overall pattern, the chronology in terms of the composer's production of both symphonies and total works and basic key. These point to specific content. The program title, Pastorale, refers to poetic content, to mood and atmosphere: in this instance, one of a "woodsy," country flavor. In addition to the initial titles, each successive movement is titled, giving clues to the progressively changing mood and atmosphere of the work.

Just as in the absolute symphony, in which there is extraordinary diversity in the working-out of patterns and designs, so are there different kinds of poetic content in the program symphony. Sometimes the program suggests action with a fairly clear plot, as in the Fantastique by Berlioz. In the Fantastique, the poet-hero is involved in various episodes beginning with dreams of love and ending with a nightmare in hell. Despite the striking originality of this sort of program, such an "action" symphony is rather rare. "Action" programs are seen much more often in the symphonic poem, such as Till Eulenspiegel by Strauss, or in the program overture, such as "Romeo and Juliet" by Tchaikovsky.

Much more common, and perhaps more appropriate to the essentially abstract nature of symphony, is the loosely programmatic symphony, in which the separate movements are linked in a very general way. Typical is the Pastorale. Each tableau-- the arrival in the country, the gentle brook, the happy peasants, the storm, and the final common rejoicing--reflect Beethoven's intense love for and association with the woods and fields. The Faust Symphony by Liszt, suggested by Goethe, depicts the personalities of the main characters of the play--Faust, Gretchen, and Mephisto-- rather than the plot.

Often, individual movements do not carry descriptive titles, and the initial title of the symphony implies very little except a certain oneness of mood. Such is the Winter's Dreams Symphony by Tchaikovsky. Others include the La Passione and Trauer symphonies by Haydn; the Eroica by Beethoven; the Spring Symphony by Schumann; the Romantic Symphony by Howard Hanson

A surprising number of these loosely suggestive works deal with geographical location, aiming to capture the atmosphere of the land as well as the spirit of its people. Mendelssohn's delightful Italian and Scotch symphonies are what we might call "souvenir" pieces, resulting from his prolonged and fruitful travels. In this general category come Schumann's Rhenish Symphony, Tchaikovsky's Little Russian and Polish symphonies, Ralph Vaughn Williams' London Symphony, Dvorak's Symphony from the New World, and the Alpine Symphony by Richard Strauss.

Though symphonies with extramusical content are del ightful in themselves, one should keep constantly in mind that poetic content is as frosting is to the cake: charming, ornamental, and pleasing but not absolutely essential for the eating. Any symphony--absolute or programmatic--must stand on its inner structural strength and beauty. Any one of the descriptive works mentioned above can be enjoyed by the listener with no knowledge of its titles. And further, any of the above can be shown to be a superb example of formal design and structural cohesiveness. Because music, of all the fine arts, is the most abstract, most intangible, made up of tones progressing in time, flaming and then perishing, it must be experienced and perceived directly. In short, the listener's imagination can be sparked by the program of a symphony, but full appreciation is possible only when he becomes aware of the purely musical values underlying the whole.

THE DRAMATIC SYMPHONY

A symphony is dramatic when important things seem to be happening; when the music suggests conflict, tension-relaxation, catharsis; when we feel that the individual musical statements are important and serious and have a potential meaning beyond themselves. The dramatic symphony often starts with materials which seem to ask questions or pose problems that need to be solved. The perfect example of this type of material is the opening passage of Beethoven's Symphony No. 5: eight tones, ending on a long held note, suggesting all at once suspense, search, quest, adventure.

Strong contrast is often heard in the opening section of a dramatic work. Themes of a strongly contrasted nature are juxtaposed, just as characters introduced in the first act of a play often come into conflict.

Movements tend to be in sharp contrast with one another. In Berlioz' Fantastique, this is decidedly the case. What could be in stronger contrast than a second movement representing an elegant ball, a third movement depicting a scene in the country complete with shepherds and a distant storm, a fourth presenting the terror of the guillotine, and a finale containing all the shrieks and horror of a witches' sabbath?

There also tends to be a great use of dissonance with unusual chords and harmonic progressions. Dynamic range tends to be wide: more louds, more sudden softs, great crescendos. Development sections in such works are of utmost importance. Many dramatic themes are created not so much for their lyric quality as for their potential; for what they may become under the stimulus of development. It is probably safe to say that in Beethoven's Symphony No. 5, no lyric theme is heard outside of the second movement.

Finales tend to be climactic in the dramatic symphony. Ultimately, denouement is achieved: There is often an immense sense of fulfillment. Very common in this type of symphony is a major key in the finale answering a minor key in the first movement.

The cyclic technique leads to dramatic style in symphony. The very fact that themes presented early in the work come back in successive movements works for drama. When these themes carry over into later movements, they have often strikingly changed and evolved. Through them the work can achieve great unity and cohesion while affording opportunity for enormous contrast.

And finally the 19th century dramatic symphony often contains great variety of instrumentation. Unique combinations were used and new instruments were added to the score for dramatic purposes. The added Janissary music (bass drum, triangle, cymbals) in the finale of Beethoven's Symphony No. 9 is typical. Cymbals are commonly and very effectively used in the great climaxes that occur toward the end of many dramatic symphonies. The pipe organ, with its capability for enormous volume and color contrast, sometimes joins the orchestra. Such is the case in Saint-Saens' highly dramatic and effective Symphony No. 3 in C minor.

THE LYRIC SYMPHONY

Melody, often singable and easy to remember, is the hallmark of the lyric symphony. Grace, elegance and simplicity are paramount. Dramatic moments do occur, but they act primarily as a foil to the predominant melodiousness, just as lyric moments occur in basically dramatic works. Many early Classical symphonies, such as the ones by Mozart, Haydn, and the young Beethoven fall into the lyric category.

Often there is a suggestion of the country: Folk songs or quasi-folk songs and dances are common as in Dvorak's Symphony No. 8, Beethoven's Symphony No. 6, Mahler's Symphony No. 1, Sibelius' Symphony No. 2, Mendelssohn's Symphony No. 4, and Haydn's London Symphony.

Humor is also often present in the lyric symphony. Beethoven's Symphony No. 6, in the third movement, depicts a country band trying to play in time, but with the oboist constantly coming in one beat too late (see Part 3). Prokofiev, in his lyric Classical Symphony lampoons an early gavotte in the third movement. Haydn delights in stimulating all kinds of sounds in his lighter symphonies--a clucking chicken, a bear, a ticking clock--and the good fun of the surprise in Symphony No. 94 is well known. Beethoven has the woodwinds imitate the tick-tock of the newly invented metronome in the second movement of his Symphony No. 8.

THE SYMPHONIC POEM

Related to the symphony is the symphonic poem, often cast in sonata allegro form. Its extra-musical content places the symphonic poem in the category of program music and relates it to the 19th century program symphony. The symphonic poem's extra musical subject matter is far ranging. Geographical locations (Borodin's Steppes of Central Asia, Smetana's The Moldau, Resphighi's The Pines of Rome) and other subjects are sometimes seen, but most often the symphonic poem derives its program from literary works. The works of Shakespeare, Dante, Goethe, Cervantes, Byron, Vergil, Nietzsche, and many others have been expressed in musical terms through the symphonic poem.

Eleven Representative Symphonic Poems Based on Literature

1. Liszt, Mazeppa, (Victor Hugo).
2. Liszt, Les Preludes, (Lamartine)
3. Tchaikovsky, Romeo and Juliet, (Shakespeare).
4. Tchaikovsky, Francesca da Ramini, (Dante).
5. Saint-Saens, Danse Macabre,
6. R. Strauss, Also sprach Zarathustra, (Nietzsche).

7. R. Strauss, <u>Don Quixote</u>, (Cervantes)
8. Dukas, <u>The Sorcerer's Apprentice</u>, (Goethe)
9. Debussy, <u>Prelude, To the Afternoon of a Faun</u>, (Mallarme)
10. Sibelius, <u>The Swan of Tuonela</u>, (the Kalevala)
11. Schoenberg, <u>Pelleas and Melisande</u>, (Maeterlinck).
12. Loeffler, <u>A Pagan Poem</u>, (Vergil).

THE SINFONIETTA

The sinfonietta is a symphony of reduced dimensions; it normally is shorter in length, lighter in style, and uses a smaller orchestra. The sinfonietta is to the symphony as the sonatina is to the sonata. Two well known examples are: the <u>Sinfonietta</u> (1926) by the Czeck composer Leos Janacek, and the <u>Swing Sinfonietta</u> (1936) by the American composer, Morton Gould.

Chapter II

PERFORMANCE FORCES IN THE SYMPHONY

Perhaps the most striking aspect of the concert orchestra as a performance medium is its inclusiveness of instrumental forces. At one time or another a great variety of instruments, traditional and exotic, have been used in the realization of symphonic thought: bells in the fifth movement of Berlioz' Fantastique; the oboe d'amore, representing the "dreaming child" in Strauss' Sinfonia Domestica; the organ in Saint-Saens' Symphony No. 3. The concert orchestra has then undergone a significant evolution in the number and variety of instruments.

It is possible, however, to discuss a basic orchestra that grounds the instrumental combinations that occurred in the symphony's approximately 200-year history. If we peel away instruments added to the traditional orchestra for amplification or special effets, we find a basic concert orchestra at the core of symphonies from Haydn to Stravinsky.

This core orchestra can best be understood from the viewpoint of its group organization. The beginning listener, when first confronted with symphonic sound, tends to be lost aurally in the maze of instrumental sonority. Close attention will later reveal that certain related instruments play together for a time, or join other homogeneous groups for fuller ensemble. These groups of instruments are called choirs or families. There are three primary orchestral choirs: woodwind, brass, and strings. Woodwind and brass playing together are often simply called the winds. Percussion instruments, late-comers in the evolution of the concert orchestra, when sufficient in number, are grouped into what is called the percussion section, or, as the French say, batterie.

It is important to see that each of the three orchestral choirs is sufficient to produce a complete register of pitches: high, low, and middle. In other words, each family of instruments in the full concert orchestra includes members representing soprano, alto, tenor, and bass registers: Each choir can realize a full register of sound. There are enough instruments to play either all of the notes of chords spread through the highs, middles, and lows; or contrapuntal textures that require a full register of pitches.

In symphonic practice, the composer will not only use these choirs separately for monochrome effects, but will mix choirs and instrumental timbres at will. He may wish to realize a particular chordal texture by having the cellos, bass viols, and bassoons carry bass elements; french horns and violas play middle-range pitches; and violins, oboes, and flutes, the soprano parts.

This ability of instrumental families to cover the complete range of musical sounds is partly true even for the percussion section. The timpani and bass drum anchor the total sound at the bottom, snare drums suggest a middle-range sound, while the triangle and others cover the soprano area.

Certain other instruments not basic to the core orchestra but often cropping up in late

23

Romantic and contemporary symphonies, such as the piano, harp, and xylophone, offer within themselves a complete range of pitches. Others often seen, such as the english horn, contrabassoon, and piccolo, are actually either smaller and higher, or larger and lower versions of standard instruments. For example, the english horn is really a lower oboe; the piccolo is a high flute; the snare drum exists both in standard size and a larger, tenor size.

The core orchestra contains the following instruments in order of range for each group from soprano to bass:

Woodwind choir:	Flute
	Oboe
	Clarinet
	Bassoon

Brass choir:	Trumpet
	French horn
	Trombone
	Tuba

String choir:	Violin
	Viola
	Cello
	Bass viol

Percussion:	Triangle
	Cymbals
	Snare drum
	Timpani
	Bass drum

EVOLUTION OF THE ORCHESTRA

Not all of the above instruments were in use in the early stages of the development of the symphony. Nor were they present in as large numbers as they are in 20th-century concert orchestras. Haydn's orchestra at Esterhazy in 1783 numbered perhaps 25 players; the Salomon orchestra at London, composed for and conducted by Haydn, listed a roster of nearly three dozen players.

A review of instrumentation for symphony for the last two centuries would have to begin with an orchestra of near-chamber music proportions. Mozart, on visiting the famous Mannheim orchestra in 1777, reported its size and disposition as follows: "On either side 10 or 11 violins, 4 violas, 4 violoncelli, 4 contrabassi, 2 flutes, 2 oboes, 2 clarinets, 4 bassoons, 2 horns, with trumpets and drums." This was one of the largest resident orchestras of the time, and smaller aggregations were common. Beethoven, in a letter to Archduke Rudolph, hoped that there would be no less than eight violins for the performance of his Symphony No. 7 (1812)! It seems incredible that he would have even considered the small orchestra requested for the performance of the powerful work. But though some concert orchestras at Vienna apparently were lamentably small, it is known that other musical centers boasted much larger groups. The orchestra at Munich in 1815 contained a string choir of near-20th-century proportions: 24 violins, 8 violas, 12 cellos, 8 bass viols. Wagner's original enthusiasm for Beethoven was fanned to fever pitch when he heard Habaneck's large Paris orchestra rehearse the Symphony No. 9. We can safely assume that his enthusiasm was due not only to the fine performance standards of the orchestra, but to the fact that its size was adequate for the rendering of Beethoven's cosmic musical thoughts.

In the 18th century, horns and trumpets had little melodic flexibility and were used primarily to reinforce climaxes or to sustain harmonies behind more active instruments. Valves for these instruments did not appear in the symphony orchestra until the second quarter of the 19th century. Haydn, Mozart, and Beethoven relied on the natural trumpet and the hand horn for their brass force. Because chromatic tones were difficult to achieve and unsatisfactory when they were achieved, their parts were largely diatonic and melodically simple, (example 1). A continuo part played by the harpsichord helped to "fill" middle-range

EXAMPLE II-1 Filtz, Sinfonia a 11, first movement

parts until approximately 1760 (example 2). The keyboard player reading the figured bass part added chords and melodic figuration in the middle range and served to bind and balance the overall orchestral sound. Often this continuo player acted as conductor, directing the players from his seat at the harpsichord. With the writing of more interesting cello, bassoon, and viola parts, and the entrusting of harmonic elements to trumpets and horns, the basso continuo was abandoned. And it was just as well, for the harpsichord's timbre did not blend well with the rapidly evolving three-choir system of instrumental organization. It would be difficult to conceive of a harpsichord or pianoforte intruding into the characteristic woodwind, brass, and string choir structure of the Beethoven symphonic scheme.

As it had done in earlier times, the string choir of the Classical period carried most of the melodic activity, with flutes either doubling or occasionally sallying forth on their own. Mozart and Haydn, especially in their later symphonies, gave much more important

EXAMPLE II-2 Johann Stamitz, <u>Sinfonia a 8</u>, first movement

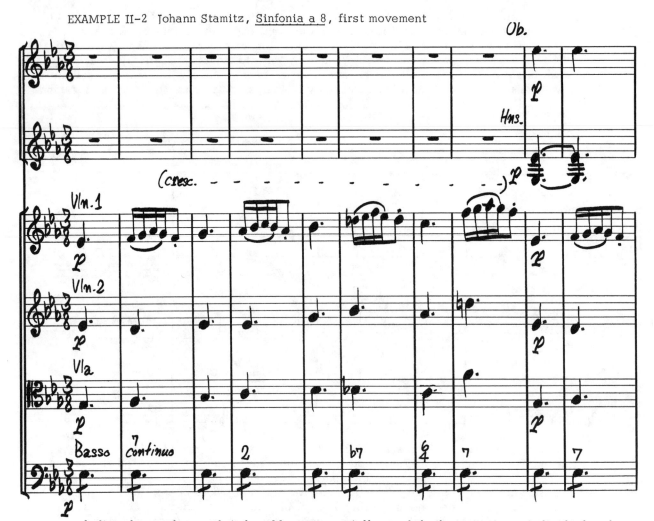

melodic roles to the woodwinds. Mozart especially used the bassoon in an individual and arresting manner (example 3).

EXAMPLE II-3 Mozart, <u>Symphony No. 40</u>, K. 550, first movement

It should be noted that the winds were usually used in pairs: two flutes, two oboes, etc. With Beethoven we begin to see a grouping in three's. The Symphony No. 5 adds a piccolo to the two flutes, and a contrabassoon to the other two bassoons. Trombones start out in three's: an alto, a tenor, and one bass. The Eroica introduces a third horn.

Despite the large orchestra of late Beethoven, some Romantics were content with a lean orchestration. Mendelssohn, for example, scored the Italian Symphony for two flutes, two oboes, two clarinets, two horns, two trumpets, timpani, and strings: a traditionally Classical instrumentation. However, as the musical concept in the Romantic period became enlarged, the winds became more numerous. The piccolo was often present; the english horn was added to the oboes, the bass clarinet to the clarinets. Trumpets as a rule remained a pair, though Berlioz in 1830 added two cornets to the paired trumpets in the Fantastique. Occasionally several trumpets are heard in late Romantic symphonies. The tuba joined the three trombones regularly after 1850, making that section a foursome. The percussion section became much larger, adding instruments such as the cymbals and bass drum with the ability to point up large climaxes.

This increase of winds and percussion came about for two reasons: first, because of the greater variety of timbre that they offered; and second, because of the increase in total string forces. The concert orchestra grew in number from approximately 20-40 in the 18th century to a massive juggernaut in the late 19th century, consisting of over 100 players. This increase of number was primarily in the strings. It was therefore necessary that the winds and percussion add to their number to allow better tonal balance.

The following listing of the typical modern symphony orchestra shows a balanced disposition of tonal forces:

Woodwind choir:
    Piccolo--1
    Flutes--2 or 3
    Oboes--2
    English horn--1
    Clarinets--2 or 3
    Bass clarinet--1
    Bassoons--2
    Contrabassoon--1

Brass choir:
    French horns--2 to 4
    Trumpets--2 to 4
    Trombones--2 tenors and 1 bass
    Tuba--1

Percussion:
    Timpani--2 to 4
    Bass drum--1
    Snare drum--1
    Cymbals
    Xylophone, bells, celesta, gong, tambourine, etc.
    Triangle

String choir:
    Violins--14 to 20 firsts, 12 to 18 seconds
    Violas--8 to 12
    Cellos--8 to 10
    Basses--8 to 10

Miscellaneous:
    Harps--1 or 2
    Piano
    Organ

A listing of representative instrumentation of symphonists for the Pre-Classical era to the present shows a varying and constantly evolving conception of balance in the concert orchestra:

Pre-Classical Orchestras

Sinfonia—Sammartini (1701-1775)
    Violin 1
    Violin 2
    Viola
    Basso (continuo)

Sinfonia in C Major (1755)--C.P.E. Bach (1714-1788)
    2 Flutes
    2 Horns
    Violin 1
    Violin 2
    Viola
    Basso (continuo)

Sinfonia in D Major—Stamitz (1717-1757)
    Timpani
    2 Trumpets
    2 Horns
    2 Oboes
    Violin 1
    Violin 2
    Viola
    Basso (continuo)

Sinfonia in B-flat Major—Cannabich (1731-1798)
    2 Horns
    2 Clarinets
    2 Bassoons
    Violin 1
    Violin 2
    Viola
    Basso (continuo)

Classical Orchestras

Symphony No. 88 (ca. 1787)--Haydn (1732-1809)
    1 Flute
    2 Oboes
    2 Bassoons
    2 Horns
    2 Trumpets
    2 Timpani
    Violin 1
    Violin 2
    Viola
    Violoncello obbligato, Contrabass

<u>Symphony No. 1</u> in C Major (1799-1800)--Beethoven (1770-1827)
  2 Flutes
  2 Oboes
  2 Clarinets
  2 Bassoons
  2 Horns
  2 Trumpets
  2 Timpani
  Violin 1
  Violin 2
  Viola
  Violoncello, Contrabass

Romantic Orchestras

<u>Faust Symphony</u> (1854)--Liszt (1811-1886)
  2 Flutes (Piccolo)
  2 Oboes
  2 Clarinets
  2 Bassoons
  4 Horns
  3 Trumpets
  3 Trombones
  1 Tuba
  Timpani
  Cymbals
  Triangle
  Harp
  Organ
  Tenor solo
  Men's chorus
  Violin 1
  Violin 2
  Viola
  Violoncello
  Contrabass

<u>Symphony No. 2</u> (1877)--Brahms (1833-1897)
  2 Flutes
  2 Oboes
  2 Clarinets
  2 Bassoons
  4 Horns
  2 Trumpets
  3 Trombones
  1 Tuba
  2 Timpani
  Violin 1
  Violin 2
  Viola
  Violoncello
  Contrabass

Post-Romantic Orchestra

Symphony No. 2 in C minor (1890-1894)--Mahler (1860-1911)

    4 Flutes (Piccolo)
    4 Oboes (English horn)
    5 Clarinets (bass clarinet)
    4 Bassoons (Contrabassoon)
    10 Horns
    8 Trumpets
    4 Trombones
    1 Tuba
    2 Timpani
    Triangle
    Tam-tam
    Cymbals
    Bass Drum
    Bells
    2 Harps
    Organ
    Violin 1
    Violin 2
    Viola
    Violoncello
    Contrabass
    Soprano solo
    Alto solo
    Mixed chorus

Contemporary Orchestras

Symphony in Three Movements (1945)--Stravinsky (1882-1971)

    2 Flutes (Piccolo)
    2 Oboes
    3 Clarinets
    2 Bassoons (Contrabassoon)
    4 Horns
    3 Trumpets
    3 Trombones
    1 Tuba
    Timpani
    Bass Drum
    Piano
    1 Harp
    Violin 1
    Violin 2
    Viola
    Violoncello
    Contrabass

<u>Symphony No. 4</u> (1955)--Henze (1906-   )
  2 Flutes (Piccolo)
  2 Oboes (English horn)
  2 Clarinets (Bass clarinet)
  2 Bassoons (Contrabassoon)
  4 Horns
  3 Trumpets
  2 Trombones
  1 Tuba
  Timpani
  Cymbals
  Triangle
  Glockenspiel
   Vibraphone
  Harp
  Piano
  Celeste
  Violin 1
  Violin 2
  Viola
  Violoncello
  Contrabass

You will note in the above listing that the three self-sufficient choirs and the percussion section did not evolve all at once. The string family was the earliest to achieve fullness and balance and was actually complete long before the genesis of symphonic form in the 18th century. This was possible because of the early perfecting of the string family at the hands of the master craftsmen--Amati, Stradivarius, and others-- centered in Cremona, Italy.

Toward the end of the 18th century, in the high Classical period, the woodwind choir achieved its essential, homogeneous, balanced shape with the addition of clarinets to the old standbys, flutes, oboes, and bassoons.

As we have seen, trumpets and horns, because of certain technical limitations, played an important but nevertheless complementary role in the 18th-century symphony. Two trumpets and two horns, limited largely to quite simple diatonic melody, could hardly be considered a self-sufficient choir. It was in the 19th century, when valves and pistons were added to these instruments, and when the trombones and tuba joined in, that the brass properly became a full-fledged orchestral choir.

The percussion, like the brass, was a buttressing and amplifying force in the 18th-century concert orchestra. This was true despite its occasional enlargement, as in Haydn's <u>Military Symphony</u>. Timpani were sufficient. In the next century, especially in its latter half, timpani were often supplemented by triangle, cymbals, snare drum, and bass drum. It was then that the percussion gained an essential role as a full section, capable of integration into the symphonic texture.

With the advent of more varied percussion instruments, including pitched instruments such as piano, xylophone, and celeste, 20th-century composers have tended more and more to use the separate <u>batterie</u> sound itself to carry the full compositional load. This technique occurs in certain portions of orchestral compositions, as in Britten's <u>Young Person's Guide to the Orchestra</u>, or in pieces designed specifically for percussion, such as Varese's <u>Ionization</u>.

Perhaps it remains for the 20th century to see the percussion section attain "choir" status in the symphony. If this becomes fact, we then might view the growth of the orchestrally self-sufficient but integrated choirs cumulatively:

17th century:	String choir (with miscellaneous instruments)
18th century:	String choir plus woodwind choir (with horns, trumpets, timpani)
19th century:	String choir plus woodwind choir plus brass choir plus percussion section
20th century:	String choir plus woodwind choir plus brass choir plus percussion choir (?)

	Woodwinds	Brass	Percussion	Strings
Production of Tone	Wind through reed(s), or edge blown as in flute	Wind through mouthpiece	Striking, scraping rubbing, shaking etc.	Scraping, Plucking, hitting
Dynamics	Medium	Strong	Strong	Light
Function (in order of frequency)	1. sustaining 2. melodic 3. rhythmic	1. sustaining 2. melodic 3. rhythmic	1. rhythmic 2. sustaining 3. melodic	1. melodic 2. sustaining 3. rhythmic
Position on stage	Middle	Rear	Rear	Front (except basses)
Position on score	Top	Upper-middle	lower-middle	bottom
Organization of players	Into sections by instrumental type. First chair leads.	Same as Woodwinds	1 section only (timpanist leads)	same as Woodwinds. First chair (violin I) is concertmaster

VOICES IN THE SYMPHONY

A somewhat unusual, yet highly effective technique is the use of voices in an ordinarily instrumental medium. The stunning introduction of solo quartet and full chorus in Beethoven's _Symphony No. 9_ is so well known that discussion of it is almost superfluous, except to note that this innovation strongly influenced later symphonic style. Mahler, perhaps more than any other Romantic, effectively integrated voices into his symphonies. Symphony No. 2, _The Resurrection,_ uses two female solo voices and a massive chorus to reach a climax in a finale of near-cosmic proportions. _Symphony No. 8_, the _Symphony of the Thousand_, uses voices throughout. At an early performance, the massed vocal forces numbered 850, with 8 soloists. The orchestra numbered 146 players.

Other symphonies with added vocal forces include the tautly dramatic _Faust Symphony_ by Liszt, and the _Symphonie funebre et triomphale_ by Berlioz, which, besides using chorus shows an unusual instrumental scoring for strings and military bands.

The following chart shows contrasts and similarities between instrumental and vocal media. When both media are present in the symphony a very wide range of tone color is available to the composer.

PERFORMANCE MEDIA

INSTRUMENTAL	Registers	VOCAL
Special Advantages		Special Advantages
–Wide range	Soprano	–Sustaining power
–Flexibility	Alto	–Expressivity
–Wide dynamic	Tenor	–Explicit expression
Scope	Bass	through text
		–Multiplicity of timbres
MEDIA		MEDIA
–Solo		–Solo
–Chamber ensemble		–Chamber ensemble
–orchestra		–Massed chorus
–band	any	–Any mixture
–any mixture	Mixture	of above
of above		

THE CONDUCTOR

From the time of Beethoven, the symphony has featured one nonplaying soloist: the conductor. His role is to shape the communication that is in the music: to transmit the thoughts of the composer to the listener. His interpretation of these musical thoughts is of first importance. He must analyze the music and commit himself to one interpretation, one that will fulfill himself as well as realize the artistic purposes of the composer. His role then is subjective. Berlioz suggests: "The orchestral conductor should see and hear; he should be active and vigorous, should know the composition and the nature and compass of the instruments, should be able to read the score, and possess . . . other almost indefinable gifts, without which an invisible link cannot establish itself between him and those he directs."

Today the conductor is seen on the podium, in front of the players, with or without a baton, articulating certain gestures that are meant to elicit specific musical responses.

He often serves as musical director as well. This means that he assumes responsibility for all programming, choice of soloists, auditions, and development of the orchestra as a whole. Sometimes he becomes educator as well. The position of Music Director of the Boston Symphony Orchestra typifies this situation. Aside from his immediate duties as conductor, the Director also often guides the Summer Music School at Tanglewood in Lenox, Mass., which is also the site of the orchestra's summer performance activities.

In our time, the conductor is a specialist: an artist-executive. But it was not always so. In early performances, the leader was not a specialist: He was either a composer or a player who also conducted.   The composer often sat at the harpsichord and led the ensemble; at other times the first violin led with the bow. The Harvard Dictionary of Music tells how, "During Haydn's visits to London in 1791 and 1794 control of the orchestra was divided between Haydn at the piano and Salomon with his violin."

The orchestra was led primarily by aural means, with perhaps a signal of the bow, head, or hand to set the tempo, start the music, or steady the group in difficult passages. Communication was achieved largely by listening rather than by looking at regular signals from the leader. This aural communication was most pronounced at the 18th-century Paris Opera, where since the days of Lully the beat was produced by the stamping of a large stick or cane on the floor.

In the 18th-century orchestra, communication from leader to players was both simple and obvious. It sufficed for the patent reasons that the orchestra was relatively small and the music played was almost invariably organized rhythmically around strong, regular metric beats. Later, in the era of the mature Beethoven in the early 19th century, highly sophisticated musical compositions performed by quite large orchestras necessitated the emergence of a nonplaying leader. It was then that a simple roll of paper or a baton made its appearance. Communication from the leader to the players in performance became basically visual. Berlioz categorically states: "An orchestra which does not watch the conducting-stick has no conductor."

As conducting techniques developed, many composers became renowned as conductors: Weber, Spohr, Mendelssohn, Berlioz, Wagner. As an indication of things to come, certain composer-conductors never attained or desired high instrumental skills themselves. Berlioz and Wagner were typical. They were in strong contrast to the 18th-century composer-leader who was usually a fine player and often a superb one.

At present, the normal role of the conductor has come to be divorced from either active solo performance or composition. There are exceptions to this, of course. Major composers such as Stravinsky and Copland conduct extensively, but conducting is not a primary role for them. Leonard Bernstein--conductor, composer, performer--seems to represent a return to the inclusive role of the 18th-century musician.

Whatever the few exceptions, the first role of the specialist conductor in the 20th century will probably remain in the area of overall artistic direction rather than that of active composition or solo playing.

THE SCORE

In concert, the conductor on the podium usually uses a full score representing all of the sounds reproduced by his players. The musicians of course play from their part only. You have seen in earlier chapters several fullscore pages from the pre-Classical and Classical repertory. Though completely sufficient for the music at hand, instrumentation for early symphonies shows a limited aray and quantity of instruments.

In the following examples from Tchaikovsky's <u>Pathetique Symphony</u> you will see a full-blown instrumentation typical of the late Romantic period.

Example 4 shows a full score representing a portion of the third movement. Note that each choir, represented by a grouping of staves, has its own place on the score page: woodwinds on top, brass at the upper middle, and strings at the bottom. Staves for the <u>batterie</u> lie immediately above the strings. Within each choir grouping individual instruments are seen according to their register: soprano instruments on the higher staves, alto and tenor instruments in the middle, and bass instruments at the bottom. Thus, within the woodwind choir (placed at the top of the score page), flutes are highest, oboes and clarinets are lower, and the bassoons are at the bottom. This placement of instruments according to register within the choir holds for the strings, but an exception occurs in the brass, where the alto horns are seen higher than the soprano trumpets.

By looking at the full score page one can not only see the work's instrumentation--the total actual forces for its performance--but the division of these forces into choirs, and the placement of instruments within these choirs according to register. Not as obvious to the eye but infinitely more important to the ear is the way the score reflects the composer's orchestration.

EXAMPLE II-4 Tchaikovsky, Symphony No. 6 in B minor, Pathetique, third movement

EXAMPLE II-5

ORCHESTRATION

Orchestration is the art of presenting musical ideas effectively through the medium of the instruments in the concert orchestra. But it is more than that. In the hands of master orchestrators such as Mozart, Berlioz, Tchaikovsky, and Debussy, orchestral color becomes a structural element itself: a component as important as melody, rhythm, and harmony. In all of the examples from the Tchaikovsky symphony, orchestral color is indeed inseparable from the overall musical idea. Since the days of Haydn and Mozart, when the newly balanced orchestra made the art of orchestration possible and necessary, matters of orchestral timbre, texture, and sonority have been integral to the process of composition.

Example 4, above, shows a _tutti_ passage from the coda section of the _Pathetique's_ third movement. The effect desired here is one of massive brilliance. A march-like melody is carried by the upper strings doubled by the flutes and piccolo. This doubling by the flutes provides the string sound with precisely the edge it needs to cut through the heavy supportive elements. The bass line is seen represented by five staves: those for bassoons, bass trombone and tuba, cello and contrabass. The horns, trumpets, and upper trombones flesh out the orchestral texture with powerful eighth-note chords. There is both clarity and heaviness. Melodic and harmonic elements are dispersed throughout the instruments in a way that allows everything to be heard that should be. Each instrument is given a role that will clarify and enhance the overall idea.

In this instance the orchestral sonority achieved comes from a heterogeneous mixture: Selected instruments within a choir work together with other instruments in other choirs. For example, the bassoons, lower brass, and lower strings all carry the bass line.

Example 5 shows a different sonority brought about by a homogeneous use of choir against choir in antiphonal style. The dialogue is between all of the strings in unison and all of the woodwinds in unison.

The coda to the first movement of the Pathetique (example 6) shows another example of the homogeneous use of choirs. Here the strings again are in unison as they play a descending B Major scale eight times. By the second measure the brass are dispersed in a homophonic spread, with the first trumpet carrying the chorale-like melody. Next, the woodwinds--also in homophonic formation--take over from the brass. Toward the end, the four horns begin a cadence and give way to the trombones and tubas with soft timpani as they play the final tonic chord. As the tonic chord approaches, the strings are thinned out so that only the cellos and contrabasses play the last two repetitions of the scale pattern. When the tonic chord sounds, the strings have vanished, leaving only the lower brass and timpani to end the musical thought. The effect planned by the composer for the close of the first movement is one of unwinding tension and the relief found in the quiet resolution into tonic major harmonies. Accordingly, Tchaikovsky arranges his orchestra into juxtaposed instrumental blocks working together to project simple melodic, rhythmic, and harmonic ideas.

In 19th-century orchestration, often texture is thinned and the sound softened sufficiently so that a solo instrument can be featured. This is evident in example 7, in which the solo clarinet plays a veiled reminiscence of the principal lyric theme while the timpani and divided strings (without contrabasses) provide a soft chordal cushion.

EXAMPLE II-6

41

EXAMPLE II-7

PART II
The Evolution of the Symphony

Chapter III

THE CLASSICAL SYMPHONY, ANTECEDENTS

A symphony is like a building divided into several rooms. The architect designs his edifice as he will. It may be large or small; ornate or simple. The building derives its unity and style from the designer: there will be a harmony of planes and building materials.

Each room is like a movement, with its own individuality and function yet integral to the purpose and style of the whole structure. If we extend the analogy a bit further, and imagine that our symphonic building is a house, then certainly the slow introduction is like an entrance or foyer, the slow comtemplative second movement is like a study, the scherzo is the game room and the minuet is the ballroom.

You will now see the symphony begin as a small, simple structure, change in style from composer to composer and from period to period. Through the decades it will grow in length and performance mass, and it will gradually broaden its expressive scope.

The word symphony has been extensively used for at least four centuries. By derivation it simply means, "a musical ensemble." It therefore might have been used to describe any ensemble, whether the performers were instrumentalists, singers, or both. (There actually exists ensemble music for various vocal and instrumental combinations by Heinrich Schutz called "Symphoniae Sacrae.")

The sense in which symphony is considered in this book is inclusive of a multiple-movement instrumental form which crystallized in the 18th century and then continued to evolve until the present day.

Pre-Symphony Forms of the Baroque

Though its actual origins are somewhat shadowy, it is possible to trace the embyonic form of the symphony to the canzone alla francese, an early sectional instrumental form consisting primarily of vocal-like polyphony. This led to the Baroque sonata da chiesa, in which clearly separated and contrasted movements were used.

The Baroque Sonata.

The sonata da chiesa a tre was written for a chamber combination of 2 treble instruments with continuo: 2 violins, cello, or bassoon and keyboard (harpsichord or organ). This instrumentation was much favored by Arcangelo Corelli as indicated by his set titled, 24 Sonate da chiesa a tre. Sonatas for fewer or more instruments such as the sonata a due, or the sonata a cinque were also common. In each case, the keyboard part, doubling the cello or gamba bass line, and providing harmonic body to the texture, was an "extra" instrument, making the total ensemble one more than the title indicates.

These Baroque sonatas were cast in aggregate form, consisting of several contrasted movements. The usual tempo plan of the sonata da chiesa was: slow-fast-slow-fast (Adagio, Allegro, Adagio, Allegro).

The above clearly shows that the Baroque sonata anticipated important features of the later symphony. Both Baroque sonata and symphony were multiple movement forms, each movement in contrasted tempo. The sonata da chiesa's opening Adagio leading to an Allegro pre-figures perhaps the later classical symphony where a slow introduction often preceded the first movement of the sonata allegro form.

As we saw in chapter 2, Performance Forces in the Symphony, the orchestra for the pre-classical symphony usually included a harpsichord, realizing the figured bass as it had previously done in Baroque sonata. A further connection with the symphony is the fact that the early sonata a quatro, or a cinque might occasionally have been played by a small orchestra where players "doubled" the individual melodic parts. This principle of collectivity is absolutely basic to the symphony. In fact, some of these sonatas were actually titled as "symphonies", Guissepe Torelli, in 1687, introduced sonatas under the title of Sinfonia a 2,3,4, instrumenti.

The Baroque Concerto.

Like the sonata, the baroque concerto was cast in successive movements, contrasted in tempo and style. Francesco Geminiani's use of concerto grosso form followed the same tempo plan as did Corelli in his sonata da chiesa (slow-fast-slow-fast).

The dramatic principle within the concerto grosso was the juxtaposition of a small group of instruments (concertino) with massed strings (ripieni).

On the other hand, the solo concerto was organized through three movements, (fast, slow, fast). Typical of this was Antonio Vivaldi's set of four solo violin concertos, Fall, Winter, Spring, Summer collectively titled, The Seasons. Each of the four concertos was set in three contrasted movements.

The Baroque Dance Suite.

The dance suite, scored either for solo instrument, various chamber combinations, or orchestra, consisted of several individual dances such as the allemande, courante, minuet, sarabande, and gigue. Each of these dances functioned as a kind of "movement". Prefacing the suite was a "movement" in non-dance style such as a prelude or toccata. One obvious connection of the suite with the symphony is exemplified by the minuet. A regular member of the dance suite in the baroque, the minuet - expanded and idealized - often was included as the third movement of the symphony until Beethoven.

Another connection, not so obvious but very important, was in the inner structural pattern of the baroque dances. With J. S. Bach especially, the structure of his longer dances pre-figured the most important movement pattern within the symphony, sonata allegro form.

Bach's allemandes, courantes, etc., were organized in two parts, which can be labelled: A-B, each repeated. Within the A part, after the entrance of the first subject, a modulation to the dominant key occured together with an incipient second subject. In a limited sense, this is like the exposition section of sonata allegro form.

The B part began in the dominant key, with the first subject, often in an inverted position. Finally, towards the end of the B part, the tonic key returned.

The Baroque Overture

A strong link exists between the opera overture of the Baroque and the symphony of the Classical period. In fact, it was the late Baroque Neapolitan Overture that _became_ the pre-classical symphony.

The French Overture

It was with Lully at the French court of Louis XIV in the middle of the 17th century that the opera overture took its mature form. This structure, prefacing the many operas and ballets written by Lully for the Court of Louis XIV, is now known as the French Overture.

Played by an orchestra, the Lully Overture consisted of two or three contrasted sections played without pause. A typical example is Lully's Overture to the Opera, Armide (1685). It begins in a slow, stately tempo, then moves to a fast tempo where much melodic imitation is heard. The last section is again in slow tempo. Thus, its tempo scheme is: slow-fast-slow. Occasionally Lully ended his overture with a quicker section in minuet style.

The Overture style is often heard in the later music of Handel and J. S. Bach. Here, the dotted rhythmic figure of the opening grave is greatly emphasized and the imitation in the following fast movement suggests the fugue.

The Italian Overture

The opera overture in Italy developed along different lines. Instead of using the slow-fast-slow plan of the French, Italian composers used an opposite sequence of tempos: fast-slow-fast. This is the Neapolitan Overture of the early 18th century.

It was at this point in music history that the symphony began. The Neapolitan opera overture (sinfonia) was written essentially in a homophonic style rather than in the polyphonic style of the earlier French Overture. As you will see, basic to the evolving symphony is a _homophonic_ style of writing, where a leading melodic idea supported by subsidiary harmonic elements is paramount.

The Italian operatic overture (sinfonia) in three sections (fast-slow-fast) mostly in homophonic style, was the transitional form that led to the fully developed symphony. Often it was separated from opera production and performed independently along with other instrumental pieces for concert audiences. Gradually, composers wrote sinfonias directly for the concert stage, with no thought of opera. Thus, the symphony as one of the most important of large instrumental structures had its genesis.

A leading exponent of this overture style was the opera composer, Alessandro Scarlatti. His son, Domenico, best known for his numerous sonatas for cembalo (exercizi), also wrote operas including overtures of the Neapolitan type.

Domenico Scarlatti's Sinfonia in G (Italian Overture) scored for flute, oboe, strings, and continuo, is a short work in three sections. The first section is essentially homophonic featuring some imitation. The second section, in slow tempo is very short and features a lovely solo for the oboe. The last section moves in moderate tempo and is the minuet dance style. Another of his Sinfonia, also in G, shows the tempo plan as: fast-slow-moderate (minuet)-fast. This is a direct anticipation of the late classical sequence of tempos in the four movement symphony.

The following table shows the relationships among Baroque aggregate instrumental forms and the late 18th century classical symphony.

RELATED BAROQUE AND CLASSICAL AGGREGATE FORMS

Form		Number of Movements or Sections	Key Scheme	Tempo Scheme	Texture	Example
Baroque Sonata da Chiesa		4	All or most movements in tonic	Slow-fast-Slow-fast	Polyphony emphasized	J. S. Bach, Trio Sonata in Musical offering
Baroque Concerto	Solo	3	Tonic/Other/Tonic	Fast-Slow-Fast	Homophony/Polyphony	Handel, Organ Concerti
	Grosso	Early, 4 or more, (later 3)	All or most mvts. in tonic	Slow-Fast-Slow-Fast	Homophony/Polyphony	Corelli, Concerto Grossi
Baroque Suite		Indeterminate. Often includes 4 core dances	All or most Mvts. in tonic	Varied	Homophony/Polyphony	Couperin, "Le Grand" Ordre No. 8 From premier Livre
Baroque Overture	French	3	Tonic	Slow-Fast-Slow	Homophony/Polyphony	Lully, Overture to "Armide"
	Italian	3	Tonic	Fast-Slow-Fast	Homophony	D. Scarlatti, Sinfonia in G
Late 18th Century Classical Symphony		3 or 4	Tonic-Other-Tonic-Tonic	Fast-Slow-Moderate-Fast	Homophony	Mozart, Symphony #41, K. 551, in C Major

THE PRE-CLASSICAL SYMPHONY

When Haydn and Mozart came into the musical scene in the last half of the 18th century, there already existed a large body of symphonies containing the essentials needed to build a musical art of the first order. These essentials were:

A new orchestral style of playing featuring colorful dynamic effects, especially the crescendo

An orchestra organized around three choirs with percussion: woodwinds, brass, strings, and timpani

A fully developed homophonic style; clear primacy of single melody supported by chords in logical progression, the whole suffused by simple but effective rhythmic patterns

The inclusion of the minuet on a regular basis

The crystallization of sonata-allegro form as one of the sturdiest patterns for inner organization, especially in the first movement

The importance of a clearly articulated second theme within a clearly articulated new key area, usually the dominant

Sammartini in his sinfonias contributed rhythms that were varied enough to permit the building of extensive movements without the danger of their becoming redundant and bland. Individual movements in Sammartini's symphonies featured well-defined and articulated second key groups suggesting occasionally a second theme. It should be noted here that a contrasted second theme, in a contrasted key, used in dramatic justaposition to the first, was not common in the earlier Baroque period. The structure of the typical fugue--and many other Baroque forms--was monothematic. Drama and interest here was ordinarily produced by a sustained polyphonic elaboration of one, all-pervasive melodic subject.

Composers of the Mannheim School, Johann and Carl Stamitz, Cannabich, Toeschi, Holzbauer, and others provided expressive harmony, forceful rhythm, formal unity, and clear definition of thematic groupings, as well as the above-mentioned expressive dynamic effects. Burney, writing on the scene, describes this new experimentation with dynamics as follows: "It has long seemed to me as if the variety, taste, spirit, and new effects produced by the contrast, and the use of crescendo and diminuendo in these symphonies had been of more service to instrumental music in a few years than all the dull and servile imitations of Corelli, Germiniani, and Handel had been in half a century." And again: ". . . it was here (Mannheim) that crescendo and dimuendo had birth; and the Piano, which was before chiefly used as an echo, with which it was generally synonymous, as well as the Forte, were found to be musical colours which had their shades, as much as red or blue in painting."*

The Sinfonia a 12 (with 12 instrumental parts) by Christian Cannabich (1731-1798), and the Sinfonia a 11, Op. 3, by Johann Stamitz (1717-1757), are typical Mannheim works. The Cannabich piece because it features the newly emerging clarinets, and because it displays quite advanced and characteristic orchestral scoring, is particularly useful for an understanding of the later 18th-century orchestras of Haydn and Mozart. Mozart had heard the orchestra under Cannabich and had been strongly impressed, both for the precision of its ensemble, featuring uniform bowing in the strings, and for the subtle orchestration used by the Mannheimers.

The Cannabich sinfonia, in B-flat Major, is cast in three movements and is scored for two horns, two clarinets, two bassoons, and strings. There is no minuet.

The first page of the opening allegro shows a delightful dispersement of instrumental forces. Note how the main theme (example III) is divided in alternating measures between the second and first violins. Both are often given independent parts throughout. This rather democratic usage of the first and second

* Charles Burney, A General History of Music

51

EXAMPLE III-1 Cannabich, <u>Sinfonia a 12</u>, first movement, Theme 1

EXAMPLE III-2

violins is clearly evident in the transition to theme 2, where each is given double stops as well as brilliant figurative passages. The resulting sound is very rich.

In measure 8 of example 1, the clarinets assume complete authority with the second phrase of the theme, while the strings play inconspicuous chords on the second beat and the horns and bassoons quietly sustain the harmony. Apparently either Cannabich was determined to explore to the full the timbre of the clarinets or he had two superb clarinetists with whom to work; both the second and the third themes are carried by them. Theme 2 finds the clarinets in sixths and thirds supported by bassoons, a most felicitous combination and one which was to become standard in later works.

Sonata-allegro form, without introduction or coda, serves to organize this first movement. The three themes of the exposition show distinct variety, both melodically and rhythmically. Their clear-cut individuality decidedly points to later Classicists. From this type of innocent juxtaposition of contrasted but quite compatible melodic ideas was to emerge the trenchant, dramatic clash of symphonic themes by Beethoven. Cannabich's development shows unusual sophistication. Thematic fragmentation is clearly to be seen.

This section begins with a spare, thinned-out version of the clarinet motive, this time in the strings (example 2). At the fourth measure, the clarinets in turn give out the opening motive of theme 1, originally given to the second violins. The bassoons answer with the little grace-note figure previously taken by the first violins. Later on in the development the figure in example 3 is seen followed by another (example 4) in the bass. Both of these figures had occurred as part of transitions separating the main thematic ideas in the exposition. Thus melodic fragments representing most of the exposition are woven into a compact, dynamic development section. In the hands of Beethoven, this very process was to become the vehicle for surging dynamism and drama in the early 19th century.

EXAMPLE III-3

EXAMPLE III-4

The Sinfonia a 11 by Johann Stamitz is cast in four movements, with a conventional da capo minuet. It is scored for oboes or flutes, trumpets, horns, drums, and strings. The famous orchestral crescendo is abundantly present, beginning with the very first theme (example 5).

The piece begins with the typical premier coup d'archet (first strike of the strings) which influenced Mozart in his Paris Symphony. After these bold and powerful forte chords for full orchestra, at measure 5 the strings start softly on a low d and eight bars later crest into a crashing forte. The score is liberally covered with piano, forte, and crescendo indications. According to Reinhard G. Pauly, in his Music in the Classic Period,

EXAMPLE III-5 Johann Stamitz, <u>Sinfonia a 11</u>, Op. 3, first movement

crescendo effects so startled audiences that, "On at least one occasion it made them literally rise out of their seats."

At measure 17 a remarkably colorful passage occurs, showing combined use of contrasted dynamics and expressive chromatic harmony. The basses plunge to the low seventh of the dominant seventh chord in measure 18. One would expect a heavy accent here, emphasizing the dissonance. But instead there occurs a sudden <u>pianissimo</u>. This process is repeated until F-sharp minor is touched upon at measure 26. A sketch of the harmonic progression in this passage (example III-6) illustrates the bold harmonic originality shown by the elder Stamitz.

EXAMPLE III-6

The second theme of the exposition is of the type later heard in Mozart and Haydn. It is delicately etched by the violins alone, featuring the downbeat grace notes so typical of the Classical period.

Other Pre-Classical composers who contributed to the form were Monn and Wagenseil in Vienna; C. P. E. Bach, perhaps the greatest of J. S. Bach's sons; two composers in London, Boyce and J. C. Bach (another son of J. S. Bach); the Bohemian, Rossler, who wrote under the name of Rosetti; and Gossec in Paris.

C. P. E. Bach

b. Weimar Mar. 8, 1714   d. Hamburg Dec. 15, 1788

Characteristic areas of composition:

Over 600 works; 2 oratorios, 16 cantatas, various other religious and secular vocal works; keyboard and chamber works, concerti for violin, flute and keyboard, symphonies.

Important Life Facts:

Second son of J. S. and Maria Barbara Bach. George Philipp Telemann his god parent.

Early education from father in Leipsig.
1734 University of Frankfort, law student.
1737 Performs for Friedrich Wilhelm I.
1740 Friedrich II succeeds father, appoints K. P. E. as cembalist.
1742 Prussian sonatas.
1744 Marries Johanna Maria Dannermann.
1750 Applies for father's position in Leipsig, turned down.
1753 &
1762 Publishes "Essay on the true art of playing keyboard instruments" To have strong effect on Mozart and Haydn, and earn him title "father of modern pianoforte playing".
1767 Unhappy at Potsdam, Godfather dies. Resigns, yet appointed non-resident Kapellmeister. Moves to Hamburg as concert performer and music director in five churches.
1788 Dies in Hamburg.

Burney quotes C. P. E. Bach as feeling that contrapuntal music was, "learned music . . . dry and despicable pieces [canons] of pedantry that anyone might compose who would give his time to them." He might have agreed heartily with Mozart's quip in later years, "I compare a good melodist to a fine racer, and counterpointists to hack post-horses."

To C. P. E. Bach as to the Mannheimers, the new, expressive, homophonic style was much more exciting. It was simpler, more direct, enabling them to explore rich chordal sonorities, persuasive melody, and bright instrumental coloring. It is in the keyboard sonatas of C. P. E. Bach that these characteristics are forged into the dramatic style that so profoundly influenced later composers, particularly Beethoven. This is perhaps understandable if we consider that he was a superb player, with a most important book on the keyboard to his credit, An Essay on the True Art of Playing Keyboard Instruments.

The C. P. E. Bach sinfonias are historically significant because they so strongly herald the approaching mature Classical style, but also because they show unmistakable traces of the "old" manner of scoring. The Sinfonia in C Major stems from Potsdam and was written in 1755. It forms an ideal illustration of the transitional symphonic style. There are three movements, without minuet. The orchestra is one that would have been quite familiar to composers of the Baroque period: flutes and horns in pairs, with strings and figured bass. The winds are conservatively used, the flutes generally doubling the violin parts and the horns used to flesh out the harmony and to provide rhythmic accent and dynamic body to the whole.

But though the scoring is not particularly advanced for a composer who struck new ground in other areas, the use of form is. The first movement is built on a sturdy and compact sonata-allegro pattern. A theme, marked allegro assai, given out by the violins gets things started abruptly and strongly (example 7). Its disjunct contour, with pre-

EXAMPLE III-7 C.P.E. Bach, Sinfonia in C, first movement, theme 1

carious leaps in the first violin, is typical of the virile melodic posture of the composer and suggests the sort of acrobatics often seen in Haydn symphonies and quartets.

With very little preparation, a contrasted second theme appears, more yielding and elegant than the first and thus serving as an admirable foil. A short passage in unison strings leads to a positive and strong cadence in the dominant key (G Major).

The first theme reenters as the first thematic occurrence of the development section, still in the dominant key. Soon after, the second theme appears softly, but upside down, in inversion. The key feeling becomes restless as D minor, E minor, and F Major are heard. Toward the end of the development a striking passage occurs. The second theme, at this moment in E minor, rises by sequence, and tails off to a whispered pianissimo on a high g-sharp-a. Suddenly, all forces but the flutes crash in on a diminished seventh chord, fortissimo. This is precisely the kind of dynamic switch that can be seen in a great many sinfonias of the Mannheim and Viennese schools. Here, C. P. E. Bach clearly looks ahead.

The recapitulation displays no surprises. All themes come back in the original order, though there is a transition passage between first and second themes that did not occur at the outset.

A brief coda begins with a trenchant triadic figure that soon tapers off to soft suspensions and a soft half-cadence in the key of the next movement, F Major. Here we are reminded of the Baroque concerto and suite movements that end on a chord leading to the following movement; for example, the second movement of the sixth Brandenburg Concerto by J. S. Bach. The Baroque overture also showed such linked sections. (See above)

The orchestra in this period was fairly well standardized. Most of the instruments found in later scores of Mozart and Haydn were in use, though they were not used in the diversified manner that was to come. The essential orchestra early in the 1700s consisted of strings, flutes, oboes, bassoons, and horns. Later came trumpets, drums, and clarinets. The winds were used primarily as sustaining instruments, most of the melodic activity being given to the strings.

HAYDN, MOZART

The symphony matured in the hands of Haydn and Mozart. With them it also became a vehicle for sublime music. Many technical changes occurred. One was the consistent insertion of a minuet between the usual second and third movements. The late Classical symphony thus often consisted of four movements.

58

It is true that occasionally Baroque instrumental music ended with a dignified minuet, a practice not conducive to dramatic effect. A case in point is the Royal Fireworks Music by Handel. Haydn in one of his last clavier sonatas retained this practice, as did Beethoven, who placed a minuet at the end of his Variations on a Theme of Diabelli, Op. 120, for piano.

The insertion of the minuet between the meditative slow movement and the brilliant finale acted as a moment of diversion before the excitement of the finale. It provided the contrast of a dance-oriented movement and extended the scope of the work in general.

In the hands of Haydn and Mozart, the woodwinds became increasingly important. The bassoon, which earlier often simply doubled the bass viols, now was assigned important melodic functions, especially in Mozart's later works. The flutes, which had sometimes been used as substitutes for the oboes, were given their own vital melodies. Clarinets, though they had been used by Rameau and others much earlier, were recognized for their marvelous tone color possibilities and began to play a leading role, again especially in Mozart.

Trumpets, horns, and drums played a lesser role. Horns, however, were often assigned important melodic functions in the trio sections of minuet movements.

Of much greater importance than the above changes was the high development of dramatic and coherent unifying forms within the individual movements. Forms such as sonata-allegro, rondo, theme with variations, and minuet with trio, were raised to a very high level. Especially important was the emphasis placed on development sections within the various movements. It was here that the composer could explore to the full the dramatic potential latent in themes presented earlier in the movement. As seen above, it is usually in the development sections that the greatest intensity is felt. Great climaxes build; marvelous transformations of motives and rhythms occur; great ingenuity is shown in modulation and in harmonic color. In addition, there also occurred a refinement of melody and a strengthening of the overall harmonic scheme.

FRANZ JOSEPH HAYDN

b. Rohrau, Austria Mar 31–April 1, 1732
d. Vienna, May 31, 1809

Characteristic Areas of Composition: 18 operas, 14 masses, over 100 symphonies, 16 overtures, over 270 chamber works, 15 keyboard concerti, 22 other solo concerti, 52 + keyboard sonatas, numerous songs and folk song arrangements.

Important life facts:
  Second child of Matthias Haydn, master wheelwright and Maria Koller, a cook.
  1738 Taken by father to Johann Mathias Franck's school in Hainburg for voice lessons.
  1740 Georg Reutter hears Haydn and takes him to St. Stephen choir School in Vienna as Chorister. Singing, violin and clavier lessons.
  1745 Brother Michael comes to St. Stephen's.
  1748 Voice changing, leaves St. Stephen after punishment for a practical joke. A chorister from St. Michael's, Spangler, offers him shelter. Practices violin and clavier. Studies sonatas of K.P.E. Bach.
  1751 Composes Mass in F.
  1752 Composes comic opera Der Krumme Teufel, music now lost. Gives music lessons.
  1755 Invited to country house of Karl Joseph Edler von Fürnberg.
        Composes first twelve string quartets.
  1756 Returns to Vienna a successful teacher and composer.
  1759 Appointed music director and chamber composer of Count Ferdinand Maximilian Merzin. Begins writing four-movement symphonies for his 12-16 player orchestra.

Gives music lessons to two daughters of Keller, a wigmaker. Falls in love with the younger, who enters a convent. Father persuades him to marry the older, Maria Anna.

1760 Marries Maria Anna at St. Stephens, an unhappy marriage.
1761 Dismissed by Count Morzin and hired by Esterhazy in Eisenstadt to join Werner as music director.
1762 Paul Anton Esterhazy dies, is replaced by brother Nicholas, who increases musical resources for Haydn and Werner.
1766 Werner dies. Haydn sole Kapellmeister.
1768 Lo speziale.
1772 Farewell Symphony #45.
1773 Maria Theresa visits Esterhaz, Symphony #48 in her honor.
1776 Composes opera La Vera Costanza for Court theatre of Vienna. Opera of Anfossi by the same name preferred. Haydn withdraws his and produces it at Esterhaz.
1780 New theatre at Esterhaz built to replace one destroyed by fire. "Russian" quartets opus 33.
1781 Meets Mozart in Vienna.
1785 Mozart dedicates six quartets to Haydn.
1790 Prince Nicolas dies, his successor Anton dismisses orchestra and retires Haydn on pension. Residence in Vienna. No longer able to use Esterhaz as excuse, is persuaded by Salomon to tour England. First trip to England. Lessons to Mrs. John Schroeter.
1792 Leaves London highly successful, on way to Vienna meets Beethoven.
1794 Second journey to London, takes up residence near Mrs. Schroeter.
1795 Again highly successful, returns to Vienna, now reaches his height of fame in Vienna also.
1797 Writes song "Gott erhalte Franz den Kaiser", also found in Kaiserquartett Opus 76 No. 3
1798 The Creation.
1801 The Seasons, last major composition. Health begins to fail.
1804 Honorary citizen of Vienna.
1805 Mozart's son Wolfgang composes a cantate in his honor.
1808 Last public appearance at a performance of his Creation, conducted by Salieri.
1809 Upon news of his death, mourning throughout Europe.

The symphonies:

Over a period of nearly forty years, Haydn wrote over one-hundred symphonies. Rather than list each of these works, they are categorized below into three periods - early, middle, and late. Several of the most original and/or finest of these symphonies is listed for each period.

First period: (c. 1757-1765) Early works written while Haydn was in the employ of Count Morzin and, later, Prince Esterhazy.

Symphony No. 1, D major, (c. 1757)
Symphonies No. 6, 7, 8; D major, "Le Matin"; C major, "Le Midi"; G major, "Le Soir, et La tempesta" (c. 1761)

Symphony No. 30, C major, "Alleluja", (1765) First movement theme based on Gregorian Chant for Easter, "Alleluia".

Symphony No. 31, D major, "Hornsignal", (1765) Four horns in instrumentation.

Middle period: (1766-1784) Works of the mature master written during the Esterhazy appointment. Includes the Sturm und Drang symphonies.

Symphony No. 26, D minor, "Lamentatione", (c. 1767-68) "Sturm und Drang" style.
First and second movements use melodies based on Gregorian Chant.

Symphony No. 49, F minor, "La Passione", (1768) "Sturm und Drang" style.
One of several symphonies cast in baroque sonata da chiesa style. Opening movement in slow tempo; all movements in tonic key.

Symphony No. 41, C major. (c. 1770)

Symphony No. 44, E minor, (c. 1772) "Trauersymphonie"

Symphony No. 45, F sharp minor, "Farewell" (1772)

Symphony No. 48, C major, "Maria Theresia", (1772) One of several symphonies in C major, with trumpets and drums in the composer's festive style.

Symphony No. 60, C major, "Il distratto", (1775?)

Late period: (1785-1795) Includes the Paris Symphonies written for Comte d'Ogny the Tost symphonies and the twelve London Symphonies.

Symphony No. 85, B flat major, "La Reine" (1785-86) (Paris)
Symphony No. 88, G major, (c. 1787) (Tost)
Symphony No. 92, G major, "Oxford", (c. 1788)

Symphony No. 94, G major, "Surprise", (1791) Second of the London Symphonies.
Symphony No. 95, C minor, (1791)
Symphony No. 100, G major, "Military", (1794)
Symphony No. 101, D major, "The Clock" (1794)
Symphony No. 103, E flat major, "The Drum Roll" (1795)
Symphony No. 104, D major "London", (1795)

Paul Bekker, in his book The Orchestra, says of Haydn that, "His appreciation of life was based upon the conviction that this world is founded upon a good and right order which is not to be disturbed even by the suffering of the individual. This classic rationalist ideology assumes a harmonious order of all forces, obedient to the rules of reason." And later, "The instrumental language seemed an especially suitable medium for such ideology. It had proved itself capable of representing all human feelings. . . . From this point of view instrumental language seemed to be superior to words: the instrument might be described as the voice elevated to a higher degree. . . . Such was the inner law of Haydn's art. From it sprang his form, his orchestration, his treatment of the instrument individually and in the mass."

In the view of Bekker, Haydn's symphonic style is based on a luminous rationality. Within the confines of logic, symmetry, and order, were articulated a wide gamut of musical ideas, representing a panaroma of emotional states--the humorous, tragic, melancholy, and serene. The sobriquet "Papa Haydn" of course is too well known; it suggests to the layman a jolly composer who delighted in writing melodious, frolicsome tunes. This is partly true. Many of the movements in Haydn symphonies are permeated with frolic. But this musical levity is always buttressed by utter logic of presentation and constant compositional freshness and invention. The rondo from the Symphony No. 88 illuminates this aspect of the Haydn style. (See the discussion of this symphony below). Here is a movement which is ripe with infectious gaiety: It dances along with blithe hedonism. Yet superb invention, subtle contrast, ever-evolving freshness of presentation can be seen constantly in its few pages. The main theme (example 8), a saucy, folk-like tune, keeps cropping up. The middle section

EXAMPLE III-8 Haydn, <u>Symphony No. 88</u>, fourth movement

of the rondo suddenly finds this tune treated to the tightest polyphonic technique imaginable in development style. It is as if Haydn had said, "See how even my gayest melodies can be made to produce drama and excitement." The scoring is utterly pellucid. Every idea, all harmony and rhythm, are as neatly set out as a formal French garden. Everything can be heard clearly from soprano to bass. Thus, Haydn always tempers the loquacious with superb craft and seriousness of purpose and design. This is especially true when we examine a Haydn movement whose intent is essentially dramatic, as in the <u>Symphony No. 45</u>, the <u>Farewell</u>. Here is a first movement showing tautness and trenchant expression within the frame of a relatively brief, 216-measure sonata-allegro structure.

The main themes of the exposition (example 9) are bold, uncompromising, almost violent.

EXAMPLE III-9

The expressive interval of the augmented second heard in the first measure of the second theme is typical of the intensity that permeates the exposition section. The development reflects the dramatic flavor of the whole movement: It develops both of the above themes with constant dramatic thrust and excitement. But suddenly, at a moment when the drama is at its tautest, and with the second theme pausing expectantly on a half cadence in the key of B minor, the key switches abruptly to D Major, the dynamic level drops to piano, and a blithe new theme takes over. The contrast is sublime. With Haydn one can always look to the unexpected, the sudden swerve from the established mood, the twist in the road that presents fresh new vistas.

62

Haydn found a true instrumental voice for the symphony, with each choir and section contributing significantly to a perfectly proportioned whole. Adam Carse in his The History of Orchestration, notes that, ". . . Haydn's sense for orchestral effect was still continuously, although slowly, expanding even after middle age had passed."

Perhaps nowhere can the balance of forces, the democratic utilization of wind and string timbres be better seen than in the Symphony No. 101, the so-called Clock Symphony. The second movement is scored for the typical late Haydn orchestra: flutes, oboes, clarinets, bassoons, horns, trumpets, timpani, and full strings. It begins with the steady accompaniment figure in the bassoons and low strings that has given the symphony its nickname (example 10). Above is an enchanting melody carried initially by the first violins,

EXAMPLE III-10 Haydn, Symphony No. 101, Clock, second movement

Haydn follows up with a middle section that is quite stormy, functioning as the perfect foil to the first part (the structure of the movement is ternary, ABA). Here, brass and drums play an important role.

When it is time for the first theme to reenter, subtle changes occur: The blend of woodwinds and strings is a new one. Instead of bassoons and low strings giving out the perky accompaniment, it is taken by the first bassoon joined by the first flute, two octaves above. The first oboe, not to be outdone, joins in with five notes in respectful pianissimo at measure 4. Nine measures later it takes heart and volunteers seven notes. Ultimately it joins in regularly, adding a piquant obbligato to the main idea in the violins. The flute, which at the outset occasionally diverges from its "clock" figure, adds slight melodic fragments of its own. The bassoon does the same and is particularly piquant at measure 20 where it bounces up and down a D octave. Throughout this restatement of the theme Haydn makes do with the sparsest of forces, omitting all but the first violins, flute, oboe, and bassoon. In characteristic fashion he follows with a sudden break of key, and repeats the theme again beginning in E-flat Major. He adds a crescendo and soon after fleshes out the texture to full orchestra for a variation of the main theme, forte. Curiously, the clarinets here receive perfunctory treatment: They serve only to sustain the harmony and double other parts.

Haydn, through a significant span of his creative life, had at hand his own orchestra with which to experiment. His long residence at Esterhazy, where he was expected to turn out symphonies with nearly the frequency that J.S. Bach had produced cantatas at his various posts as organist, challenged him to experiment constantly. Thus there are light symphonies and heavy symphonies, tragic ones and gay ones. There is a thunderstorm in No. 8; No. 26, La Lamentione, uses a Gregorian chant; and there are four horns in No. 31, the Horn Signal. The two sets of six London symphonies show him as having reaped the benefits of this constant experimentation. A work such as the Clock (No. 101), the third of the second set of London symphonies, shows that he could express exactly what he wished with perfect mastery of the orchestra.

ANALYSIS AND COMMENTARY

SYMPHONY NO. 88 IN G MAJOR

ORCHESTRA

The orchestra in this symphony is usual for the late Classical period. There are: one flute, two oboes, two bassoons; two horns, two trumpets; timpani; and strings. The trumpets, which may have been added in later editions, do not make their appearance until the second movement.

GENERAL STYLE

This work shows Haydn at his very best. It is a supreme example of control and logic in form, the whole informed with high good spirits and elegance of style. Many of the themes resemble folk song and folk dance, suggesting perhaps the composer's peasant origins. The second movement, however, does not suggest folk music; its serene, <u>cantabile</u> melody soars with solemn majesty. Beethoven much admired it.

MOVEMENT 1

Key:	G Major
Meter:	Triple, then duple
Tempo:	<u>Largo</u>, then <u>allegro</u>
Form:	Slow introduction leading directly to a fast sonata-allegro structure
Orchestra:	Trumpets, timpani--<u>tacet</u>

INTRODUCTION (Meas. 1-16)

Typically, Haydn establishes a mood appropriate for an important musical structure by presenting a solemn, dignified introductory theme. The music proceeds in a deliberate gait and finally settles on a dominant chord. After a brief pause the strings sally off with the first theme of the exposition (example 11).

EXPOSITION (Meas. 16-102)

EXAMPLE III-11   Theme 1

The first theme is clearly in the "hunt" style. The "hunt" intervals of the perfect fifth, major third, and major sixth set the mood, while the generally light, <u>staccato</u> character of the theme underlines the feeling of joyful expectation. The full orchestra repeats theme 1 with the addition of a strong, supportive rhythmic figure in the lower strings and bassoon. This supportive figure is suddenly transferred to the violins and assumes the lead as the first transition begins. As in so many connecting passages from the quick movements of the Classical symphony, there is little tunefulness but much sparkle. At measure 51, an important note is emphasized: c-sharp, the leading tone of the new key soon to be heard, D Major. The leaping bustle suddenly subsides as the second major theme of the exposition arrives (example 12).

EXAMPLE III-12 Theme 2

Though there is still buoyancy and verve, the contour of this second theme is gentler than that of the first. It provides a moment of respite. The figure from the first transition asserts itself and the orchestra builds to a climax. Again, the excitement abruptly ebbs and a saucy little descending theme is given out by the oboes.

Instantly, the violins answer with essentially the same idea, going up. Almost before this little badinage has a chance to make its effect, the full orchestra jumps in with the powerful closing theme of the exposition section.

DEVELOPMENT (meas. 102-179)

The action begins quietly enough. A little trill-like figure in 3rds is played p and drops to pp. It then rises, touching on an e-flat before giving way to the essential motive from theme 1 in the surprising key of A-flat Major. These thematic materials suffice for a considerable time as several new keys are suggested. At measure 147 theme 2 breaks in, but it is soon crowded out by an intense imitative dialogue built on the motive from theme 1. The closing theme from the exposition, theme 4, takes over, plumping itself on the dominant of the home key, G Major, and a short rest leads to the recapitulation section.

RECAPITULATION (Meas. 179-253)

Theme 1 returns in the tonic. But there is a charming difference. This time the two violins play softly, while the flute comments with a jaunty obbligato figure above. As in the exposition, the transition follows, but its harmonic course is altered so that it will lead easily to the second theme, this time to be heard in the home key, G Major. The theme does enter in the tonic, as does theme 3. Only theme 4, the original closing theme of the exposition, is left out. Instead, a brilliant coda (example 13) brings the movement emphatically to a close.

CODA (Meas. 253-265)

EXAMPLE III-13

MOVEMENT 2

Key: D Major
Meter: Triple
Tempo: Largo
Form: Additive; has elements of variation and rondo structure, because the first
            theme is heard six times in all, and is each time different
Orchestra: Full

Theme 1, a lovely cantilena melody (example 14), is carried initially by the solo oboe and the solo cello playing an octave apart. The use of these solo instruments for the presentation of the first theme is unusual for the period and anticipates similar scoring in the Romantic symphony.

EXAMPLE III-14   Theme 1

After the first rich, leisurely presentation of this idea, the tonic minor harmony is touched upon, after which theme 1 returns, again given to the solo oboe and solo cello. But this time delicate, drooping figures in the first violins join in while the second violins play soft double stops, pizzicato. After a quiet, demure cadence in the tonic key, the full orchestra bursts out with a remarkable theme. Over a tonic pedal, three powerful strokes of a dominant seventh chord are heard. Immediately, the oboes answer with a timid, bare interval of the third played p (example 15).

EXAMPLE III-15   Theme 2

The hammer strokes are repeated, after which oboes and strings modulate gently to the key of A Major. Here the flute and first violins take up theme 1 in the new key. As it turns out, the purpose of this passage is to lead back to the first theme in the original key as played by the original solo instruments, cello and oboe. Haydn, showing inexhaustible invention, now writes charming staccato scales for the first violins.

Theme 2 suddenly interrupts, this time in the tonic minor. Following closely, theme 1 appears in F Major, an exotic key for a movement in D Major.

The sixth and last appearance of theme 1 finds the oboe again in the lead but with all of the cellos and first violins joining in. All the while, the second violins murmur softly with broken chords. The coda is strong and virile, featuring the crashing dissonances of theme 2.

MOVEMENT 3--Menuetto

Key:	G Major
Meter:	Triple
Tempo:	Allegretto
Form:	Three-part ternary: minuet with trio
Orchestra:	Full

67

Here the structure is traditional. The first section begins with an elegant but energetic theme played by full orchestra (example 16).

EXAMPLE III-16 Theme 1

At measure 44 the texture thins considerably as the second, or trio section begins. Obvious in this theme is the peasant influence. Not only are the melody and accompaniment close to the country dance called the Ländler, but the drone fifths played by the bassoons and violas are highly suggestive of the musette, an early bagpipe-like instrument. Particularly Haydnesque are the syncopations toward the close of the trio section. Menuetto da capo at the end of the trio indicates that the whole of the first section is repeated.

MOVEMENT 4

Key:	G Major
Meter:	Duple
Tempo:	Allegro con spirito
Form:	Rondo with development section
Orchestra:	Full

This movement is a gem; Haydn is at his sparkling best, showing incredible structural sophistication. The principal theme (refrain) keeps coming back as in any rondo, but always with a piquant twist.

REFRAIN (Meas. 1-32)

The theme of the refrain (example 17) is glib, zesty, yet simple and plastic enough to be easily recognized as it recurs throughout the movement. Also, its basic simplicity allows Haydn to use it effectively in the development section toward the middle of the movement.

EXAMPLE 17 Theme 1

At measure 8, Haydn stands the motive from his theme on its head (inversion). It is answered very brusquely by the full orchestra asserting that the motive is really supposed to go down. Shortly before the entrance of the first episode, the full orchestra presses heavily on the dominant minor, giving momentary relief to the rather steady use of major harmony throughout.

EPISODE I (Meas. 32-84)

This section is rather extensive. It begins with furious activity in the strings (example 18),

EXAMPLE III-18

which continues until the motive from the refrain interjects a quiet note, first in the dominant key (D Major), and immediately after in the dominant minor (D minor). One almost believes that the refrain has returned, but doubt is soon dispelled as the bustling figuration continues on its way, leading to an insistent stamping on the dominant chord. This signals the true return of the refrain.

REFRAIN (Meas. 84-108)

This section is similar to the opening one, except that the instrumentation differs (example 19). This time the flute and violins give out theme 1, while the lower strings supply pizzicato chords and the bassoons and horns bounce about with staccato chords.

EXAMPLE III-19

EPISODE II: (Developmental; Meas. 108-158

   This section is unmistakably developmental in character. Haydn writes a dense imitative
section built on the motive of the refrain. The dynamic level, <u>ff</u>, is kept until measure 142,
emphasizing the section's dramatic nature. At measure 142 the fury subsides as we are
deftly led back to the final presentation of the refrain.

REFRAIN (Meas. 158-190)

Theme 1 is as it was at the beginning, except that the flute joins the strings and bassoon.

CODA (Meas. 190-221)

At measure 190 the music pauses for a moment. A martial rhythmic figure is heard, then a brief fermata holds back the momentum. Without further ceremony, Haydn impatiently plunges into characteristic figures taken from episode I and the whole symphony closes on a note of great joy.

Wolfgang Amadeus Mozart

b. Salzburg, Austria Jan. 27, 1756
d. Vienna, Austria Dec. 5, 1791

Father Leopold Mozart, performing musician, composer, and author.
Mother Anna Marcia Pertl of St. Gilgen.

Characteristic areas of composition:
17 operas, numerous church compositions including 18 masses, numerous arias, 7 cantatas and oratorios, ca. 40 symphonies, numerous collections of dances, 47 concerti including 12 for violin and orchestra and 24 for piano and orchestra, 17 sonatas for organ and orchestra, 6 string quintets, 23 string quartets,   sonatas for violin and piano, numerous other chamber works, numerous piano solo works.

1761 First performance at 5 1/2 years old.
1763 First efforts at composition by imitation of sister Maria Anna's manuscript book.
       Performs for Emperor of Austria and Court of Versailles.
1762 First tour of Munich, Linz, and Vienna with his sister.
1764 Trip to London, tested by the King of England with compositions of J. C. Bach and
       Handel, sight-reads with ease. Composes first two symphonies.
1765 Arrives at the Hague, prolonged illness.
1766 Six sonatas for Piano and Violin. Returns to Salzburg.
1767 Two Symphonies K. 43 & 76.
1768 First opera La finta simplice.
1769 Made Konzertmeister by Archbishop of Salzburg. Composes two masses K. 65 & 66
       and Te Deum K. 141. Leaves Salzburg for Italy, meets Martini (church composer).
       Arrives in Rome where he writes down entirely from memory Allegri's Miserere
       after second hearing. Three symphonies K. 81, 97, & 95. Accorded "The Order of
       the Golden Spur" by the Pope.
1771 To Bologna, made a member of the Accademia Filarmonia, first as compositore, then
       Maestro di Cappella
1772 Returns to Salzburg, employed by Archbishop.
1773 Composes Missa "Pater Dominicus".
       "Little" G Minor Symphony K. 183
1775 La finta giardiniera (opera).
1776 Missa Brevis K. 175.
1777 Resigns from employ of Archbishop, leaves with strained relations. Goes to Mannheim;
       includes clarinets in compositions. Falls in love with Aloysia Weber.
1778 Journeys to Paris with his mother, who is in poor health. Concerto for flute and harp
       K. 299. Mother dies in his arms. J. C. Bach visits him. Returning to Salzburg, but
       stops at Nancy and Strasbourg. In Mannheim, visits Webers, composes grand aria
       for Aloysia K. 316. Father commands him to return "immediately".

1779-
1780 In Salzburg, composes <u>Coronation Mass</u> K. 317, Symphonies K. 319 & 338.
1781 Commissioned to write opera for Carnival at Munich, <u>Idomeneo</u> K. 366.
   Summoned by Archbishop of Vienna and hired as "domestic Virtuoso", forbidden to
   play alone in any home but the Archbishop's. Dismissed by Archbishop after argument,
   and lodges with the Webers. Meets Haydn.
1782 Opera <u>Die Entführung aus dem Serail</u>. Marries Constanze Weber at St. Stephen's in
   Vienna.
1783 Journeys to Salzburg to present Constanze to father. Cool reception for Constanze.
   Returns to Vienna, stops at Linz, <u>Symphony #36 "Linz"</u> K. 425.
1784 Joins Freemasons.
1785 Father journeys to visit son in Vienna. Six quartets dedicated to Haydn, meets
   Lorenzo da Ponte.
1786 <u>Le Nozze di Figaro</u> K. 492 (opera) performed with great success.
1787 In Prague, composes opera <u>Don Giovanni</u> K. 527. Gluck, chamber composer for
   Maria Theresa, dies. Still no court appointment for Mozart.
1788 Composes Symphonies # 39, 40, & 41 between June 26 and August 10.
1789 Tours Dresden, Leipzig (J. S. Bach's St. Thomas Church), Berlin, Potsdam (offered
   position of Kapellmeister, turns it down).
1790 <u>Cosi Fan Tutti</u> (opera). Meets Haydn for last time, tells Haydn that it will be the
   last time he will see him. <u>Die Zauberflöte</u> (opera). Contacted by stranger to compose
   a Requiem. Opera <u>La Clemenza di Tito</u> K. 621.
1791 Dies, probably from exhaustion leading to nephritis. Requiem unfinished, preoccupied
   with the idea that the Requiem was for himself. Buried in a pauper's grave.

The symphonies:
   Mozart's first symphony (Eb major, K. 16) was written either in late 1764 or early 1765,
his last, the "Jupiter" in 1788. Thus his first was composed when the composer was but a
child, and the last three years before his death at the age of 35. Although Mozart wrote
symphonies throughout most of his short life, those selected below, beginning with Symphony
No. 25, show that he achieved great mastery of the form.

```
Symphony No. 25, G minor (1773) Ko. 183.
Symphony No. 29, A major (1774) Ko. 201
Symphony No 31, D major, "Paris", (1778) Ko. 297.
Symphony No. 35, D major, "Haffner", Ko. 385 (1782)
Symphony No. 36, C major, "Linz" Ko. 425 (1783)
Symphony No. 38, D major, "Prague", Ko. 504 (1786)
Symphony No. 39, E flat major, Ko. 543 (1788)
Symphony No. 40, G minor, Ko. 550 (1788)
Symphony No. 41, C major, "Jupiter", Ko. 551 (1788)
```

   Like Haydn's, Mozart's later symphonies show consummate workmanship and the perfect
blend of content with form. But the total body of Mozart's works in symphony form does not
show the same kind of diversity in style. There are no incipient program symphonies such as
Haydn's <u>Symphony No. 8, Le Soir</u>; no charming tricks, as in the finale of Haydn's <u>Farewell</u>
where the players exit one by one; and no surprises as in Haydn's <u>Symphony No. 94</u>.
Mozart had no resident orchestra which he could call his own. The titles given to his
symphonies, such as the <u>Paris Symphony, No. 31</u>, written in Paris in 1778; the <u>Linz Symphony</u>,
written in 1783; the <u>Haffner Symphony</u>, written for the Haffner family at Salzburg in 1782;
and the <u>Prague Symphony</u>, done in 1786, attest to his placing the symphonies wherever they
might be heard. The greatness and unique quality that informs the mature Mozart of the
symphonies lies in the area of melodic and harmonic content, rather than in structural experiment for its own sake. Bekker says, "The cast and special technique of Mozart's orchestra
represent no such innovations as Haydn's. Rather was he supreme. . . from his ability to
reveal each instrument as a singing and acting individuality, an ability he had acquired and
developed in his experience with the opera orchestra." And further, "Haydn had established

the independence of the instruments and combined them into a rational unity. Mozart had inspired this orchestral unity with the singing qualities of the human voice."

Let us see if this is true. The second movement from Mozart's last symphony, Symphony No. 41, the Jupiter should make Bekker's point if it is a valid one. Not only is it representative of the mature Mozart, written after his great operas, but it is an acknowledged masterpiece, considered a paragon of the lyric, cantabile style of the period.

The second movement, marked andante cantabile, follows the sonata-allegro pattern. The first violins, muted, begin with a serene theme (example 20). Though this theme is eminently lyric, it is not especially vocal in style. Indeed it is not unlike the theme given

EXAMPLE III-20

above from Haydn's Clock Symphony. Its range and rather florid configuration stamp it as being conceived in terms of its instrumental presentation, obviously in terms of the violin. However, a second theme enters (example 21), which is this time of a character that could

EXAMPLE III-21

easily pass as an aria from a Mozart opera. We can assume that this is what Bekker is
talking about. He is quite correct.

He is again correct when we consider the harmony in certain passages of this movement.
The transition (example 22) that separates the two themes   given above is startling in its
pathos and intensity of feeling. Oboes and clarinets initiate the thought in a suddenly

EXAMPLE III-22

darkened harmony with a rising broken chord in C minor. The first violins turn back down
with the same chord and land on poignant dissonances caused by a c-sharp grating against a
c-natural in the bass. This idea is repeated immediately a step higher and is followed by a
rising sequential passage of an intensity and passion matched only in certain passages found

in Beethoven. Note the bold dissonance on the third beat of the seventh full measure. Here is a D-flat Major triad in first inversion (the Neapolitan sixth chord of the key) that clashes with the note c-natural, a minor second away from its root tone. Again we see the influence of opera. Passages of similar harmonic intensity abound in Mozart's operas. An example that quickly comes to mind is the orchestral music that accompanies the dialogue between the Don and the statue of the Commendatore in Don Giovanni.

Whatever the cause may be, the plain fact remains that Mozart excelled Haydn in matters lyric and harmonic in the symphony. His melodies sing more and his harmony and counterpoint have a naturalness and expressive power seldom seen in Haydn.

In the area of counterpoint, Mozart is superb. In the coda to the Jupiter Symphony (fourth movement), five separate motives are combines in a polyphonic texture of consummate mastery. The elaborate combination of these motives suggests J. S. Bach. The effect is completely nonpedantic and perfectly in keeping with the natural buoyancy of the music that precedes it. In short, Mozart's craft never obstructs the simple universality of his music. Every bit of subtle compositional "play" in the form is camouflaged by natural melodiousness and matching pellucid textures. One can only think of the exquisite Renaissance painter Botticelli, about whose art it has been said that it is " . . . full of [his] characteristic poetic yearning and vehemence of expression, his half-childish intensity of vision; exquisite in lightness of touch and in swaying, rhythmical grace of linear composition and design."*

SYMPHONY NO. 40 IN G MINOR K 550

ORCHESTRA

The orchestra for this work consists of: one flute, two oboes, two clarinets, two bassoons; two horns; and strings. (Basses double cellos throughout.) There are no trumpets or drums in this work, a somewhat unusual practice in late Classical orchestration. The two clarinets were added and oboe parts modified by the composer in the revised version.

GENERAL STYLE

This symphony, one of the great symphonic triptych including symphonies No. 39, 40, and 41 is unique. It is held together by an incisive sense of musical logic that is one of Mozart's main attributes. Yet the music is personal, subjective, and entirely winning on the strength of its beauty of sound alone. The development sections of movements 1, 2, and 4 are intensely dramatic and point clearly to Beethoven. Melodic and harmonic elements point ahead even further, to the music of Chopin and other Romantics.

MOVEMENT 1

Key:	G minor
Meter:	Duple
Tempo:	Molto allegro
Form:	Sonata-allegro
Orchestra:	Full

EXPOSITION (Meas. 1-100)

There is no introduction: The piece is immediately taken up with a theme informed by a true quality of pathos (example 23). This quality is partly brought about by the descending intervals of the minor second at the beginning (example 24) and the downward use of the harmonic minor scale (example 25). The harmonic minor scale contains the exotic interval of the augmented second (fifth and sixth notes of example 25).

*Encyclopaedia Britannica (1957).

EXAMPLE III – 23 Theme 1

EXAMPLE III – 24

EXAMPLE III – 25

Ordinarily the harmonic minor scale is used in an upward direction. Apparently Mozart desired the peculiar intensity of the augmented second, even though the shape of his melody required that it occur in a descending scale passage.

The first theme glides gently along until suddenly, at measure 16, all the winds cry out with a searing dissonant diminished seventh chord over repeated string octaves on the dominant.

Thus very early in the work we are given notice by Mozart that this is to be a searching, dramatic symphony. The first theme begins again, but this time quickly modulates to the relative key, B-flat Major, which prepares for the entry of a sturdy transition idea. Here there is sturm und drang (storm and stress), a violent quality sometimes seen in the high Classical style.

77

After a clear and incisive cadence on the dominant of the new key, B-flat Major, a grace-ful, yielding theme begins (example 26). Aside from this theme's controlled equanimity and Hellenistic symmetry, it is a superb example of Mozart's work with the woodwind choir.

EXAMPLE III-26 Theme 2

Strings and woodwinds share alike, and all sound at their finest. At measure 58 another episode occurs, building in intensity through a crescendo and ultimately leading to the third theme. (example 27)

EXAMPLE III-27

Theme 4 (example 28) is derived from a motive taken from theme 1. Note how this remembered

EXAMPLE III-28 Theme 4

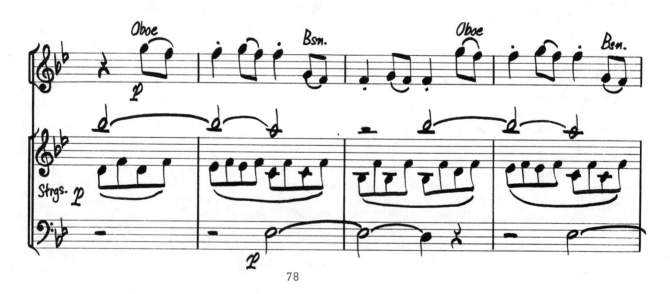

78

fragment is tossed back and forth from clarinets to bassoons, who then give way to the strings for a forceful cadence. At the conclusion of theme 4, the momentum already built up is carried to the end of the exposition by active scale-like figures in the strings, reinforced by the woodwinds. .

DEVELOPMENT (Meas. 101-166)

The high dramatic action of the development is built on materials from theme 1. An extremely tight, trenchant modulation from the key of B-flat Major (at the close of the exposition) to the distant key of F-sharp minor inaugurates the first appearance of theme 1 in the development (example 29).

EXAMPLE III-29

Several other keys are touched upon, with theme 1 heard successively in the high and low strings. Ultimately the tension subsides somewhat and imitative fragments from theme 1 are heard in the woodwinds. At measure 160 the horns hold on to the dominant of the home key while the upper woodwinds sift down in sequence to a cadence in the tonic. Here one would normally expect to hear theme 1 enter on cue at the tonic chord for the beginning of the recapitulation. But Mozart has slipped the theme in before its time. Making its entrance unobtrusively, the first few notes of the theme are heard before the woodwinds complete their cadence in the tonic. The effect of elision here is magical, for one never really knows when the development ends and the recapitulation begins. The seams are hidden.

RECAPITULATION (Meas. 164-285)

All themes from the exposition come back in the same order as before. As is expected, themes 2, 3, and 4 are not in the tonic key, G minor. The transition from theme 1 to theme 2 begins as in the exposition, but is extended considerably and is like a second development.   It is as if Mozart felt that his regular development were not quite long enough to carry the potential for drama suggested by his themes. He therefore simply extends the transition (which featured a powerful motive anyway) to give added drive and scope to the movement as a whole.

CODA (Meas. 285-299)

This added section begins quietly with reminiscences of theme 1 and then builds to a strong figure in the strings built around alternating tonic and dominant chords.

MOVEMENT 2

Key: E-flat Major
Meter: Compound
Tempo: <u>Andante</u>
Form: Sonata-allegro
Orchestra: Full

EXPOSITION (Meas. 1-52)

   The gentle repeated notes of the initial part of the first theme are carried from violas,
up to second violins, and then up to first violins, who carry forth the rest of the idea. Note
the tiny nodding figure in measure 7 (example 30), built on two slurred thirty-second notes.

EXAMPLE III-30 Theme 1

These short notes take on increased importance as the movement progresses. After a solid
cadence in the tonic key, a new, more robust transition theme enters at measure 20 in the
dominant, B-flat Major.

   Initially there is a dramatic surge as a high b-flat, <u>f</u>, is followed by three syncopated
b-flats an octave lower. This gives way in the next measure, where the tiny nodding figure
trips about in the strings and then in the flute. This figure assumes increasing importance

80

as the music takes on the character of a transition. During this bridging section, exotic keys are touched upon and a suggestion of the repeated notes from the first theme is also heard. All of this leads to an intensification and thickening of the texture.

At measure 36, the music is hushed once again as theme 3 enters. At first one expects that it will fulfill the role of a typically well-mannered third theme for the exposition: simple, clear, and unambiguous. But once a complete statement has been made extraordinary things happen: The whole orchestra interrupts with a chromatic passage of great persuasive power, a harmonic interjection of the kind Sir Donald Tovey called a "purple patch", i.e., a sudden shift into unexpected, colorful harmony.

The exposition ends quietly with an elegant fourth theme. The tiny thirty-second-note fragment from above continues to comment on the main idea.

DEVELOPMENT (Meas. 52-73)

The development is terse. For the most part, Mozart relies on a juxtaposition of the repeated-note idea from theme 1 and the nodding figure mentioned above. The opening measures show the general trend of this section. Mozart wastes little time in injecting pathos; he requires the strings immediately to rise to a c-flat, the sixth degree of the minor tonic (E-flat minor). The key feeling throughout is fluid, informing the section with a feeling of expectancy.

RECAPITULATION (Meas. 73-123)

This section is orthodox, with the theme heard in the tonic as at the outset. Themes and transitions come back as before, but in the tonic. There is no coda.

MOVEMENT 3

Key:	G Minor
Meter:	Triple
Tempo:	Allegretto
Form:	Da capo ternary; minuet with trio
Orchestra:	Full

Wonderful things happen to the dignified minuet in this movement. The first section is starkly dramatic and displays considerable syncopation.

SECTION A (Meas. 1-42)

EXAMPLE III-31 Theme 1

The theme (example 31) is quite unusual. The tied notes over the bar lines give rise to strong syncopation. The true meter of this first theme is mixed. Example 32 shows how it can be logically notated in alternating duple and triple measures. Apparently Mozart was quite taken with the general contour of this theme, for we encountered a similar effort in his earlier Symphony in G minor (See Chapter 1).

EXAMPLE 32

At measure 14, theme 1 takes on added force as the lower strings and upper woodwinds carry it against a jagged new melodic idea in the violins and bassoons. All this builds through close imitation and strong dissonance. Before the close of the section, however, the energy slackens as the woodwinds cadence softly on the tonic chord.

SECTION B (Trio: Meas. 42-84)

After the stormy originality of the A section the trio comes as a refreshing change. The key is in the parallel major throughout (G Major). Also providing freshness is an orchestral texture much less dense than in the A section. The woodwinds are entrusted with considerable melodic activity and the two horns have their moment too.

REPEAT OF SECTION A

The direction, D. C. Menuetto, at the very end of the trio indicates that all of the first section is to be repeated. As we have noted, it has become traditional in many symphonies for the inner repeats of this returning section to be omitted. Its duration then is considerably shorter.

MOVEMENT 4

Key: G minor
Meter: Duple
Tempo: Allegro assai
Form: Sonata-allegro
Orchestra: Full

EXPOSITION (Meas. 1-124)

Action begins with the very first note of theme 1 (example 33). The strings give out the skyrocketing first motive p and are immediately joined by the full orchestra for an answering

EXAMPLE III-33 Theme 1

82

eighth-note motive, _f_. This alternation of contrasted motives continues for 30 measures, at which point the transition begins, consisting of highly figurative material heard mostly in the strings.

At measures 65 repeated _f_-naturals (the dominant of the new key) in the lower instruments signal the arrival of theme 2 in the upper relative, B-flat Major. This is taken at first by violins and violas, but soon the clarinet and bassoon take over to finish the thought. At measure 101 energetic figures enter in the strings and the full orchestra plunges on to the close of the exposition.

DEVELOPMENT (Meas. 125-206)

This section is one of the most compact ever written by the composer. Strings and wood-winds play in stark unison, outlining diminished seventh chords which give a feeling of incipient eruption and drama. What follows completely satisfies the call for stern, important happenings. Thematic materials used are mostly taken from the first theme of the exposition. These shoot back and forth from different sections of the orchestra in dense contrapuntal texture.

Note the close imitation in the string choir. The harmony is chromatic and adventuresome throughout, adding immeasurably to the feeling of excitement and headlong drive.

RECAPITULATION (Meas. 206-308)

The materials from the exposition return in the expected order. The second theme is now heard in the tonic key, G minor. Mozart, perhaps wishing to inject a fresh note in this rather regular section, alters the second theme considerably. The first violins' line is embroidered by the use of chromatic steps, and expanding chromatic intervals occur shortly afterwards. Adding a particularly poignant touch is the outlined Neapolitan chord at measure 267. Again, the writing for winds is superlative, illustrating the advance that this choir had made towards the end of the Classical period. There is no coda.

Chapter IV

BEETHOVEN AND THE EARLY ROMANTICS

        Ludwig van Beethoven was a transitional composer; his work as a whole is representa-
tive of both 18th century classicism and 19th century romanticism. In that sense he is like
the Scarlattis at the end of the Baroque period, and like Debussy at the end of the Romantic
period.

        Because Beethoven was a Janus figure in music history any attempts to place him within
either a "classic" or a "Romantic" category is fruitless. He was in both at the same time
throughout his creative life. All of his important works show the utmost sensitivity to and
imaginative use of structure and idea as a prime force in composition. On the other hand, such
was the power of subjective emotion and color in his compositions that all important composers
in the Romantic period looked to Beethoven as a generative force in their own creative efforts.

LUDWIG VAN BEETHOVEN

b. Bonn Dec. 16, 1770   d. Vienna March 26, 1827

Characteristic areas of composition:
    Composed in a wide spectrum of instrumental and vocal genres. 9 symphonies, 7 concerti,
9 overtures, 16 string quartets, and other chamber works. 32 piano sonatas, 10 sonatas for
violin and piano, 5 sonatas for violoncello and piano, 20 sets of variations for piano, 1 opera,
2 masses, and 75 lieder.

Important life facts:
    Second son of Johann and Maria Magdalena van Beethoven
1778 First public appearance as performer in Cologne.
1781 Taken out of school to travel, with mother, as child prodigy.
1782 Takes lessons on organ with Neefe and substitutes for him as organist. Publishes
        "Variations on March of Dressler".
1784 Appointed court organist.
1787 Travels to Vienna, mother dies. Meets Mozart.
1789 Member of Court Orchestra in Bonn. Wins petition to have half of father's salary for
        education of his brothers. Father is ordered to leave Bonn.
1792 Leaves Bonn for Vienna. Father dies.
1793 Lessons with Haydn, Albrechtsberger, and Salieri. 3 Piano Trios. Opus 1.
1798 Piano Concerto #1 in C Op. 15.
1800 Performance of Symphony #1 in Hoftheater, Prince Lichnowsky becomes patron.
1801 6 String Quartets, Opus 18, Piano Sonatas Opus 22, 26, and 27, Third Piano Concerto Cm, ballet
        Prometheus, and Christ on the Mount of Olives. Teaches Ries and Czerny.

85

1803 First performance of Kreutzer Sonata, Eroica Symphony. Heiligenstadt Testament.
1804 Napoleon proclaimed Emperor, occupies Vienna where Fidelio is performed.
1806 Nephew Karl born. Violin Concerto, Piano Concerto #4
1807 Mass in C Opus 86, Violin Concerto arranged as piano concerto, Symphony #5
1808 Symphony #6, King Jerome offers appointment in Kassel.
1809 Refuses appointment. Piano sonatas Opus 79 and 81, "Emperor" Piano Concerto.
1811 Patron Lobkowitz declared bankrupt
1812 Symphony #7 and 8, brother Johann marries, patron, Prince Kinsky, dies.
1813 Wellington's Victory Symphony.
1814 Last public appearance as player of chamber music. Meets Anton Schindler, Prince Lichnowsky dies. Third version of Fidelio, Fidelio overture.
1815 Financial settlement with Lobkowitz and Kinsky's estate. Brother Karl dies in Vienna, cantata Meeresstille und Gluckliche Fahrt.
1816 Assumes guardianship of nephew Karl, Lobkowitz dies. Piano Sonata Opus 101.
1817 Lawsuit over Wellington's Victory Symphony with Maelzel settled in Beethoven's favor.
1818 Start of battle with Karl's mother, Karl runs away to mother.
1819 Guardianship changes between Beethoven, von Tuscher, and Karl's mother.
1820 Again Beethoven wins guardianship of Karl from mother.
1821 Beethoven arrested as vagrant. Piano Sonata Opus 110
1822 Rossini visits Beethoven in Vienna. Stops conducting a rehearsal of Fidelio because of his deafness. Missa Solemnis.
1823 Karl returns to live with Beethoven during university studies. Diabelli Variations and Symphony #9
1826 Karl attempts suicide, Beethoven seriously ill. Karl joins Stutterheim Regiment. Sketches for Symphony #10, also to be choral symphony.
1827 After four operations, receives Last Sacrement and dies two days later.

The Symphonies:
Symphony No. I, C major, Op. 21, (1799-1800)
Symphony No. II, D major, Op. 36, (1802)
Symphony No. III, E flat major, Op. 55 "Eroica", (1803)
Symphony No. 4, B flat major, Op. 60, (1806)
Symphony No. 5, C minor, Op. 67, (1805-07)
Symphony No. 6, F major, Op. 68, (1807-08)
Symphony No. 7, A major, Op. 92 (1812)
Symphony No. 8, F major, Op. 93 (1812)
Symphony No. 9, D minor, Op. 125 (1817-23)
   (with chorus and soloists)

With Beethoven comes summary and fruition. Beethoven was close enough to the persons and the music of Haydn and Mozart to imbibe both the tradition and spirit of the late 18th-century symphonic style. He was there, and he looked, heard, and received inner direction for his coming role as synthesizer.

With Beethoven there was also prophecy. As he wove the threads left by his great predecessors into the unique fabric of his art, patterns began to emerge that prefigure much of what was to come in the Romantic age.

Chronologically, there is a rather neat line of descent among the three great figures of the Classical period. Their creative lives are separated by 20 years, more or less: one generation. Haydn reached maturity in the early 1750's; Mozart, in the middle 1770's; and Beethoven, around 1790. There is almost a familial relationship: In a sense they were as spiritual father, son, and grandson.

Symbolic of the "generation gap" operating among the great triumvirate is the matter of the wigs. Haydn, in the employ of the aristocracy for the major part of his adult life, seldom appeared in public without donning the formal wig. Portraits of the boy composer Mozart showed him nattily costumed with wig. He used it most of his life, but the unfinished painting of the composer done by his relative, Lange, in the last year of his life shows him unwigged. The lion-maned Beethoven was wigged only in his youth.

Of more importance were their contrasting attitudes toward the ruling aristocracy. Haydn was quite satisfied with his semi-menial position at Esterhazy. Grove quotes him as saying, "My prince was always satisfied with my works. . . ."*He is also known to have said, " . . . I was eventually given a position as music director to Count Morzin, and following this as Kapellmeister to His Highness Prince Esterhazy; there it is my desire to live and to die." The ever-humble Haydn, mindful of his peasant origins, was grateful for his creative gifts and for the favor shown by his patrons.

Mozart, though he depended somewhat on the nobility, chaffed constantly under them and was quite capable of speaking his mind. Once, when the Emperor Joseph spoke of his music as being overly refined and containing too many notes, Mozart said, "Just as many notes as are necessary, your Majesty." It is doubtful that Haydn would have dared to utter this.

Beethoven himself had many relationships with the aristocracy, but mostly on his own terms. They were allowed to patronize his work. He came to them as an equal.

This marked contrast in the composers' positions and attitudes toward their essential role in society, of course, has its parallel in their music. Haydn expressed his own self; but that self was generally in harmony with its environment. Therefore, there is more serenity and acceptance than there is agony of the soul. Mozart's career was a checkered one. He and his family often suffered agonies of want and deprivation. He died at the age of 35 while writing the Requiem, which he knew was to be his own. He was an easy prey for unscrupulous friends like Stadler, the clarinetist, lending money which he did not have, while at the same time depriving his family of bare necessities. The stories of his procrastination and last-minute flurries of work are charming but typical of the naive disorder that afflicted him always. It was not unusual for him to delay writing out orchestral parts to the overtures of his operas almost up to the moment of performance.

Mozart's music, especially in the late years, often reflects spiritual travail and restless gloom. The Symphony No. 40 is typical. Other tragic moods can be heard in the C minor Fantasie and Sonata for piano, K. 457, and in the second movement of the A Major Piano Concerto, K. 488. In short, we often find a depth, an intensely subjective element in Mozart, which is entirely Romantic.

Beethoven, first and foremost, expressed his self. The music is always subjective, directly representative of his singular personality. The immediate emotion, or the long-sought ideal, of the deeply felt philosophical idea--these were grasped with eager impetuosity and fervor and transformed into the quartets, the concertos, the sonatas, and the nine great symphonies.

With Beethoven, the symphony attains greater scope, both in range of expression and in physical size. The Beethoven symphony is a 19th-century form: The first was finished in 1800, the last in 1826. In fact, very nearly every innovation of the 19th-century symphony can be seen to have had its origin in the Beethoven Nine. Individual symphonies in the Romantic age might be said to equal Beethoven in one respect or other--Brahms in sophistication of form; Mahler in intensity of feeling; Berlioz in instrumentation--but no one composer ever did so much with the form as a whole. Beethoven anticipated cyclic organization in his fifth and ninth symphonies; No. 6 is a program symphony; No. 3 revolutionized the whole concept of symphonic structure by breaking nearly every canon of form extant up to that time. The ninth adds a chorus, a practice with enormous implications for symphonists of the 19th century.

*Encyclopaedia Britannica, Vol. 3 (1957).

Beethoven expands the orchestra through the addition of new instruments and by requiring more players. For all practical purposes, the instrumentation of <u>Symphony No. 9</u> is that of the Romantic symphony. Here Beethoven adds to the standard early Classical orchestra a piccolo, a contrabassoon, two more french horns (making a total of four), three trombones, and a Janissary ensemble of percussion instruments in the finale.

<u>Analysis and Commentary</u>

SYMPHONY NO. 3 IN E-FLAT MAJOR, OP. 55

ORCHESTRA

The orchestra is composed of two flutes, two oboes, two clarinets, two bassoons; three horns, two trumpets; timpani; strings. Except for the third horn, it is no different from that of Haydn and Mozart. However, the sound and concept of the Eroica clearly outdistance the parameters of the Classical orchestra. Obviously this symphony made a true expansion of the orchestra in later Beethoven symphonies absolutely necessary.

GENERAL CHARACTERISTICS

This symphony is totally original for its time. Its formal structure is everywhere fresh and full of surprises, though Classical principles survive. Bold modulations abound and Beethoven does not spare the use of dissonance. Syncopation is consistently heard, giving the rhythm in movements 1, 3, and 4 and unsettled, restive character.

MOVEMENT 1

Key: E-flat Major
Meter: Triple
Tempo: <u>Allegro con brio</u>
Form: Sonata-allegro with coda
Orchestra: Full

EXPOSITION (Meas. 1-155)

Two massive chords replace the slow introduction found in Beethoven's two earlier symphonies. Following these the cellos immediately sally forth with the first theme (example 1). Once the cellos have reached the well-known, disturbing c-sharp in the fifth measure, violins join in with a syncopated motive building to a climax. Meanwhile, the cellos go on to develop the initial motive. Listen for this abrupt flowering of two-part counterpoint after a seemingly innocuous beginning.

The triadic first motive is then quietly sequenced in an upward direction mostly in the winds, leading to a resplendent passage for full orchestra. Here Beethoven seems to be doing his best to stamp out all reference to the basic triple meter. Powerful accents are placed on weak parts of the measure in such a way that groups of two beats are heard instead of the expected three. Making for further turbulence, some of the chords are quite dissonant.

EXAMPLE IV-1 Theme 1

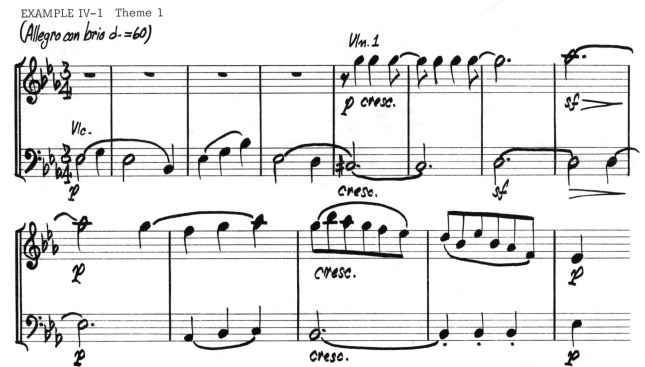

Passages such as this   are a major feature of this movement. There is no question that they exist for a specific purpose. Beethoven seizes every opportunity to wrench the comfortable triple meter asunder, to grind the ear with stark dissonances, to foil every expectation of traditional formal processes. Why? To renew and to liberate. The time had come to reject earlier successful formulas and patterns. What was needed was to inject new content into the aggregate sonata structure, breaking most of the rules, but adhering steadfastly to underlying Classical principles. As we will see, the essential principles of symphonic writing are always rigorously kept: Each movement is cast in a time-honored pattern. And within the movement unity and contrast constantly operate to maximum advantage. The total effect is new, essentially expansive and homogeneous, giving direction and inspiration to many significant composers of the Romantic period.

Once the syncopated passage above has run its course, the full orchestra gives out the initial motive from the first theme, fortissimo. Then there is quiet. A new theme is heard (example 2). Over a dominant pedal of the new key soon to arrive (B-flat Major), a tiny

EXAMPLE IV-2 Theme 2

three-note motive is tossed back and forth in the woodwinds and first violins.

The sunny mood is then rudely broken up as the full orchestra strides down a fortissimo scale leading to another important theme. Here the clarinets play a gently rising line mirrored by the bassoons and lower strings. Soon a powerful new figure enters in the violins built on clipped sixteenths and eighths in sequence. Backing this up, the winds and lower strings play staccato

89

chords which emphasize the strong beat of every second measure. All of this builds to a climax when yet another theme arrives (example 3). Shortly after, Beethoven builds up another violent climax. The strings play <u>staccato</u>, syncopated chords, and finally evolve a scale figure that

EXAMPLE IV-3 Theme 5

rises to the entrance of a new, majestic theme for the full orchestra. Once more the music is shot through with strong accents on weak parts of the measure. The excitement here is tremendous, but more tension lies ahead. The shock in the chords of theme 6 is near-cosmic in scope; Beethoven poses questions and challenges for all men and all time.

After being shaken and prodded by these Herculean gestures, one is tempted to say, "It is enough." But two more themes are yet to appear before the exposition has run its course. Theme 7 is particularly interesting from the harmonic point of view. The chords are chromatic and suggest a certain piquancy often found in Schubert. Theme 8 (example 4) is graphic and

EXAMPLE IV-4 Theme 8

uncompromisingly rough. Note the violent dissonance produced by the superimposed contrasted chords.

EXAMPLE IV-4a

Obviously there are an unusual number of themes in this exposition section. Rarely if ever would eight distinct and contrasting themes be found in the expositions of Haydn and Mozart. One is struck also by the brief, succinct nature of these themes. All of this is quite unusual and underlines the revolutionary character of the work as a whole. By writing themes that are simple and plastic, and transitions that become highly potent dramatic links, Beethoven obliterates the old differentiation between theme and transition. Every note is suffused with interest: everything is transition. In that sense Beethoven anticipates Wagner and his concept

of continuous melody in the lyric drama. Also anticipating Wagner is the use of a true
<u>steigerung</u>: The music moves with a wavelike motion, achieving crest after majestic peak.

DEVELOPMENT (Meas. 152-398)

The scope of this section is vast. Considering its length, 248 measures, surprisingly few
themes from the exposition are utilized: the first, the second, and the fourth. Of these, only
the first can be considered a theme in the traditional sense, at least in terms of extension and
phrase structure. In addition to these, however, Beethoven introduces an entirely new theme
midway through the development. It is highly lyric--in fact, the only truly lyric theme of the
whole movement. This idea serves as a rest point, an island of peace in the churning sweep
of sound.

The section begins very quietly with a dragging fragment derived from the rhythmic pattern
of theme 1. Soon the motive from theme 2 is heard. But injected into the polyphonic texture
is a new figure consisting of an accented long note followed by a rising <u>staccato</u> scale.
The mood is light and airy.

The first motive from theme 1 enters in the minor and is sequenced up with <u>crescendo</u>,
culminating in the first stormy passage of the development. Here one begins to see a further
reason for the motivic character of the themes in the exposition. Beethoven creates a mood
of crushing intensity by combining the first motive from theme 1 with the motive from theme 4.
As we shall see throughout this section, only plain, plastic motives allow for the kind of
contrapuntal mosaic Beethoven intends. The basic motive from theme 1 is heard in diminution;
it begins softly but leads to a repetition of the passage, this time a fourth higher, in the key
of G minor.

At measure 220 the opening passage of the development section is heard again, at first in
A-flat Major but soon modulating to and reaching the key of F minor. Here begins what is perhaps the most powerful passage in the whole work. The motive from theme 2, which up to now
has been the vehicle for rather playful music, becomes the basis for a fugato. The dynamic
accent on the second beat adds to the feeling of imminent eruption. Comparing the use of the
motive here with its original shape we see that Beethoven has stretched the original interval
of a second to that of a sixth. As the tension builds, the interval is stretched further to an
octave, and this, grafted onto syncopated chords in the full orchestra, continues to build
relentlessly to a climax. The climax comes with shrieking chordal dissonances. Note how
Beethoven seizes upon the interval of the minor second, the most dissonant of intervals, as
the vehicle for his climax.

Typically, Beethoven swerves away from the expected crash in the tonic (here E minor) and
ushers in <u>p</u>, for the first time, his new theme (Th. x). Its grace and charm, being totally unexpected,
is magical in this context. The peaceful mood so beautifully achieved is short lived. Inter-
rupting, <u>forte</u>, is the basic motive from theme 1 with a new motive grafted on. The transformation of this motive into something remembered but somehow new illustrates the fecundity of
Beethoven's melodic thought. Theme x reenters in the exotic key of E-flat minor, slips on in

EXAMPLE IV-5 Theme x

G-flat Major, and exits quietly to make way for the final buildup of the development. While the winds play imitative passages built on the principal motive from theme 1, the lower strings mount sequentially with a broken chord figure, _staccato_.

Here one fully expects an increase in intensity, with the section going straight to its goal, and a powerful restatement of theme 1 in the recapitulation. But no. The music drops to a hushed whisper as a fragment of theme 1 in diminution is heard. Finally, dominant harmonies are heard, but unaccountably very softly. All this is due to Beethoven's dramatic purpose. As the strings dissolve into the root and seventh of the dominant seventh chord, the first horn surreptitiously sounds the principal motive underneath in the _tonic key_. This is a clear example of the use of a polychord, and again shows Beethoven as a revolutionary and prophet. As it turns out, this "false" entry of the motive is only a last-minute, breathless anticipation of the full statement of the first theme, which appears three measures later. There is no question that Beethoven with this anticipation wished to blur the normal passage of the development into the recapitulation, to hide the seams of his structure. Again he destroys comfortable formulas in the sonata-allegro structure and gives us instead a massive, continuous, unbroken stream of melos.

RECAPITULATION (Meas. 398-557)

Except for a solo by the first horn near the beginning, the recapitulation is formally regular. All of the themes come back in the expected order and most of the music is in the home key, E-flat Major. The transitional passage between first and second themes is shortened considerably, but otherwise this section provides a respite from the wild happenings of the development.

CODA (Meas. 558-691)

The role of this coda is unusual. Before Beethoven the coda often served quite simply to punctuate the music with an emphatic statement of the principal theme supported by dominant-tonic harmony. It usually had been short and to the point, a strong close. But in this coda Beethoven creates an epilogue, an afterstatement, a second development fully as important as anything heard in the three sections before. Starting with the soft, bare tonic octave at the conclusion of the recapitulation, the music suddenly sags down a whole tone to a D-flat Major chord. This is precisely the sort of whole-tone shift that is so often heard in music at the turn of the 20th century. Again, prophecy.

Theme 1 sounds in the strings. Then, another sag into C Major with another sounding of the motive, this time forte. At this point, the second violins carry the motive while a brand new skittering motive is combined above it in the first violins. Soon theme x enters, first in the supertonic key, F minor, and then in the tonic minor, E-flat minor. Theme 1 returns, this time in the solo horn with yet a new counterpoint derived from theme 4 above.

From this playful badinage the music grows into a mood of grandeur, with theme 1 in the lower strings and the counterpoint carried by all the woodwinds. This would have provided the usual composer with a tight, ready-made ending. But there is yet one more surprise. The music quiets and Beethoven, as if he were telling us that all of his themes are important, brings back the rather inconspicuous theme 3 just before the final crashing chords.

MOVEMENT 2--MARCIA FUNEBRE

Key: C minor
Meter: Duple
Tempo: _Adagio assai_
Form: Large ternary, ABA, with coda
Orchestra: Full

92

PART A (Meas. 1-68)

EXAMPLE IV-6 Theme 1

The first violins play the first three notes of theme 1 at the lowest possible pitch of their range. This passage is perhaps symbolic of the "out of the depths" mood of the movement as a whole. Listen for the intense harmony, with diminished seventh chords supporting the melody at strategic places. Also note the rhythmic figure in the lower strings, suggestive of the death march.

Once the theme has been presented by the violins, the solo oboe gives it out an octave higher. At the peak of the oboe's wail, on its climatic note, a-flat, the lower strings drop to a significant b-flat, initiating a turn into the relative key, E-flat Major. The strings start a new theme, suffused with a feeling of quiet faith. But at the fourth measure, a sharp dominant seventh chord shatters this mood, and leads to a return to the original somber key of C minor. A new figure takes over in the cellos and ushers in a modulation to the subdominant key. Theme 1 is begun by the first violins, but soon falters and again gives way to the peaceful theme 2, this time in the woodwinds led by the solo oboe.

So far, what we have heard is a kind of pensive dialogue between the two given themes, as if the forces of life and death, hope and despair, were vying for supremacy. The outcome of the struggle is soon settled. Theme 1 returns in the oboe, which in its turn gives way to another tragic theme, the last of part A (example 7). The stark, uncompromising cadence consists of

EXAMPLE IV-7 Theme 3

bare, descending octaves, jolted by syncopated accents.

PART B (Meas. 69-104)

Treading very softly, the cellos and basses rise on a scale from the dominant to the tonic of the new key, C Major, and theme 4 enters. If the prevailing effect of part A is that of brooding melancholy, that of part B is certainly one of release. Though the thematic materials of this theme are very slight and unassuming, the texture is nevertheless intricate. Note the imitation on two levels at once. Oboe and flute interchange on the triadic motive, while the lower strings dialogue on an even plainer idea. All the while, gently undulating triplets in the violins propel the movement forward.

Suddenly at the eighth measure, powerful blasts in the full orchestra shatter the mood of serenity. Theme 4 returns, altered and leading on in an extended, relaxed passage. Towards the close of part B, the orchestra again interrupts violently, this time dispelling all hope of peace. Bleak octaves, similar to those at the close of part A, peremptorily usher in the return of part A and theme 1.

PART A (Varied Return; Meas. 106-209)

Here Beethoven fulfills the traditional ternary pattern by bringing back the materials heard in the first part of the movement. But there are immense and significant modifications. Perhaps feeling that part B, in its sunny optimism, endangered the ultimate tragic mood of the whole movement, Beethoven greatly expands the return of part A.

Injected soon after the return of theme 1 is a passage of extreme intensity and pathos. Built on a new, short seminal motive, there begins a fugato (example 8). For inexorable, crushing power, this passage can hardly be matched in the Beethoven literature.

EXAMPLE IV-8

The motive from theme 1 enters in G minor. It is carried by the first violins, who find themselves perched on a bare high a-flat. The cellos and basses stamp heavily on the same note four octaves below, and are then joined by the rest of the strings who introduce triplets in sixteenths. As it turns out these will provide a new background for the full presentation of theme 1 in the tonic, C minor. Note how these triplets accented on the off-beat add to the pathos inherent to the theme itself. Further note the accompaniment figure in the bass. This provides the degree of unity needed for the new texture.

All of the other materials return, each modified by the addition of new background figures.

94

CODA (Meas. 209-247)

The coda begins very quietly with <u>staccato</u> notes in the violins. An elegiac, soft theme is heard. It soon becomes rhythmically disjointed and dissolves into delicate sequences. Further agonized wails sound in the oboe and clarinet playing octaves over triplets in the first violins. Ultimately, theme 1 returns--as it must (example 9). But this time it is itself dissolved and fragmented. It begins, tortured and torn, and finally settles on the doleful tonic--at rest.

EXAMPLE IV-9

MOVEMENT 3--SCHERZO

Key: E-flat Major
Meter: Triple
Tempo: <u>Allegro vivace</u>
Form: Ternary, ABA (scherzo with trio)
Orchestra: Full

The sap of life runs strong in this movement. At the outset of the work, near the very beginning of the first movement, when a trembling c-sharp is reached by the cellos, we already know that quest, challenge, and search will come. We know that, at the time this work was composed in Heiligenstat, there could be no question of Beethoven's approaching deafness. We know too that his spiritual travail and inner search led him to contemplate suicide, such was the agony wrought by his realization of his incipient loss of hearing.

The second movement the "Funeral March," is a lyric soliloquy, symbolizing Beethoven's and everyman's certain confrontation with death. Through it, Beethoven peers into the abyss and faces the ultimate terminal fact common to all. In terms of his life experience there is no question that this movement holds the key to his continual spiritual development. Perhaps it was in this Funeral March that he became convinced of the potential glory and transfiguration possible for all men through suffering and a fearless, positive contemplation of death. With Montaigne he would have agreed that "to philosophise is to learn to die."

The scherzo symbolizes Beethoven's supreme discovery that human creativity indeed might possibly increase in depth and intensity in inverse proportion to personal tragedy and suffering.

PART A (Meas. 1-163)

Beethoven marks his first idea, <u>sempre pianissimo e staccato</u>. Springing mysteriously

95

out of a void, the strings give out an indeterminate, oscillating figure. The actual rhythmic grouping is in twos, not threes as the time signature indicates. Not until measure 7 do we hear a clear-cut melody, in the solo oboe and first violins. Beethoven has begun with a nervous tremor, a hint of the springing vitality and surge that soon will come.

At measure 31 the skittering begins anew, in a new key and this time with the flute joining the first violins in the wispy tune. The last part of this is then tossed about in imitation from violas to second violins, but soon the indeterminate skittering returns. This time the music picks up momentum as more and more instruments join in. A sudden, one-measure crescendo finds the wisp of a tune now ecstatically trumpeted by the full orchestra (example 10).

EXAMPLE IV-10

This climax is what Beethoven has been aiming at from the first measure. There is further imitative work in the strings until all of the strings, in fiercely syncopated octaves, plunge down an arpeggiated tonic chord. Woodwinds and horns answer. Once this is stated again in the full orchestra, part A closes on a note of triumphant joy.

TRIO (Meas. 167-260)

Though he has added a third French horn, Beethoven retains the traditional thinning out of instruments in the trio. The three horns at first play by themselves and are answered by light fragments in the strings and oboes. Trumpets and drums are entirely absent.

After the full presentation of the quasi-hunt style theme (example 11), the action turns to the woodwinds and the strings. Much of the time open actaves sound, again pointing to a

EXAMPLE IV-11

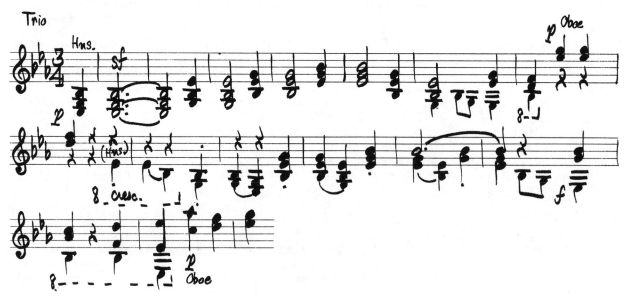

96

thinned texture.

PART A (Return of Scherzo; Meas. 254-422)

This return is nearly a carbon copy of the first part. The only change occurs at measure 381, where the meter abruptly changes to duple and the plunging figure strides straight downhill without the previous syncopated hobble. The insertion of four measures of slightly different music obviates the possibility of a straight <u>da capo</u> structure. (See the minuets of Haydn's No. 88, and Mozart's No. 40). Undoubtedly it would have been much easier to indicate a rereading of the initial A section. It attests to Beethoven's superb sense of vital detail that the changed four measures in duple meter <u>had</u> to come, despite the necessity for more paper.

CODA (Meas. 423-442)

This is brief and to the point; the three horns lead the way via emphatic dominant-tonic chords.

MOVEMENT 4

Key:	E-flat Major
Meter:	Duple
Tempo:	<u>Allegro molto</u>
Form:	Theme and variations
Orchestra:	Full

If the scherzo of this symphony represents rejuvenation and vitality, the finale represents creative power of cosmic force. The basic structure--theme and variations--was a form well used by most of the giants before Beethoven.

At this point in the <u>Eroica</u> Beethoven faced a great artistic challenge. The problem was one of success. The first three movements were thoroughly original, each one reaching the limits of human creative potential. The massive first movement posed questions and hurled challenges; the second bared ultimate reality and the final private truth; the third was a shout of joy, an hallelujah. What then for a finale? Would it be possible to express greater viatality than that of the scherzo? Would it be possible to write another sonata-allegro form with a force equal and even superior to that of the first movement? No. Beethoven grasped that what was needed was a different structure, one that represented the fundamental compositional process of identity with change: theme and variations. It would be in this form that Beethoven's Protean fecundity of musical thought could range the farthest, could fulfill the mighty strivings heard in earlier movements.

INTRODUCTION (Meas. 1-11)

Without ceremony strings alone charge down electric scales to stop on dominant chords, thus announcing massive happenings to come.

MEASURES 12-43

A theme is heard, plastic and unassuming, in unadorned octaves (example 12).

EXAMPLE IV-12 Theme 1a

VARIATION 1 (Meas. 44-59).

Variation 1 is quiet. Above and below theme 1a, now fleshed out in halfnotes, short obbligato figures are subtly woven.

VARIATION 2 (Meas. 60-75)

Considerable motion informs the second variation. A new counterpoint is added to theme 1a.

VARIATION 3 (Meas. 76-107)

Variation 3 introduces what at first seems to be a new theme. Indeed it is new--but not entirely. A glance at the bass to this new idea (example 13), shows that theme 1a is sounding at the same time. It is not that the new theme (which we will label 1b) is cast as a newly created counterpoint to theme 1a. Rather Beethoven now reveals to us for the first time the complete theme. What was heard at the beginning was simply the bass of the total idea.

EXAMPLE IV-13

One suspects a joke. Did Beethoven deliberately give the bass followed by two variations to fool his listeners? Is this a bit of musical mischief? Is the composer introducing a surprise theme (theme 1b), one that his listeners perhaps had known from his previous compositions? (Beethoven had used this same theme before in the ballet, The Creatures of Prometheus, and in the Piano Variations, Op. 35)   No. Rather is he exposing separately essential constituent elements of his theme--soprano and bass--so that later developments of both will be clearly understood.

To Beethoven, all structural elements were of equal importance: melodies, basses, transitional figures, rhythmic patterns, chordal progressions. Beethoven had no intention of examining with variation techniques the ornamental possibilities of a simple strand of tune, as he had done several times earlier and as innumerable composers had done before. Here he examines the total texture of the theme and derives from it those elements that suit him best to elaborate his masterful formal design.

VARIATION 4 (Meas. 117-174)

The first of two contrapuntal variations then begins. It starts as a fugato built on a subject derived from theme 1a. Against it is heard the fragment introduced in the first variation. A climax is gained leading quickly into variation 5.

VARIATION 5 (Meas. 175-210)

    After the thick web of sound achieved in variation 4, Beethoven thins out the texture for a light, homophonic section. At first the solo flute and first violins lead with theme 1b in the remote key of B minor. Then brilliant scale and arppeggio passages pass from the first violins to the solo flute. In turn, these give way to eighth-note triplets in all the strings, effecting a modulation to G minor.

VARIATION 6 (Meas. 210-256)

    Again the listener is faced with a puzzle. A brand new theme enters (example 14), swash-

EXAMPLE IV-14

buckling in character and reminiscent of the "Turkish" music much favored by Haydn and Mozart. At first hearing one fails to perceive the relevance of this strikingly contrasted melodic idea. But as one listens deeper, one recognizes clearly the basic motive from theme 1a sturdily underlining the new theme. It is as if Beethoven were saying, "You see, this bass theme is so fundamental to all harmonic experience that I could invent any number of new themes for it to accompany." Throughout this variation there is immense storm and stress, the theme leaping ahead with wild abandon.

VARIATION 7 (Meas. 257-276)

    This variation is very slight, serving really as a bridge to variation 8, which is long and dense with counterpoint. It is based on theme 1b.

VARIATION 8 (Meas. 277-348)

    This variation consists of another fugato using the same subject as the fugal fourth variation. This time, however, the subject is inverted and is accompanied by running scale passages.

99

Also, theme 1b is now heard as a counterpoint, once in the flutes and later in the horns. As in variation 4, much excitement is generated.

At the pinnacle of its drive the variation settles on a strong half cadence in the tonic key, E-flat Major. There is a pause and then variation 9 begins.

VARIATION 9 (Meas. 349-380)

Here there is a total change of mood: Calm and serenity reign for a long span. The graceful music of theme 1b now is transformed into a passage of great depth. The woodwinds, led by the oboes, carry the idea at first, but then strings and horns take over. Note the close harmony permeated with tense diminished seventh chords. Again the music builds through crescendo and the next variation arrives.

VARIATION 10 (Meas. 381-430)

The music continues in the sedate tempo of the previous variation. Horns lead in a presentation of theme 1b, which in melodic contour is much the same as it was when originally presented in variation 3. But, because of the tempo change and new luxuriant accompaniment, the mood is one suffused with great majesty. At the termination of theme 1b, the variation is extended considerably, with the sixteenth-note triplets from the beginning of the variation arching on and on. At measure 420 the texture thins out, the sixteenth-note triplets are heard staccato and syncopated over a pedal on the note g. Everything becomes hushed, tremulous, and expectant. At measure 430 the final explosion arrives.

CODA   (Meas. 431-473)

The tempo indication here is presto, suggesting that Beethoven conceived this concluding variation to be a coda. (It had become almost conventional in the Classical period for the final variation in these forms to be played in a quicker tempo than any before, giving a feeling of summation.) The rushing scales from the beginning of the movement are heard again and serve to usher in the final sounding of theme 1b. The horns, prominent in the whole symphony, now lead. The mood is ecstatic. Twenty-one measures of tonic harmony signal that the symphony has ended.

EARLY ROMANTIC SYMPHONISTS

Changes of attitude and of expression from period to period do not occur in an environmental vacuum. A composer and his work reflect and complement the total web and texture of his time. The age of Romanticism saw unique developments in many areas.

Jacques Barzun in Darwin, Marx and Wagner, defines Romanticism as ". . . a constructive effort after a great revolution which had leveled off old institutions and old nations-- including the mechanical materialism of the eighteenth century. Romanticism . . . valued individual freedom, subjective feeling, human reason, social purpose, and above all, art."

Individual freedom was indeed a leading motive in the 19th century. The French and American revolutions had occurred in its name. Later, in the 1800's. Garibaldi was to strike again and again for freedom in Italy.

Beethoven symbolized all of this, both in his life and in his music. He brought to climax and fruition everything before him and in that process strewed about important clues for those following. Four early symphonists picked up these clues: Schubert, Mendelssohn, Schumann, and Berlioz.

Franz Peter Schubert

b. Vienna January 31, 1797
d. Vienna November 19. 1828

Characteristic areas of composition:
   13 operas and operettas (4 incomplete), 7 masses and other religious works including
2 Stabat Mater's, and Magnificat, 9 cantatas, other choral works with piano accompaniment,
28 unaccompanied male choral works, 8 symphonies, 10 overtures, concertstück for violin
and orchestra, 21 string quartets, plus other chamber works, 61 works for solo piano including
22 sonatas, numerous works for piano duet, and over 600 songs.

Father, Franz Theodor Schubert, schoolmaster
Mother, Elisabeth Vietz, domestic servant

Taught violin by father and piano by elder brother

1807 Taught by Michael Holzer, organist in Liechtenthal, piano, violin, organ, singing
        and harmony.
1808 Choir boy in court chapel and scholar in Imperial and Royal Seminary. Made concert-
        master of student orchestra, Salieri his teacher.
1812 Mother dies. Early string quartets and overtures for orchestra.
1813 Leaves Royal Seminary. Symphony in D major. Enters training school for teachers.
1814 Teaches at father's school. Mass in F, song Gretchen am Spinnrade.
1815 Symphony in Bb, Symphony in D, Mass in G and Mass in Bb. Operettas, song Erlkönig.
1816 Symphony in C "Tragic", Prometheus cantata, first commissioned work, Symphony 5 Bb,
        Mass in C, 3 Sonatas for Violin and Piano. Der Wanderer.
1817 The Erlkönig sent to Breitkopf and Hartel, confused with a Franz Schubert of Dresden
        who emphatically denies composing it. Six Piano Sonatas. Returns to teaching at
        father's school. Overtures "in the Italian Style", Der Tod und das Mädchen and Die
        Forelle. Accepts offer as music-master to the children of Count Johann Esterhazy,
        including Karoline, at Zseliz in Hungary. Composes Deutsche Trauermesse, brother
        Ferdinand receives credit for the composition. Esterhazy family, with Schubert,
        returns to Vienna.
1819 Journeys with Vogl to Steyr, Austria. Trout Quintet commissioned. Journeys to Linz.
1820 Arrested with a group of students at Johann Senn's (a friend) house.
1821 Twenty songs published by Cappi and Diabelli including Erlkönig, Der Wanderer,
        Der Tod und das Mädchen and Gretchen am Spinnerade. Meets Weber in Vienna.
1822 Writes a variation for Diabelli's set of variations on an original theme. Wanderer
        fantasy. Symphony in B minor "unfinished". Contracts syphillis, lives with father
        at Rossau. Opera Alphonso und Estrella.
1823 Sells all rights Opus 1 to Opus 14 to Diabelli. Breaks away from firm. Admitted to
        Vienna General Hospital. Elected honorary member of Linz Musical Society. Die
        Schöne Mullerin. Incidental music to Rosamunde.
1824 Returns to Zseliz for summer. String Quartet Dm "Death and the Maiden".
1825 Mass in C, Piano Sonata in Am. Reliquie". Songs from Scott's "Lady of the Lake"
        including Ave Maria.
1826 Song "Sylvia." Vogl marries.
1827 Sixty songs are given by Schindler to Beethoven. Schubert visits Beethoven, a week
        later Beethoven dies, Schubert is one of the torch bearers in the funeral procession.
        Resumes negotiations with Diabelli. Elected as representative to the Vienna Philharmonic
        Society. Winterreise, Impromptus Opus 90 and 142, Moment Musicaux Opus 94.
1928 Symphony in C "Great", Auf dem Strom. Dies of typhoid, many works to be published
        posthumously.

The symphonies:

1813 Symphony No. I, D major
1815 Symphony No. II, in B flat major
1815 Symphony in D major
1816 Symphony in C minor (Tragic)
1816 Symphony in B flat Major
1818 Symphony in C major
1822 Symphony in B minor. This is the "Unfinished" Symphony. It was not performed
        until 1865, many years after Schubert's death.
1828 Symphony in C major, The Great

SCHUBERT

Franz Schubert, though a younger man, was actually a contemporary of Beethoven. He was born in 1797, at the time when Beethoven had reached artistic maturity, and died in 1828, only one year after the master. Schubert was awed by Beethoven, though the latter approved of the music of the younger man.

The element that distinguishes the symphonic thought of Schubert is the lyric. The structure of his symphonies, with the exception of the finely balanced Symphony No. 5 in B-flat Major, suffers somewhat from redundancy and prolixity. But there is always an abundance of tunefulness and harmonic color.

A good example of this is the Symphony in C Major, The Great, in which Beethoven's influence is patent. Witness the basic theme of the scintillating scherzo (example 15).

EXAMPLE IV-15   Schubert, Symphony in C, third movement

Here is truly Beethovenesque verve and dynamism. At the counterstatement of this theme Schubert twists abruptly from the initial tonal path, C Major, and veers toward an unexpected B-flat Major.

Soon afterwards Schubert's irrepressible urge toward the lyric asserts itself and we find the violins gamboling about with a tune strongly suggestive of the Landler, a country waltz. The cello, at the third measure, answers with a fragment of the tune while the winds back it up with wisps of the initial melody.

The second movement, a surprisingly long andante con moto, begins with an introductory tune (example 16) that might easily pass for the main tune, except that the true theme (example 16a) soon assumes the lead at measure 8. In Schubert even introductory material is charmingly lyric.

102

EXAMPLE IV-16

EXAMPLE IV-16a

Felix Mendelssohn (Jakob Ludwig)

b. Hamburg February 3, 1809
d. Leipzig November 4, 1847

Characteristic areas of composition:

8 operas (5 unpublished and 1 unfinished), religious works including Te Deum and nine cantatas and oratorios (4 unpublished), 7 concert overtures, 4 piano concerti (2 unpublished), 2 violin concerti (1 unpublished), 2 concerti for two pianos, 1 concerto for violin and piano, 3 smaller works for piano and orchestra, 3 piano quartets, 7 string quartets, 2 string quintets, 2 piano trios, string octet, 4 sonatas for piano and cello, 3 sonatas for violin and piano, numerous solo works for piano and organ, 93 songs including 12 duets, 17 symphonies (12 unpublished).

Grandfather, Moses Mendelssohn, merchant, literarian and philosopher.
Father, Abraham Mendelssohn, prosperous banker
Mother, Lea Salomon
Sister, Fanny Cecile Mendelssohn, amateur composer and pianist.

Early music studies from mother.
1816 Journey to Paris, piano lessons for Fanny and Felix
1818 First public appearance in a piano trio at Berlin
1819 Enters Singakademie in Berlin

103

1821 Three one act operettas, meets Goethe. String Symphonies.
1822 Journey with family to Switzerland. C minor Quartet Opus 1.
1823 Concerto for two pianos and orchestra.
1824 Confirmed. Symphony #1 Cm.
1825 To Paris, meets Cherubini, Halevy, Rossini, and Meyerbeer. String Quartet in B minor Opus 3, dedicated to Goethe, returning from Paris meets Goethe and plays quartet for him. Octet for Strings, Trumpet Overture premiered, Mendelssohn plays piano in Beethoven's Choral Fantasie on same program. Opera Die Hochzeit des Gamacho Opus 10.
1826 Midsummer Night's Dream Overture.
1827 Attends University of Berlin lectures by Hegel. Mendelssohn aware of "historical role of Teutonic race."
1828 Studies Handel. String Quartet in A Opus 13.
1829 Presents revival of Bach's St. Matthew Passion, a success. Fanny engaged to Hensel (painter). Journey to England and Scotland--to the Hebrides. Reformation Symphony, opera Die Heimkehr aus der Fremde Opus 89.
1831 To Italy meets Mozart's son Wolfgang. G minor Piano Concerto Opus 25. First version of Die erste Walpurgisnacht Op. 60. Goethe dies. Second journey to London.
1832 Final version of Hebrides Overture. Meeresstille und glückliche Fahrt, Op. 27.
1833 Italian Symphony.
1834 Elected to Berlin Academy of Fine Arts. Rondo Brilliant for Piano and Orchestra Opus 29.
1835 Accepts offer to conduct at Gewandhaus in Leipzig. Father dies.
1836 Receives honorary doctorate for University of Leipzig. St. Paul Oratorio.
1837 Marries Cecile Charlotte Sophia Jeanrenaud, daughter of deceased minister of French Reformed Church. Six Preludes and Fugues for Piano Opus 35, and Three Preludes and Fugues for Organ Opus 37, Piano concerto in D minor Opus 40. Third trip to England.
1840 Appointed Kapellmeister in Berlin. Variations Serieuses.
1841 Partially resigns from Leipzig, to London.
1842 Scottish Symphony dedicated to Queen Victoria. Mother dies.
1843 Commissioned by Frederick Wilhelm to compose Te Deum for one thousandth anniversary of empire. Final version of Die erste Walpurgisnacht.
1844 Six Organ Sonatas Opus 65.
1846 Elijah. Through overwork from conducting, composing, and performing, health deteriorates.
1847 Fanny dies, a severe blow. String Quartet in F minor, Opus 80, memorial to Fanny. Mendelssohn dies, national mourning.

The symphonies:

11 symphonies
These are early works, unpublished in Mendelssohn's lifetime but now available on discs.
Symphony No. 1, C Minor, Op. 11 (1824)
Symphony No. 2, "Hymn of Praise", Op. 52 (1840)
Really a symphony-cantata. Chorus and orchestra.
Symphony No. 3, A Minor, Op. 56, "Scottish" (1842)
Symphony No. 4, A Major, Op. 90, "Italian", (1833)
Symphony No. 5, D Major, Op. 107, "Reformation", (1831)

Felix Mendelssohn wrote five symphonies, frequently adding a descriptive title, as in No. 4, the Italian, and No. 5, The Reformation. All are informed with a masterful sense of logic and structural coherence. Whereas Schubert was at his best in smaller forms such as the lied, Mendelssohn possessed superb intellectual capacity for marshalling large structures into balanced wholes. His was a mind of universal scope. The scion of a

104

wealthy, erudite, highly cultured Jewish family, he was given every advantage to develop
his critical and creative faculties. He was a classical scholar, spoke and read several
languages, could draw exceedingly well, and was noted for the verve and polished erudition
of his conversation. Added to this was a strong native musical talent. Like Mozart, he
was a prodigy in both performance and composition. The Violin Sonata in F minor, written
when he was 16, is incredibly sophisticated, suggesting that he attained his true life
style at an early age. The overture to his Midsummer Night's Dream, written the following
year, is acknowledged as an unsurpassed piece of its kind.

Mendelssohn was at his greatest in gossamer pieces, such as the scherzo from his
Octet in E-flat for Strings, Op. 20. The Symphony No. 4, the Italian, shows the composer at
his finest, with a precise blend of elegance and deftness. There is no attempt at deep
probing or questing. But there is dash, charm, and vivacity.

The Symphony No. 5, the Reformation, attempts to achieve high drama and to communicate
important, serious things. Its orchestra is larger than that of No. 4: three trombones and
contrabassoon are added to the usual winds in pairs. The outer movements show a most
serious mien, and it is in them that two melodies associated with the early Lutheran Church
are heard: the Dresden Amen and "Ein feste Burg." The Dresden Amen (example 17) is
heard for the first time in the piece toward the close of the introduction in the first move-

EXAMPLE IV-17 Mendelssohn, Symphony No. 5, Op. 107, Reformation, First movement

ment. This is followed by a stormy, sturdy theme in D minor, showing rock-like force and
determination (example 18).

EXAMPLE IV-18

Following is a closely knit sonata-allegro form in the Classical tradition but dis-
playing little of the dynamism and drive found in the Beethoven symphonies. The finale is
built around the familiar Lutheran hymn, "Ein feste Burg." Clad in rather chaste colors,
it first appears in the woodwinds (example 19). Progressively the hymn tune permeates all

of the orchestra until the initial theme of the main body of the movement enters (example 20).

EXAMPLE IV-20

Throughout the movement the sturdy hymn tune crops up, adding an element of homogeneity and oneness to the form. At the end, the whole orchestra trumpets out the hymn, lending a grand dignity and a kind of ecclesiastical sobriety to the whole.

ANALYSIS AND COMMENTARY

Symphony No. 4, A major, Op. 90, "Italian", Movement 1

Orchestra:
2 flutes, 2 oboes, 2 clarinets, 2 bassoons; 2 horns, 2 trumpets; timpani; strings.

The orchestra here is the same as the one used by Beethoven in his first two symphonies. It is essentially a classical orchestra; modest by the standards of most romantic composers.

General Style:
This blithe, elegant work is one of the masterpieces of the romantic century. It is as clear and pellucid in texture as the best Mozart and Haydn. Without revolutionizing musical form, it nevertheless attains complete freshness within traditional structural molds. It also is as lyric as anything written in the period. Though it is labelled "Italian," it is not a nationalistic symphony. It does, however, capture the spirit of Italy through its rhythms and quasi-folksong melody. J. Wolff, one of the composer's biographers, considered that

this work was, "drenched in the splendour of the southern sun."

MOVEMENT 1

Key: A major
Meter: Compound
Tempo: Allegro vivace
Form: Sonata-allegro with coda
Orchestra: Full

EXPOSITION: (Meas. 1-186)

This happy movement has no slow introduction; it begins in bright tempo, allegro vivace. The first thing you hear is a tonic chord in the strings, pizzicato, followed by swift, repeated notes in the high woodwinds. At measure 2, to the accompaniment of the woodwinds, the violins play Theme 1:

EXAMPLE IV-21

Shortly you hear Theme 1 again, but this time much louder. Then begins an important structural event, the transition from Theme 1 to Theme 2. Listen for three things:
  1. Dialogue between woodwinds and strings
  2. Modulation, preparing for the new key (E major), the dominant.
  3. The basic motive of Theme 1 heard first in the cellos and basses, then in the violins.

107

Quiet and lyric, Theme 2, arrives, played by the clarinet and bassoon. Once Theme 2 is repeated by the violins, a very brief transition leads to the closing theme of the exposition section, Theme 3.

Though not exactly the same, Theme 3 is similar to Theme 1. They both are built on the same three-note motive (do-mi-so). Compare Theme 1 with Theme 3, but remember that they are in different keys: Theme 1 in the tonic (A major), and Theme 3 in the dominant (E major).

DEVELOPMENT: (Meas. 187-346)

The development section begins with the unexpected. Instead of hearing one of the ideas from the exposition section, you will hear a new theme:

EXAMPLE IV-22 Theme X

Follow the course of this march-like theme presented in different keys and in different instruments. At one point in its journey the three-note motive from Theme 1 (example 21) interrupts and then joins in. This leads to a climax where the whole orchestra thunders out Theme X. The dynamic level then drops. Again using the three-note motive from Theme 1, the composer gradually returns to the recapitulation section through a dramatic crescendo.

RECAPITULATION (Meas. 346-481)

Listen for the return of Themes 1 and 2, this time both in the tonic key, A major. After this you would normally expect to hear Theme 3 as you did in the exposition. But before it returns, Mendelssohn slips in Theme X from the development. Obviously, the composer had planned his march-like Theme X as a regular member of his thematic cast, but had omitted its entrance in the exposition in order to provide a fresh, new idea for the development.

Theme 3 (now Theme 4) does appear, in its proper place at the end of the recapitulation as it had been at the end of the exposition.

CODA (Meas. 490-563)

The coda begins immediately with the three-note motive from Theme 1 in the winds answered twice by Theme X in the strings. All of this is loud and brilliant. Then the first violins soften, drop down the scale and skitter about as an accompaniment to a fresh new theme played by the second violins. This smoothly articulated coda theme is gentle and lyric. And last, the dynamic level rises, references to Themes 1 and 2 are heard, and the movement ends with several strong tonic chords.

Robert Schumann

b. Zwickau, Germany June 8, 1810
d. Endernich near Bonn July 29, 1856

Characteristic areas of composition:
    2 operas, one unfinished, 17 choral works, 4 symphonies, requiem mass, 6 overtures,
4 piano concerti only one complete, cello concerto, violin concerto, 2 piano quartets,
3 string quartets, 3 piano trios, 1 piano quintet, 3 sonatas for piano and violin, other
chamber works, numerous piano solo works including 7 collections, character pieces and
3 sonatas, 6 organ fugues, 259 solo songs, 17 duets with piano and 72 part songs.

Father, August Schumann bookseller, publisher and author
Mother, Johanna Christiana

1816 Sent to a private school, average student, piano lessons from J G. Kuntzsch
1819 Hears Mozart's Die Zauberflöte and pianist Moscheles
1820 Pianist for evening performances at Zwickau Lyceum
1822 Composes Psalm CL for soprano, alto, piano and orchestra
1826 Father dies
1828 Studies piano with Friedrich Wieck, meets daughter Clara, nine years younger.
    Schubert dies.
1829 Moves to Heidelberg
1830 Hears Paganini at Frankfort, strongly influenced. Mother is persuaded to allow
    Schumann to try a musical career, lives with Wieck. Abegg Variations.
1832 Contemplates suicide. Death of sister-in-law Rosalie and brother Julius
1834 Falls in love with Ernestive von Fricken, begins Carnaval. Editor of "Neue
    Zeitschrift fur Musik".
1836 Mother dies. Interested now in Clara Wieck, father forbids them to see each other
1837 Secretly sees and corresponds with Clara. Kinderszenen, Novelletten Op. 21 ,
    Davidsbündlertänze, moves to Vienna
1839 Brother Eduard dies, returns to Leipzig, Clara institutes legal action to set aside
    father's consent
1840 Receives Ph.D. without thesis or examination in recognition as composer, also
    probably to influence court's decision. Returns to song, Liederkreis and Dichterliebe.
    Wieck unable to prove drunkeness charge against Schumann, court grants consent
    for marriage. Fünf lieder and Frauenliebe und-leben. Robert and Clara married near
    Leipzig. Der Deutche Rhein, patriotic song for solo, chorus and piano.
1841 Symphony #1 Bb "Spring" after a poem of Adolph Böttger.
    Symphony #2 (now #4) Dm. Tour to Weimar and Bremen.
1842 Clara very successful on tour, Robert returns alone to Leipzig while Clara continues
    to Copenhagen. Father Wieck spreads rumor of separation, Robert contemplates
    taking Clara to America. Clara returns one month later. Three String Quartets Op. 41,
    Piano Quintet Eb. In Neue Zeitschrift attack on Gustav Schilling, sentenced to six
    days imprisonment for libel, commuted to five thaler fine.
1843 Meets Berlioz who comes to Leipzig. Leipzig Conservatory opens, Schumann
    accepts professorship. Offered editorship of "Allgemeine musicalische Zeitung,"
    declined.
1844 Tours Russia with Clara, moves to Dresden.
1845 Avoids first performance of Tannhauser, hears opera one month later and changes mind.
1846 Symphony #2 C major.
1847 Album Für die Jungend Op. 68
1848 Many compositions such as Adventlied, Waldszenen, Phantasiestücke for Clarinet and
    piano, Konzertstück for four horns and orchestra. Dresden insurrection. Robert and
    Clara flee to Maxen rather than take an active part. Requiem for Mignon Opus 98b,
    Four Marches, Szenen aus Faust.

1850 First production of opera Genoveva in Leipzig. Cello Concerto. Conducts eight
      concerts in Leipzig, Symphony #3 Eb "Rhenish", overture Die Braut von Messina.
1851 Overtures Julius Caesar and Hermann und Dorothea (Goethe), revises Symphony #2 Dm,
      renumbered #4. Two sonatas for violin and piano. Der Rose Pilgerfahrt.
1852 Composes Mass Op. 147 and Requiem Op. 148, possibly due to his conducting of
      Bach's B minor Mass and St. Matthew Passion. Rheumatic attack. Violin Concerto
      written for Joachim. Meets Brahms. Last choral concert conducted by Schumann at
      Düsseldorf. Leaves position after dispute with both choir and the Musikverein
      committee.
1854 Sees Brahms again, begins compilation of a "Dichtergarten", an anthology of great
      writers' sayings on music. Pursued by aural and visual illusions. Throws himself
      into the Rhine, is rescued and sent to a private asylum in Endernich. Many visits
      by Brahms and Joachim.
1856 Clara, accompanied by Brahms, allowed to see Robert for first time in asylum.
      Dies two days later.

The symphonies:
Symphony No. 1, B flat Major, Op. 38, "Spring" (1841)
Symphony No. 2, C Major, Op. 61 (1845-46)
Symphony No. 3, E Flat Major, Op. 97 "Rhenish" (1850)
Symphony No. 4, D Minor, Op. 120 (1851) Revision of symphony written in 1841; originally
    Symphony No. 2.

    Robert Schumann in a sense exemplified traits seen in both Schubert and Mendelssohn.
Like Schubert, he was at his best in the shorter forms. Not many doubt that his finest efforts
were the suites for piano such as the Kinderscenen, Op. 15; and the Carnaval, Op. 9; and
the lieder cycles such as Dichterlieder Op 40. He was a positive force in musical society.
His writing and crusading for better music and performance, his championing of composers
such as Brahms and Chopin, his wit and eloquence, remind us very much of the gentle
Mendelssohn. Like Mendelssohn, he tried his hand at a wide gamut of compositions:
chamber music for many combinations, the concerto, sonata, program music, smaller forms,
and four symphonies.

    He married the most famous female concert pianist of the 19th century, Clara Wieck. With
her and on his own, he travelled and brushed elbows with the most important people of his
time. He was extremely emotional, and his music is always intensively pervaded by his
personality. Themes such as that in example 23 from the slow movement of the Symphony

EXAMPLE IV-23 Schumann, Symphony No. 2, Op. 61, second movement

No. 2, throb with passion and ardor. Whereas Mendelssohn in his lyric movements sometimes descends to a pretty sentimentality, Schumann's lyricism is hardier and deeper. And

his harmonic vocabulary is much more daring than Mendelssohn's, reminding us of the harmonic color heard in the Schubert symphony.

The Symphony No. 2 is also distinguished for its use of a "motto" theme (example 24).

EXAMPLE IV-24

Its appearance in the first, second, and third movements gives the work a limited cyclic structure and serves well to bind the whole. Adding further cohesion is the recurrence of a motive from the second-movement theme given above (example 23) as the second subject of the finale.

ANALYSIS AND COMMENTARY

Symphony No. 1, B flat major, Op. 38, "Spring", Movement 1

Orchestra:

2 flutes, 2 oboes, 2 clarinets, 2 bassoons; 4 horns, 2 trumpets, 3 trombones; timpani, triangle; strings. The instrumentation of this symphony is typical for an early romantic work. The use of the triangle in the first movement is unusual, but otherwise this is the basic orchestra for the early nineteenth century.

General Characteristics:

Schumann wrote this symphony in four days. (piano score) One has only to listen to the spontaneous, flooding emotion of the piece to know that this is true. The composer evidently was completely carried away with this work and finished the symphony as it were in one long artistic breath. The separate movements were originally intended to have the following titles: 1) "Spring's Awakening", 2) "Evening", 3) "Merry Playmates", 4) "Full Spring".

MOVEMENT 1

Key:	B flat major
Meter:	Quadruple
Tempo:	Andante un poco maestoso – Allegro molto vivace
Form:	Sonata-allegro with introduction and coda
Orchestra:	Full

INTRODUCTION (Meas. 1-38)

The slow introduction begins with a herald motive in the trumpets and then in the strings.

EXAMPLE IV-25

After a dark, dissonant passage played mostly by the upper woodwinds, the tension eases. Gentle, broken chords sound in the strings as the tempo gradually increases. A crescendo builds leading to the full orchestra playing Theme 1 in the exposition.

EXPOSITION: (Meas. 39-133)

EXAMPLE IV-26   Theme 1

Since Schumann originally planned the first movement to be titled, "Spring's Awakening", the symbolic meaning of this slow introduction is clear. The clarion sounds of the opening trumpets and the slow toiling harmonies that follow represent the earth about to break the long quiet of its winter. Theme 1 of the exposition, in bright tempo, represents a burgeoning into the life of spring.

The first eight notes of Theme 1 are identical in pitch with the trumpet motive (example 25) that begins the introduction. Although the tempo is now different, both Theme 1 and the trumpet motive are essentially one.

After a zestful transition the dynamic level drops and Theme 2 enters in the dominant key, F major. Theme 2 is as delicate and reticent as Theme 1 is propulsive.

112

Another transition follows, building in tension, and featuring strong syncopation. At the height of the excitement, Theme 3 enters to close the exposition section. As can be seen in example 27 this closing theme consists of little more than a rising scale for two octaves and

EXAMPLE IV-27

then a return down the scale. Simple as this idea may seem, closer listening shows an interesting structural subtlety. Its rhythmic pattern (first 8 notes) is identical with that of Theme 1. Thus there exist strong ties between Themes 1 and 3 of the exposition.

Theme 3 will play an important role in the development section to follow.

DEVELOPMENT (Meas. 134-293)

This section is long and intensely dramatic. Much of its melodic material refers to Theme 1. However, Schumann introduces a surprise, a fresh new theme in the solo oboe:

EXAMPLE IV-28 , Theme X

Listen carefully for the bass line supporting Theme X. Here the lower strings are occupied with melodic material taken from Theme 1. Theme X provides contrast; its accompaniment in the bass provides unity.

About half-way through the development, the full orchestra gives out Theme 1 complete. For the first time the triangle joins the other instruments of the orchestra, its tone color giving a vibrant edge to the tumultuous sounds.

Toward the end of the development, Theme 3 makes an extended appearance. Schumann treats it imitatively, tossing it from instrument to instrument. The resulting tension, and a crescendo signals that Theme 1 and the recapitulation are near.

113

RECAPITULATION (Meas. 293-380)

Schumann here applies an original twist to traditional sonata allegro form. Theme 1 does indeed enter as it should in the tonic key (B flat major). But now it sounds more as it did in the introduction section than it did at the beginning of the exposition section. In short, Theme 1 now is stretched back to the long note values of the introduction: the brass play the theme in half-notes rather than in eight-notes. The effect of this durational "stretch" is to usher in the recapitulation with a majestic sweep as well as to remind the listener of the close organic quality of the entire movement.

Soon the fast tempo returns. Theme 2 sounds in the woodwinds, this time in the tonic. Then comes the transition to Theme 3. But Theme 3 never appears. Perhaps Schumann felt that it had been emphasized enough at the end of the development section.

CODA (Meas. 380-515)

At any rate, instead of Theme 3, you hear a sudden quickening of pace (animato) and a strong reference to Theme 1 in the violins. This is the beginning of the coda section. Theme 1 reaches a peak of excitement with the winds joining the strings. The dynamic level then drops, and a lovely string theme appears for the first time. This fresh new theme, the loveliest of the movement, serves to hold back the rushing pace of the coda, but just for a moment.

Another crescendo, with Theme 1 in the trumpets and horns, leads to an assertive close in the tonic.

Hector Berlioz

b. La Cote-Saint-Andre, Isere Dec. 11, 1803
d. Paris March 8, 1869

Characteristic areas of composition:
    3 operas, 6 overtures, 4 symphonies, choral works including Grande Messe des Morts, Te Deum, L'Enfance du Christ, La Damnation de Faust. Songs with piano or orchestral accompaniment, 3 pieces for Harmonium, several voice and orchestra arrangements, including La Marseillaise.

Important life facts:
Son of Dr. Louis-Joseph Berlioz
1815 Falls in love with Estelle Dubeuf, 18. Early education in Classics, Medicine, and
         Music.
1818 Studies harmony
1821 Sent to Paris as medical student, but is fascinated by opera.
1824 Enters Conservatoire, studies with Lesueur and Reicha.
1825 Messe Solonelle at Saint-Roch, orchestra of 150.
1827 Enters Prix de Rome, cantata unperformable, "La Mort d'Orphee." Sees Harriet Smithson
         at Theatre de l'Odeon.
1830 Engaged to Camille Moke. Prix de Rome, goes to Rome and Moke marries Pleyel.
         Rob Roy Overture and Lelio.
1832 Unhappy, leaves Rome early, returns to Paris after stopping home.
1833 Marries Smithson
1834 Harold in Italy
1837 Grande Messe des Morts at Invalides. Conducts Harold in Italy and Fantastique before
         Paganini.
1838 Opera, Benvenuto Cellini, a disaster.
1839 Romeo and Juliette. Joins Journal des Debats.
1841 Lives with Marie Recio.
1844 Publishes treatise "TRAITE DE L'INSTRUMENTATION

1846 La Damnation de Faust.
1847 Extremely successful journey to St. Petersburg and Moscow.
1854 Harriet dies, marries Recio. L'Enfance du Christ.
1855 First performance of Te Deum (1849) at Saint Eustache.
1856 Elected member of French Institute.
1862 Marie dies.
1863 Premiere of Les Troyens (1859) in Paris, resigns from Journal des Debats. Becomes ill,
      nursed by mother-in-law Recio. Love affairs with Adele and again Estelle Duboeuf!
1865 Revises memoirs, sends copy to Estelle.
1867 Son Louis dies of yellow fever in Havana. Final concert in St. Petersburg. Health
      continues to deteriorate.
1869 Dies in Paris

The symphonies:
Symphonie fantastique, Op. 14, (1830)
"Harold en Italie" Symphony with solo viola, Op. 16, (1834)
"Romeo et Juliette" Symphony with chorus and solo voices, Op. 17; (1839)
"Symphonie funebre et triomphale", chorus, strings and military band, Op. 15, (1840)

Hector Berlioz, alone among these early Romantics, achieved high originality. It was not
that he attained what Beethoven could not or did not; rather he, more than the above composers,
fully perceived the new ground which Beethoven had mapped out and left to be explored. This
new ground lay in orchestral color, in the use of voices with instruments, and in program
music. Also, perhaps more than any Romantic composer, early or late, he followed Beethoven's
lead in the area of irregular rhythms. Berlioz' masterful use of syncopation and nonsymmetrical
phrase structure is directly descended from late Beethoven. Berlioz' two program symphonies,
the Fantastique and Harold in Italy discussed elsewhere in this book, are unique. Both utilize
cyclic form systematically and completely. The solo viola part in Harold in Italy never becomes
exhibitionistic. In this area, Berlioz follows the lead of the Beethoven of the Piano Concerto
No. 4 and the Violin Concerto, in which the solo part is integrated in a texture that is
thoroughly symphonic.

In the symphony with chorus and solists, Romeo and Juliet, Berlioz goes beyond Beethoven's
use of voices in his Symphony No. 9. Vocal parts appear throughout the form. Whereas in the
Ninth the text by Schiller adds but one dimension--that of specific meaning--to a traditionally
organized sonata for orchestra, Romeo and Juliet is basically a vocal piece buttressed by
symphonic form.

Analysis and Commentary

SYMPHONIE FANTASTIQUE, OP. 14

ORCHESTRA

The orchestra for this symphony consists of: two flutes, piccolo, two oboes, English
horn, two clarinets, four bassoons; four horns, two cornets, two trumpets, three trombones,
two tubas; two timpani, snare drum, chimes, cymbals, bass drum; two harps, strings. This
is a large orchestra for the early Romantic period. The introduction of unusual instruments such
as the chimes and harps is intended by the composer solely to realize the sounds suggested
by his program, not for sheer sensationalism. And much more interesting than the "jumbo"
proportions of the orchestra is the manner in which the instruments are used. The many unusual combinations of instrumental sonorities can be viewed as a compendium of the coloristic
devices used by later composers of the period.

GENERAL CHARACTERISTICS

This work at times attains huge proportions: The volume of sound generated by the massive orchestra is stupendous. Yet in some sections Berlioz achieves almost a chamber-music transparency. The second movement, "A Ball," is the interpolated movement in the symphony. Without this movement, it would follow a four-movement aggregate structure with the usual tempo scheme. Berlioz wrote the _Fantastique_ while in the throes of a passionate pursuit of the Shakespearean actress Harriet Smithson. Obviously the symphony is autobiographical, the "young musician of extraordinary sensibility and abundant imagination" being Berlioz himself and the _idee fixe_ representing Harriet. What is extraordinary in the music is its prophetic, though unconscious, projection of what Freud was to analyze and label as wish-fulfillment 70 years later in, _The Interpretation of Dreams_: "If the dream, as this theory defines it, represents a fulfilled wish, what is the cause of the striking and unfamiliar manner in which this fulfillment is expressed? Whence comes the material that is worked up into the dream? What causes many of the peculiarities which are to be observed in our dream thoughts; for example, how is it that they are able to contradict one another?" As we experience in the _Fantastique_, the psychological dream-saga of a young man who quests, murders, and suffers the horror of the guillotine and then the torments of hell, we feel the peculiarities and contradictions of wish-fulfillment that fascinated Freud. This music will make sense only if we forget previous symphonic models predicated on the conscious, rational mind and see it as an intuitional probing into the very stuff of the unconscious dream world. Only then will the unique use of sonata form, chordal structure and progression, orchestration, and melodic organization make sense.

MOVEMENT 1--REVERIES. PASSIONS

PROGRAMME OF THE SYMPHONY

A young musician of unhealthily sensitive nature and endowed with vivid imagination has poisoned himself with opium in a paroxysm of love-sick despair. The narcotic dose he had taken was too weak to cause death, but it has thrown him into a long sleep accompanied by the most extraordinary visions. In this condition his sensations, his feelings, and memories find utterance in his sick brain in the form of melody in his mind, like a fixed idea which is ever returning and which he hears everywhere.

FIRST MOVEMENT: Visions and Passions (Largo--piu mosso--allegro agitato e appassionato assai--religiosamente)

At first he thinks of the uneasy and nervous condition of his mind, of sombre longings, of depression and joyous elation without any recognizable cause, which he experienced before the beloved one had appeared to him. Then he remembers the ardent love with which she suddenly inspired him; he thinks of his almost insane anxiety of mind, of his raging jealousy, of his reawakening love, of his religious consolation.

Key:	C minor
Meter:	Quadruple
Tempo:	Largo, allegro agitato e appassionato assai
Form:	Sonata-allegro with introduction and coda
Orchestra:	English horn, third and fourth bassoons, trombones, tubas, cymbals, bass drum, chimes, harps--_tacet_

INTRODUCTION (Meas. 1-71)

Quiet repeated notes on the dominant ending on a hushed tonic chord are played by the winds. Muted strings then give out a lugubrious theme suggesting, in Rosa Newmarch's phrase, "the attractive luxury of woe" (example 29). The several _fermatas_ at the joints of

EXAMPLE IV-29

the theme's phrase structure perhaps convey the dislocated, checkered quality of the dream's start. One cannot understand the symphony as a whole. with its constant bizarre twists and turns and constant flouting of symphonic conventionalities, without seeing it in the context of the young artist's dream-wish.

Soon after the violins scamper up a staccato scale, gather momentum in crescendo and build to a climax (example 30). This mercurial scherzo-like passage following immediately

EXAMPLE IV-30

upon a moaning theme is typical of the sudden twists and turns to be heard throughout the work. Once the climax has been reached, with the first and second violins curling about in intense dialogue, the winds prepare the way for a return of the theme of example 1. This time the orchestral sound is thickened considerably with flutes and clarinets providing a flowing background.

At measure 46, the theme ebbs away as the cellos and basses settle on an a-flat which remains as a pedal point for 14 measures, anchoring remarkable thematic happenings above. Four markedly contrasted melodic ideas combine in an eerie, atmospheric passage. The second violins volunteer a bugle-call-like motive while the violas play an ascending broken-chord figure, pizzicato. Above, the first violins playfully comment with a fanciful staccato motive of their own, ppp. All the while the horns have their own lyric line. Ultimately the pedal point gives way and held chords played on four different dynamic levels within two measures lead to a tempo change (allegro agitato e appassionato assai). Bombastic chords in the full orchestra usher in the idee fixe and the exposition.

EXPOSITION (Meas. 71-167)

The idee fixe (example 31) is one of rare beauty. It begins chastely, carried by the first violins doubled by the first flute. Soon urgent, staccato chords in the other strings join in providing kinetic energy and propulsion. Though the theme itself is long (41 measures), only its initial motive will be basic throughout the movement.

117

EXAMPLE IV-31   Theme 1

Violent outpourings follow in the full orchestra, serving as a transition to the entrance of theme 2. Note how similar the beginning of this passionate theme is to theme 1 above. In fact, they share the same motive. With the full presentation of theme 2 in the dominant key, G Major, the exposition closes. Repeat marks at measure 167 indicate that it is to be repeated. And this is good, for the exposition is much shorter than normally would be expected in a movement of this magnitude.

DEVELOPMENT (Meas. 168-240)

Before looking at the development section, some comments about its highly unusual character should be made.

Mention has been made already of the dream quality of the work as a whole. As the form spins itself out, we are constantly aware of what might be called an alogical progression of melody, harmony, and rhythm. The scherzo-like passage from the introduction (example 30) is typical. This passage did not "figure" to follow the opening theme. It is a sudden wrench into a foreign mood, one totally unexpected. Among the German or Austrian symphonic masters such as Schumann, Brahms, or Mendelssohn, this passage would not have happened--at least not in that particular place in the structure. Instead, material from the opening theme perhaps would have gradually evolved into a consistently logical transition or bridge. There would have been <u>identity</u> and or <u>consistency</u> of materials. In fact, we can state that the fundamental procedure of the great German symphonic tradition is categorically predicated upon logical, consistent evolution of materials from what came before. We can follow a development of a Classical master as clearly as we follow the thread of thought in an essay by Locke or a novel by Sir Walter Scott. Not so with Berlioz, particularly in the <u>Fantastique</u>. Here convincing patterns are achieved just as much by the <u>juxtaposition</u> of contrasted materials as by the <u>relatedness</u> of materials. This might be called the mosaic technique--the articulation of meaning through placing side by side contrasted elements. Thus we will constantly encounter strange incursions of unexpected materials, much as totally conflicting images often mesh together in a dream. In a sense this is Impressionistic, the emerging pattern being due not to smoothly articulated lines and planes but to the atmospheric juxtaposition of colors. This mosaic treatment becomes apparent at the start of the development and throughout this work.

The motive from the <u>idee fixe</u> sounds in the bass (example 32) and then is sequenced up the chromatic scale. Soon only the first four notes of the motive continue the upward trek.

118

EXAMPLE IV-32

At this point, out of nowhere, a flatfooted passage consisting of repeated notes energized by a gallop-like rhythmic pattern takes over. This serves to introduce two presentations of the second motive from theme 2. Once these have sounded, another structural non sequitur happens: The strings in octaves give out a simple chromatic scale rising to a climax and then dropping down again (example 33). The rising and falling scale continues for several

EXAMPLE IV-33

measures until a powerful chord on the dominant seventh of D Major puts a stop to its seemingly aimless drive.

A long pause prepares for the entry of theme 1. It enters in the dominant key, G Major, with considerable change of orchestration, the winds carrying the theme while the strings provide rhythmic energy.

Once this has ended, a billiant transition strikes out toward another peak. At the apex of its climb the second motive from theme 2 plunges in, carried by the string choir. At first treated as a brief fugato and passed up from cellos to violas to second violins, it ends up played with dash and brilliance by the strings and upper woodwinds. Again the intensity diminishes as a fragment from theme 1 drifts down gradually from the woodwinds to the lower strings.

Once a peaceful mood has been attained a new theme appears in the solo oboe (example 34).

EXAMPLE IV-34

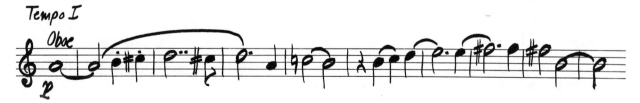

Listen, in example 34 how the initial motive from the <u>idee fixe</u> provides a unifying <u>obbligato</u> below. As this diaphony progresses we become aware that another climax is building. At this point, the listener will realize that one of the basic techniques used by Berlioz for generating excitement is the same as was used by Beethoven in the first movement of the <u>Eroica</u>: that is, a constant charging-up to Herculean heights followed by moments of quiet and gathering of energy. The particular buildup here has a very important goal--the return of theme 1 in the tonic major (C Major) for the start of the recapitulation.

RECAPITULATION (Meas. 412-452)

Theme 1 sounds in full orchestra, <u>ff</u> and syncopated (example 35). Berlioz here sounds

EXAMPLE IV-35

at his most stunning. If he does not hurl thunderbolts as does Beethoven in his tempestuous moments, he shakes the earth with enormous, quaking reverberation. One now expects to hear theme 2. But no. Instead, the motive from the idee fixe is heard dialogued in the woodwinds. Next, syncopations provided by accented chords in the brass on the second beat wrench the ear of the listener, who has already been subjected to enough excitement for a dozen symphonies. But this is the final assault; the strings sift down in quarter notes on the essential figure from the motive of the <u>idee fixe</u> accompanied by the solo oboe sighing down the chromatic scale. Quietly the first violins give out the same motive in its original shape. Rest comes with soft chords suggesting the religious consolation mentioned in the program.

MOVEMENT 2--A BALL

SECOND MOVEMENT: A ball (Valse; allegro non troppo)

In a ballroom, amidst the confusion of a brilliant festival, he finds the loved one again.

Key:	A Major
Meter:	Triple
Tempo:	Valse; <u>Allegro non troppo</u>
Form:	Ternary with introduction and coda
Orchestra:	2 flutes, 1 oboe, 2 clarinets; 4 horns; 2 harps, strings (Appropriately, the instrumentation here is the thinnest of the whole work).

INTRODUCTION (Meas. 1-34)

Again Berlioz greets us with a <u>crescendo</u> passage leading to a climax. In fact, the whole introduction is built on this device. The build-up is quite elegant, being carried mostly by strings and harps. It serves the purpose of creating a sense of expectancy for an important melodic happening. The materials used in the introduction are very simple. Over strings playing tremolo broken chords, the harps alternate with answering rising arpeggios.

The winds join in just before the arrival of the waltz theme proper. Theme 1 (example 36) is charming. It combines the sensitivity of Chopin's idealized waltz with the functional ballroom dance of the Strauss family. The harps soon provide filigree in the background. A new idea (example 37) interrupts,

EXAMPLE IV-36 Theme 1

featuring accents at the start of each measure. When the waltz theme comes back in the first violins, all the other players accompany with light chords marking the typical waltz accompaniment pattern

EXAMPLE IV-37 Theme 2

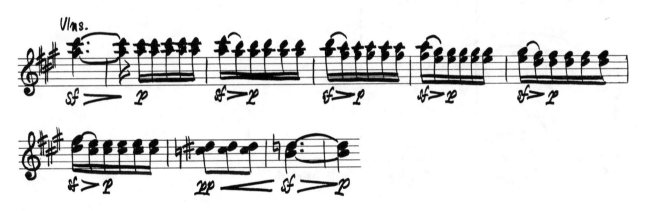

PART B (Meas. 119-173)

Part B is given over to an entry of the _idee fixe_. First heard at the beginning of the exposition section of the first movement, it is now shaped to fit into the contour of a waltz (example 38).

EXAMPLE IV-38

Compare example 38 with example 31 in movement 1. Note change of meter, key, orchestration, and accompaniment. At measure 12 of example 38, fleeting suggestions of the waltz theme itself (example 36) sound. Listen to the masterful combination of these two contrasted melodic ideas. Though it is not generally recognized, Berlioz was a master contrapuntalist. There is no question that he did not arrive at an appreciation of the fugues of J. S. Bach until late in his life (when Saint-Saëns played the _Well-Tempered Clavier_ for him), but nevertheless his music is saturated with a kind of nonacademic, natural blending of independent lines.

PART A (Return; Meas. 174-311)

The return of part A is greatly transformed. The orchestration varies considerably and the whole part is expanded. Theme 1 returns with the second violins, violas, and cellos doubling in octaves. Above, the first violins contribute a wispy obbligato figure. The idea shown above in example 37 returns, this time in the woodwinds, while the strings spatter about pizzicato notes outlining simple triads. When theme 1 returns at measure 225, it is heard in the woodwinds. At measure 250 the tempo indication, animato, indicates a quickening of pace. A new theme enters in the woodwinds. Note the tonic scale outlined in the violins. The music becomes more and more exciting until a climax with a dominant-tonic cadence brings the action to a temporary halt. Here the idee fixe in the solo clarinet enters again. It seems to dissolve into tender nostalgia as it comes to rest on a dominant octave.

CODA (Meas. 312-360)

The change of tempo to a fiery con fuoco is characteristic of what actually went on in the ballrooms of 19th-century Europe. Often the conductor would speed up the last waltz of a set so that the dancers hurtled over the floor with dizzying speed. A dazzling new theme begins the coda. At measure 330 elements from theme 1 sizzle through the string choir while the horns and clarinets give out a plain, descending tonic scale. A stringendo gives impetus toward a strong close.

MOVEMENT 3--SCENE IN THE COUNTRY

THIRD MOVEMENT: In the country (Adagio)

It is a summer evening. He is in the country musing when he hears two shepherd-lads who play the ranz des vaches (the tune used by the Swiss to call their flocks together) in alternation. This shepherd duet, the locality, the soft whisperings of the trees stirred by the zephyr-wind, some prospects of hope recently made known to him, all these sensations unite to impart a long unknown repose to his heart and to lend a smiling colour to his imagination. And then she appears once more. His heart stops beating; painful forebodings fill his soul. 'Should she prove false to him?' One of the shepherds resumes the melody, but the other answers him no more. . . . Sunset . . . distant rolling of thunder . . . loneliness . . . silence.

Key:	F Major
Meter:	Compound
Tempo:	Adagio
Form:	Modified rondo with introduction and coda
Orchestra:	2 flutes, 1 oboe, English horn, 2 clarinets, 4 bassoons; 4 horns; 4 timpani; strings

To those who would believe that Berlioz' orchestration is overblown, the study of this movement provides reason for pause. Except for the second episode, the scoring is of a most transparent character. Theme 1 (example 39) is astoundingly simple, both in construction and scoring. It begins without accompaniment and receives support only later from thin chords played pizzicato in the strings.

INTRODUCTION (Meas. 1-19)

EXAMPLE IV-39

   The theme is example 39 is cast as a melancholy dialogue between oboe and english horn.
Of great interest is the rhythmically free quality of the theme, strongly suggesting the
spontaneous blowing of wind instruments by shepherds. Rests placed at the beginning of
the alternate measures completely destroy any feeling of planned meter or sophisticated
musicianship. In short, the music perfectly represents the natural and bucolic. At measure
11, two solo violas surreptitiously enter, providing a tremolo background.

REFRAIN (Meas. 20-48)

As is often true of Berlioz and other Romantic composers, the melody (example 40) is leisurely
and long.

EXAMPLE IV-40 Theme 1

EPISODE 1 (Meas. 48-68)

EXAMPLE IV-41 Theme 2

Theme 2 consists of two highly contrasted phrases: The first finds the woodwinds in thirds pressing sequentially down a scale; the second is played by the strings, pp, articulating a delicate syncopated figure. This is heard twice, the second time a fourth higher. Following this the strings take over with an intensified rhythmic version of their previous answering phrase. The music builds in excitement.

REFRAIN (Meas. 69-81)

Theme 1 returns but exquisitely modified. It is taken by bassoons, violas, and cellos. Portions of the string choir provide soft pizzicato repeated notes for background. The first violins skitter about with a thirty-second-note figure, while the upper woodwinds and third horn interject sparse chords at every half measure. The key is now the dominant, C Major. Measure 85 shows the texture becoming much more ample as the key modulates to the subdominant, B-flat Major.

EPISODE 2 (Meas. 87-130)

It is in this dramatic episode that the idee fixe returns. The motive now is adjusted considerably, not only because of the essential structure of the movement as a whole (its key, meter, tempo, etc.), but because of the program: "His beloved appears anew, spasms contract his heart, and he is filled with dark premonition." To create the atmosphere of the lover's anxiety, the idee fixe is combined with a new theme in the bassoons and low strings (example 42). The love theme itself is yielding, while the new theme is informed with a kind of masculine assertiveness. The resulting ambivalence achieves exactly the necessary mood of apprehension and inner tension. Tension mounts and by measure 106 the orchestra in rhythmic unison underlines the anxious state of the lover. Once tension slackens, flutes and oboes in thirds rise on a quiet scale and then cadence in the home key, F Major. A delicate retransition begins. Second violins and violas, ppp, play pizzicato scale figurations. Above, the solo clarinet and solo flute carry on a gentle dialogue.

REFRAIN (Meas. 131-174)

Again theme 1 returns in new orchestral garb and with new obbligato background in the winds. At measure 150 another instance of Berlioz' superb contrapuntal skill occurs. Two motives are combined, each treated imitatively. The strings give out suggestions of theme 1, while the upper woodwinds share echoes of the idee fixe. Listen for the interval of the third perched high in the flutes and violins. Berlioz provides an incredibly wide gamut of orchestral color: from the brief, thin line of this passage to the great splashes of sound

EXAMPLE IV-42

elsewhere. At measure 160 the motive from the love theme is accompanied by trill-like figures, meant perhaps to suggest bird calls.

CODA (Meas. 175-   )

The introduction theme returns, but this time only in the english horn. We assume that the summer storm that is brewing has dampened the musical ardor of the second shepherd. Below the theme, the timpani, tuned to sound an interesting chord--a-flat, b-flat, c, f-- suggest far-off thunder (example 43).

The thunder sounds nearer. But apparently the storm will pass elsewhere for the strings give a quiet final cadence in the home key and the tableau fades.

EXAMPLE IV-43

MOVEMENT 4--MARCH TO THE GALLOWS

FOURTH MOVEMENT: The procession to the stake (Allegretto non troppo)

He dreams that he had murdered his beloved, that he has been condemned to death and is being led to the stake. A march that is alternately sombre and wild, brilliant and solemn, accompanies the procession. . . . The tumultuous outbursts are followed without modulation by measured steps. At last the fixed idea returns; for a moment a last thought of love is revived--which is cut short by the death-blow.

Key: G minor
Meter: Quadruple
Tempo: <u>Allegretto non troppo</u>
Form: Free fantasy
Orchestra: Full, chimes--tacet

127

INTRODUCTION (Meas. 1-17)

Pizzicato chords in the low strings, ominous rumbles in the timpani, and gutteral sounds in the muted horns immediately plunge the listener into an atmosphere of dread. A portentous crescendo in the sixteenth measure ushers in section 1 with its macabre first theme.

SECTION 1 (Meas. 17-61)

EXAMPLE IV-44 Theme 1

Though theme 1 (example 44) is extremely simple in intervallic structure, outlining a descending Aeolian G minor scale, it is nevertheless permeated with a sense of implacable doom. At measure 25 the theme is repeated, this time in parallel thirds and to the accompaniment of a sardonic obbligato in the solo bassoon. The intensity builds and builds until at one point the brass interject a shrieking dissonance.

SECTION 2 (Meas. 62-77)

Ascending scales in bassoons and strings introduce theme 2 (example 45). This theme, carried by the winds and giving a strong impression of the military, perhaps suggests the triumphant march of the forces of law and order. We are reminded of the gleeful mobs following the tumbrels as they carried the condemned aristocracy to the guillotine during the French Revolution.

EXAMPLE IV-45 Theme 2

Measure 77 shows repeat marks, indicating that the music is to be heard again from the beginning.

SECTION 3 (Meas. 78-123)

Elements of theme 2 begin this section. But soon a bizarre version of theme 1 is heard. Note how the orchestra chops the theme into little bits, each choir sharing in its descent. Theme 2 returns with increased fury, as does theme 1. At this point the whole orchestra mounts a cosmic crescendo that crests over into section 4.

SECTION 4 (Meas. 123-178)

The full orchestra, except for percussion, strides majestically down with theme 1 in the tonic key, G minor. But at measure 130 there is a violent harmonic wrench as theme 1 in the exotic key of D-flat Major is turned completely about to ascend in inversion.

The feeling of imminent death is charged with utter horror when the rhythmic figure shown in example 46 takes hold. The feeling of crushing dread continues until a powerful half cadence is heard. Then, in total contrast, the solo clarinet gives out the motive from the

EXAMPLE IV-46

idee fixe. The head rolls (example 47).

EXAMPLE IV-47

129

There can be no doubt that the poet's last thought is of the loved one.

MOVEMENT 5--DREAM OF A WITCHES'SABBATH.
WITCHES' ROUND DANCE

"Not green leaves were there, but of a dusky color, not smooth boughs but gnarled and tangled, not fruits but thorns with poison." Dante, <u>Divine Comedy</u>, Canto XIV.

FIFTH MOVEMENT: The witches' sabbath (Larghetto; allegro)

He dreams that he is present at a witches' dance, surrounded by horrible spirits, amidst sorcerers and monsters in many fearful forms, who have come to assist at his funeral. Strange sounds, groans, shrill laughter, distant yells, which other cries seem to answer. The beloved melody is heard again, but it has its noble and shy character no longer; it has become a vulgar, trivial, and grotesque kind of dance. She it is who comes to attend the witches' meeting. Friendly howls and shouts greet her arrival. . . . She joins the infernal orgy . . . bells toll for the dead . . . a burlesque parody of the <u>Dies Irae</u> . . . are heard at the same time.

Key: C Major
Meter: Quadruple, compound
Tempo: <u>Larghetto</u>. <u>Allegro assai</u>
Form: Free fantasia
Orchestra: Full

This diabolical, maniacal tone-scene is the touchstone for many like pieces in later years of the Romantic century. To name a few: Liszt: <u>Totentanz</u>, <u>Mephisto Waltz</u>; Tchaikovsky: <u>Francesca Da Rimini</u>; Saint-Saëns: <u>Dance Macabre</u>; Gounod: "Walpurgis Night" from the opera <u>Faust</u>; Mussorgsky: <u>Night on Bald Mountain</u>; MacDowell: <u>The Witches' Dance</u>.

Before examining the structure of this movement it would be well to become acquainted with the themes associated with the hellish situation: First, the <u>idee fixe</u>, transformed into a caricature of itself (example 48); the theme associated with the witches' dance

EXAMPLE IV-48

(example 49); and an ancient liturgical chant, <u>Dies Irae</u> ("Day of Wrath"). (Example 50).

EXAMPLE IV-49

EXAMPLE IV-50

The <u>idee fixe</u> is heard twice, and only in the first section. But the Witches' Dance and the <u>Dies Irae</u> are scattered throughout, undergoing constant transformation.

SECTION 1 (Meas. 1-39)   INTRODUCTION

The orchestration at the beginning is highly original, setting a mood of leering evil. The muted violins and violas are dispersed through a diminished seventh chord, while the lower strings play a rising scale motive. At measure 4 the divided strings slither down a chromatic scale to be answered by grumblings in the cellos and basses and <u>pizzicato</u> broken chords in the other strings. Brass comment, then the high flutes and oboes intone a primitive figure trailed by the muted solo horn echoing the same idea. This is repeated a semitone higher. As the solo horn again gives out its ghostly echo, this time <u>pppp</u>, the tempo changes and the disguised <u>idee fixe</u> lurches in, madly played by the solo C clarinet. As it is about to complete its second phrase, a cataclysmic shout erupts in the full orchestra as if all of hell's tormented were egging the witch on with high glee.

131

SECTION 2 (Meas. 40-239)

It is here that the transformed _idee fixe_ sounds complete. The orchestration paints to perfection the picture of a hideous, cackling witch. The high E-flat clarinet leads. Note how the bassoons, entering in the fun at measure 47, add precisely the ribald touch needed. (example 48).

Once the theme has run its course, wild chromatic scales in the woodwinds and strings finally plunge down a syncopated passage and pause on a half cadence in C minor, the key of the next section. Shooting out of the strings comes the motive soon to be associated with the Witches' Dance. Then cellos, basses, and bassoons fall into the lower depths and pause on a low _c_. When the _Dies Irae_ does enter it is sounded by low bassoons doubled by the tubas. At first it is heard in long note values, but successive repetitions find the chant played by the horns and trombones in diminution then by the woodwinds and _pizzicato_ strings in further shortening of note values. All of this is repeated twice with some modification of instrumentation. At measure 121 the motive from the Witches' Dance leads in a frantic crescendo that crashes into the Witches' Round Dance proper, Section 3.

SECTION 3 (Meas. 240-523)   WITCHES' ROUND DANCE

Appropriately enough, the Round Dance is presented as a fugato, with a violent syncopated measure after each entrance of the subject (example 49). This fugato spans 163 measures. At measure 304 a sudden turn into an E-flat chord inaugurates a striking episodic passage. The brass and bassoons play strong repeated chords while the upper woodwinds slip down a syncopated chromatic scale. This happens four times. All the while the strings are slipping in and out with the three-note pickup from the fugato subject itself.

Now begins another gigantic buildup to what will become one of the main events of the movement: the combination of the Witches' Dance theme with the _Dies Irae_. Over and around mysterious harmonies, transformed versions of the Round Dance sound, first outlining chords, then tracing a chromatic scale. Imitation is heard throughout. The crescendo does not actually begin until measure 363, but what a crescendo it is. At the peak of its fire, the whole orchestra grinds against itself with a dissonant chord that, for audacity, anticipates 20th-century harmony.

Example 51 shows how Berlioz combines his two major themes. Once this has run its

EXAMPLE IV-51

132

course in the home tonic, C major, the famous passage for the string choir occurs. The violins and violas turn their bows around and strike the strings with the wood in what is called col legno. The resulting scratchy twittering provides background for a new entrance of the Round Dance theme, this time in A minor and with trills.

Once the Round Dance has finished we are prepared for the final surging close, but not before the abbreviated Dies Irae injects itself into the wild melee once more. Below it the strings and bass drum lurch within each measure from a pp to a ff, adding to the spirit of cataclysmic doom. For sheer orgiastic abandon these concluding pages of the Fantastique have few equals in any art. One thinks perhaps of the 15 prints for the "Apocalypse" by Dürer three centuries before, or the Guernica" of Picasso in our time. The end of the movement comes with the whole orchestra stamping and screaming out a new version of the Round Dance.

Chapter V

LATE ROMANTIC AND CONTEMPORARY SYMPHONISTS

Of the late Romantics no less than eight composers contributed an important body of symphonies: Brahms, Bruckner, Mahler, Sibelius, Dvorak, Tchaikovsky, Liszt, and Franck.

Though there are several undoubted masterpieces in the work of these men, again little is offered that Beethoven had not either fully explored or strongly suggested. The exception to this statement is the nationalism found in the works of Dvorak, Sibelius, and Tchaikovsky.

Johannes Brahms
b. Hamburg May 7, 1833
d. Vienna April 3, 1897

Characteristic Areas of Composition: 15 accompanied and 14 unaccompanied choral works, 2 serenades, 2 overtures, 4 symphonies, a set of orchestral variations and orchestrated Hungarian Dances, 2 piano concerti, 1 violin concerto, 1 concerto for violin and cello, 3 piano quartets, 3 string quartets, 2 string sextets, 2 string quintets, 1 piano quintet, 3 sonatas for violin and piano, 2 for cello and piano, and 2 for clarinet and piano, 3 piano sonatas, 7 sets of variations for piano, 5 ballades, 18 intermezzi, 3 rhapsodies for piano, 11 organ choral preludes, four other works for organ, 203 songs, 25 duets, vocal quartets, canons, and numerous arrangements of folksongs.

Father, Johann Brahms, contrabass player.
Mother, Johanna Henrika Christiane Nissen.

Pupil of Cossel, also a pupil of Marxen (Cossel's teacher), who was a pupil of Siefried, who was a pupil of Mozart.

> Studies theory and piano with Marxen.
> Visit of USA turned down, plays for several years in taverns but discouraged by mother who feared for his health.

1853 On tour with violinist Remenyi, transposes piano part to Kreutzer Sonata at sight. Meets Joachim at Hanover and Liszt at Weimar. Meets Clara and Robert Schumann, publishes Sonatas in C and F# minor.
1854 Variations on a Theme by Schumann, 4 Ballades.
1856 Schumann dies.
1857 Music-master to Prince of Lippe-Detmold.
1858 Serenade in D op. 11, Piano Concerto #1. Love affair with Agathe von Siebold.
1859 Serenade #2 in A.
1860 Director of ladies choir at Hamburg.
1862 Visit to Vienna.

1863 Conductor of Singakademie of Vienna, settles in Vienna.
1864 Visits Baden-Baden, Clara Schumann. Piano Quintet in F minor Op. 34, several revisions ultimately scored for piano and strings at Clara's suggestion.
1865 Mother dies. String Sextet in G "Agathe".
1866 Father remarries.
1868 Ein Deutsches Requiem.
1871 Director of the Gesellschaft der Musikfreunde.
1872 Father dies.
1873 Two String Quartets Op. 51, Variations on a Theme by Haydn.
1876 Symphony #1 C minor Hans von Buelow coins phrase "the three B's".
1877 Brahms refuses Ph.d. from Cambridge. Symphony #2.
1878 Violin Concerto.
1879 Ph.d. from Breslau University for which he afterwards composes Academic Festival Overture. "Rain" Sonata for Violin and Piano Op. 78.
1880 Breaks friendship with Joachim.
1881 Piano Concerto #2 Bb Op. 83.
1882 Naenie Op. 82.
1883 Symphony #3.
1885 Symphony #4.
1887 Prussian "Pour le Merite" awarded, Knight of the Prussian Order. Concerto in A minor for Violin, Cello, and Orchestra Op. 102.
1889 Honorary key to city of Hamburg.
1890 Conferred with Order of Leopold by the Emperor of Austria.
1892 Turns down Cambridge Ph.d. second time. Three Intermezzi Op. 117.
1893 Six Pieces for Piano Op. 118, Four Pieces for Piano Op. 119.
1894 Two Sonatas for Clarinet and Piano Op. 120.
1896 Four Serious Songs Op. 121, Eleven Choral Preludes for Organ Op. 122, last composition. Clara Schumann dies, Brahms arrives too late for the funeral. Attends his last concert March 7, a performance of his Symphony #4. Dies of cancer of the liver less than one month later.

The symphonies:
    Symphony No. 1, C minor, Op. 68, (1876)
    Symphony No. 2, D major, Op. 73 (1877)
    Symphony No. 3, F major, Op. 90, (1883)
    Symphony No. 4, E minor, Op. 98 (1885)

Johannes Brahms' first symphony was hailed by its champions as the "Tenth," implying that Brahms was a kind of symphonic reincarnation of Beethoven. Indeed, it was almost as if certain generic characteristics of the Beethoven symphony skipped a generation--the early Romantics, Schubert, Schumann, Mendelssohn, and Berlioz--but were fully inherited by Brahms.

We find in Brahms an immense concern with the challenges of Classical form. He took the symphony as Beethoven left it (excepting the chorus in the ninth) and started over again. In his symphonies we find the same care for design, a similar emphasis on development, and the exhaustive search for balance between unity and contrast. Yet there is a difference. Brahms, despite his great love for Classical order and logic in music, had to deal with basic materials of music that had evolved for 50 or so years since Beethoven. Harmony had become very sophisticated; melody had changed. In a word, though Brahms chose to work in Classical forms, he had to weld these to Romantic sound. This was his particular challenge as a symphonist.

Brahms' four symphonies stand the closest scrutiny that musical analysis can offer. Not one bar simply "is." Every musical detail is in place: All is order; correct progression and musical direction is never in doubt. Yet the music abounds with beautiful sound. Melodies are saturated with twilight glow. In short, the music sings.

One need only listen to the natural lilt of the opening melody in the first movement of Brahms' <u>Symphony No. 4</u> to realize this fully. It sounds as fresh and spontaneous as a country song. Yet analysis tells us that its intervallic structure can be reduced almost to a formula. The melodic intervals can be shown to be descending thirds, which in their turn are derived from a massive thirteenth chord built on the fifth tone of the scale. Brahms undoubtedly planned this logical basis for his "spontaneous" melody, for we find a similar "formula" underlying the second theme in the first movement. The miracle is that this planned structure does not sound synthetic.

EXAMPLE V-1 Brahms, Symphony No. 4, Op. 98, first movement

136

ANALYSIS AND COMMENTARY

SYMPHONY NO. 2, D MAJOR, OP. 73

Orchestra:

2 flutes, 2 oboes, 2 clarinets, 2 bassoons; 4 horns, 2 trumpets, 3 trombones, tuba; timpani; strings. Again, as in the Mendelssohn and Schumann symphonies analysed above, the orchestra is modest in size. Only the trombones, tuba and 3rd and 4th horns distinguish it from the orchestra of late Haydn and Mozart symphonies.

General characteristics:

This is Brahms's "pastorale" symphony; it is lyric and predominantly sunny. Brahms, before its performance in 1877, was fond of telling his friends about the new work, "the new symphony is so melancholy that you will not be able to bear it." Remembering the dramatic character of the First Symphony, they may well have believed him.

MOVEMENT 3

Key: G major
Meter: triple (parts B anc C use different meters)
Tempo: Allegretto grazioso
Form: ABACA-coda (small rondo)
Orchestra: Trumpets, trombones, tuba, and timpani, tacet.

PART A: Meas. 1-32

If it were not for the piquant accents on the third beat of the first two measures Theme I might suggest the elegant atmosphere of the 18th century minuet. The cellos support the solo oboe with pizzicato, broken chords.

EXAMPLE V-2

All thematic materials in Part A flow from Theme 1 and are carried entirely by winds.

PART B: Meas. 33-106

The mood abruptly changes. The meter goes from triple to duple, tempo is geared upwards, and the upper strings enter for the first time. Instead of the nostalgic lyricism of Part A, now there is verve and excitement. The violins play an idea which at first sounds fresh and new!

137

EXAMPLE V-3

Close examination reveals however that this is a new version of Theme 1. Thus there is thematic connection between Part A and Part B. As we move through this movement you will understand that there is more subtlety than first meets the ear. Though the effect of the whole is simple, with natural flow, the form is carefully planned and organically conceived.

A sudden crescendo leads to Theme 2, a bold march-like idea played by the strings backed up with strong on- the -beat chords in the winds.

EXAMPLE V-4

This then gives way to the idea from example 2 above played back and forth from strings to woodwinds. The dynamic level gradually diminishes.

PART A: Meas. 107-125

Theme 1 returns in the original tempo and original key (G major). This time it is shortened and varied.

PART C: Meas. 126-194

Again the mood changes: the Presto tempo returns, and the meter changes to three-eight. Much staccato is heard. A short downward scale passage in the strings introduces in the fifth measure what seems again to be a fresh, new idea. It is fresh by not new.

EXAMPLE V-5

As it turns out this is but a variation of Theme 2. Brahms creates a new mood in Part C but, as he did in Part B, he relates it thematically to what came before.

The idea in example 4 above is tossed around from strings to woodwinds. Near the end of Part C listen for a brief reference to Theme 1 in the flutes. Then listen for a slackening of the pace and a change of key; this signals the 2nd return of Part A.

PART A: Meas. 194-224

Theme 1 returns in the original tempo. This time however, it is played in the first violins rather than by the oboe. It sounds in the key of F sharp major, a tonal area far removed from the tonic key, G major. This exotic new key lends exquisite tonal contrast for this part of the movement. How very effective is this contrast becomes plain when you hear what follows. Gradually Brahms eliminates the many accidentals basic to F sharp major, as he modulates back to the tonic, G major. Theme 1 is heard again in the oboe, in the tonic.

CODA: Meas. 225-240

The coda starts with a short but lovely new melodic idea high in the strings and then high in the woodwinds. A brief remembrance of Theme 1 in the oboe, a soft cadence in the tonic, and the movement ends.

Anton Bruckner
b. Ansfelden, Upper Austria September 4, 1824
d. Vienna October 11, 1896

Characteristic Areas of Composition: 8 masses, 7 large choral works including Magnificat and Te Deum, 37 motets, 11 symphonies, 13 cantatas, 1 string quartet, songs, and solo works for piano and organ.

Important Life Facts
Father, Anton, schoolmaster.
Early music schooling at St. Florian.

1836 Four Preludes.
1840 To Linz for teacher studies.
1841 Teacher at Windhaag, first Mass.
1845 Organist and assistant teacher at St. Florian.
1848 Organist at Foundation of the St. Augustine Monks, Requiem in D minor.
1856 Organist at Cathedral in Linz.
1860 Also choirmaster.
1863 Hears his first Wagnerian opera Tannhäuser, turning point. Symphony in F minor, unnumbered.
1864 Mass in D and Symphony #0
1865 Meets Wagner and Von Bülow, Symphony No. 1
1866 Mass in E minor (polyphonic 8-part chorus and brass).
1867-
1868 Mass in F minor (symphonic style), nervous breakdown. Journeys to Vienna, teaches organ and theory at Conservatory.
1871 Becomes full professor, journeys to London Exhibition and Crystal Palace, gives organ concerts.
1873 Symphony #3 "Wagner".
1874 Symphony #4 "Romantic".
1875 Symphony #5
1881 Symphony #6, first real success.

1883 <u>Symphony #7</u>, Wagner dies.
1884 <u>Te Deum</u>.
1885 <u>Symphony #8</u>, Hanslick describes success as "boisterous rejoicings".
1891 Resigns from Conservatory. Vienna University bestows honorary doctorate.
1892 <u>Psalm 150</u>, last major sacred work.
1896 <u>Symphony #9</u>, incomplete, confides to friends that if symphony should not be completed, the <u>Te Deum</u> should serve as finale. Bruckner dies.

The symphonies:
    Symphony No. 1, C minor, (1865-1866)
    Symphony No. 2, C minor, (1871-1872)
    Symphony No. 3, D minor "Wagner Symphony", (1873)
    Symphony No. 4, E flat major, "Romantic" (1873-74)
    Symphony No. 5, B flat major (1875-77)
    Symphony No. 6, A major, (1879-81)
    Symphony No. 7, E major (1881-83)
    Symphony No. 8, C minor, (1884-85)
    Symphony No. 9, D minor, (1887-96) (Unfinished)

The dates given for each symphony is the completion date for the original version. Bruckner however revised his symphonies often. In addition to the above nine works, there exists in piano score a student work, the Symphony in F minor, and the Symphony No. 0, D minor (1863-64)

In symphonic style Anton Bruckner somewhat resembles Brahms. The symphonies as a whole are conservative in form. They are absolute (The "program" to the 4th Symphony proves the rule) and they follow the standard four-movement plan. Each movement is cast in a traditional form (sonata allegro, scherzo, etc). Orchestral sonority is "thick" as in Brahms, and there is a similar sobriety of musical thought.

Beyond these structural identities however the symphonies of Brahms and Bruckner show marked differences. Brahms' working out of structure within symphonic form is utterly sophisticated, reflecting the high intellectual ability of his thought as well as a thorough academic knowledge. Structural cohesion is lacking with Bruckner; there is a tendency to say more than is really necessary.

Also different from Brahms' work is the advanced chromaticism in Bruckner's symphonies. This progressive harmonic language is derived largely from the composer's admiration for the music of Wagner.

Textures often are organ-like, reflecting Bruckner the superb church organist; a certain rambling character in the adagios suggesting his love of improvisation. The scherzos, usually suggesting the lilt and stamp of Austrian folk ländler, offer a welcome contrast to the generally somber cast of the whole.

<u>Listening Guide</u>

<u>SYMPHONY No. 7 Adagio</u>

The second movement of Bruckner's Seventh Symphony is a long, expressive Adagio in C sharp minor. The composer here is very close to Richard Wagner both in thought and musical content. Bruckner revered Wagner, considering him the leading composer of his time. Wagner died (Feb. 1883) as this Adagio was written and it is thought that Bruckner, while he wrote, had a premonition of the master's passing. Be that as it may, it is not inappropriate to consider the Adagio as a deeply felt musical eulogy.

In his turn, Bruckner was considered by Wagner supporters a leading disciple of Wagnerism and the one to carry Wagnerian aesthetics into the realm of absolute music. That he realized this hope can nowhere be better seen than in this Adagio.

Bruckner included the Wagner tuben (tenor tubas in B flat) in the instrumentation of this score, a specific instance of Wagner's musical influence. The tuben are heard in the opening measures as they and the violas give out the first phrase of the first theme:

EXAMPLE V-6

A more substantial Wagnerian influence however lies in the area of melody and harmony as can be heard in the passage following Theme 1:

EXAMPLE V-7

These five measures follow a favorite Wagnerian formula: chromatic sequences of a short melodic and harmonic pattern. In fact, the melodic and harmonic language is chromatic throughout much of the movement suggesting at once the tonal method of Wagner in the later music dramas.

Theme 2, in F sharp major, begins at measure 37 after the movement's first climax:

EXAMPLE V-8

This is one of the most lyric themes ever conceived by Bruckner. Mahler surely loved its feeling of bittersweet nostalgia, for he himself wrote similar themes over and over again in his own symphonies.

Bruckner's nine symphonies form an indispensable link in the entire development of the German romantic symphony. This symphonic tradition began with Beethoven's 3rd (1803), continued with Schubert, Mendelssohn, Schumann, Brahms, Bruckner; and culminated with Mahler's unfinished Tenth (1910).

Gustav Mahler
b. Kalist July 7, 1860
d. Vienna May 18, 1911

Characteristic areas of composition: 2 operas, (early, unpublished), 10 symphonies, and 42 songs.

1875 Enrolls in Vienna Conservatory, same year as Hugo Wolf.
1877 Studies history, philosophy and history of music at the University of Vienna
1878 Meets Anton Bruckner.
1880 Kapellmeister at Hall in Austria, Das Klagende Lied.
1883 Chorusmaster of Italian opera at Carl Theatre in Vienna, Kapellmeister at Cassel. Hears Parsifal at Bayreuth. Wagner dies.

143

1885 Second Kapellmeister at Prague under Seidl
1886 Second Kapellmeister at Leipzig under Nikisch
1888 Director at Budapest. Brahms hears his conducting and is impressed. Symphony #1,
      Des Knaben Wunderhorn.
1891 Kapellmeister at Hamburg.
1892 Guest conductor of German Opera in London.
1894 Symphony #2 from Des Knaben Wunderhorn.
1895 Becomes a Roman Catholic. Symphony #3 D minor.
1897 Upon strong recommendation from Brahms, appointed Kapellmeister at Court Opera in
      Vienna. Brahms dies.
1900 Symphony #4 in G.
1902 Marries Alma Schindler. Symphony #5 c#minor, Rückert Songs, Kindertotenlieder.
1904 Symphony #6 A minor
1905 Symphony #7, B minor
1906 Visits America.
1907 Symphony #8 in Eb.
1908 Conducts New York Philharmonic and Metropolitan Opera. Das Lied von der Erde.
1909 Symphony #9 Db.
1910 Symphony #10 unfinished
1911 dies in Vienna.

The Symphonies:
    Symphony No. 1, D major (1888)
    Symphony No. 2, C minor (1894) with chorus and vocal soloists.
    Symphony No. 3, D minor (1895) with choruses and contralto soloist.
    Symphony No. 4, G major (1900) with soprano solo
    Symphony No. 5, C sharp minor (1902)
    Symphony No. 6, A minor (1904)
    Symphony No. 7, D major (1905)
    Symphony No. 8, E flat major (1907) with choruses, vocal soloists
    Symphony No. 9, D flat major (1909)
    Symphony No. 10, (unfinished) (1910)

Gustav Mahler studied with Bruckner at the Vienna Conservatory, and there can be no question that the master's influence was felt by the younger man. Mahler, like Bruckner, wrote nine symphonies. (Nine seems to have been a significant number for the production of symphonies: Beethoven and Dvorak also wrote nine). They have common leanings: a tendency toward the episodic, serious, and grand; a penchant for rich, Wagnerian, chromatic harmony; a love of Viennese folk song and dance; and contrapuntal textures.

But in Mahler there is something else. As Berlioz had been before, Mahler was enchanted with the sound of the human voice in the symphony. In the words of Salazar, in Music in our Time, "Mahler moved from song to symphony, just as the acorn engenders the oak. In a simple melody, in a children's popular song, Mahler heard the musical murmurings of the cosmos." The Symphony No. 1 contains folklike melodies taken from his earlier song cycle, Songs of the Wayfaring Stranger; Nos. 2, 3, 4, and 8 all contain vocal music. There was precedent for this: We have already mentioned the voices in Beethoven's Symphony No. 9 and in Berlioz' Romeo and Juliet. Even Mendelssohn had contributed a sort of hybrid symphony-cantata, the Hymn of Praise. But there is a significant difference between Mahler's use of the human voice within the vast panorama of his symphonic thought and its use by his predecessors. Beethoven in the ninth saw the voice as the necessary intensifying medium for the achievement of the ultimate statement of his philosophy. The human quality of the voice was a perfect tool to express the sentiments of brotherhood, love, and universality found in the Schiller text. Berlioz' use of chorus and soloists in the Romeo and Juliet Symphony stems from his desire to make the dramatic programmatic idea very explicit. What better plan than to use important sections of Shakespeare's play in a thoroughgoing integration with symphonic style?

144

With Mahler, however, it is the microcosmic lied itself that provides spiritual motivation. Unlike both earlier masters, Mahler came onto the scene after a large body of lieder had developed. Schubert, Schumann, and Brahms had evolved the lieder cycle to such a degree that it had become one of the major forms of the Romantic century. These songs represented the very quintessence of the personal and subjective. They directly embodied the intimate, poetic, and lyric--traits of basic importance to Romanticism as a whole. Mahler, whose primary characteristic in his music is that of intense, subjective statement--the total expression of the self--grasped the importance of the folk and art song as the agent for "humanizing" the symphony. His extraordinarily agonized personal involvement in the very web of the music can best be understood by his own words written on the score of the unfinished Symphony No. 10, "Madness seizes me, accursed that I am--annihilates me, so that I forget that I exist, so that I cease to be. . . . " As one listens to the symphonies, shot through with tortured, spasmodic passages, searing climaxes, frenetic exultations, and mystic murmurings, these words come true. And often, song is very near, not only actual quotations, but in the very heart of all Mahler's lyric moments. The following melody from the adagietto movement of the Symphony No. 4 is a perfect example of the lyricism in the symphonies. It throbs with the bittersweet pungency of old Vienna and all the travail of a troubled soul.

EXAMPLE V-9 Mahler, Symphony No. 4, fourth movement

LISTENING GUIDE

Symphony No. 1, D major, Movement 2

Form: Ternary
Key: A major
Meter: Triple
Tempo: Kraftig bewegt (with a strong swing)

145

We have already seen the influence of song on the symphonies of Mahler. Selections from the composer's own cycle, Songs of a Wayfarer are present in the First Symphony as is the French round, Frere Jacques (in a minor key). What we have not emphasized is the strong attraction felt by Mahler for the countryside, its people and their music. Mahler was raised in the small Moravian village of Iglau.

"I see the blue heavens once more and the quivering flower, and my scornful laughter dissolves in tears of love. And I must love it, this world with its deception . . . and its eternal laughter."

Peasant songs and dances, military music from the local garrison, the songs of the hurdy gurdy, and especially the landler, an Austrian country waltz, influenced him deeply. Movement 2 of the First Symphony is partly in the landler style. There is a waltz swing throughout Part A but with heavy "country" accents on the first beat of the measure.

PART A Meas.

Part A begins with the cellos and basses marking the beat. Above, the other strings play an upbeat figure in a kind of "yodel" style from the Austrian mountains. The woodwinds then play the main theme:

EXAMPLE V-10

KRÄFTIG BEWEGT

It is astonishing how this simple theme is made to generate rich and varied consequences. At times the dance is ferocious, other times it is gentle; great, rough climaxes give way to mysterious scamperings.

The orchestra is treated democratically throughout; all choirs in their turn share the theme. Seldom is an instrument assigned solely to play supportive background; all lines are melodically interesting. Unlike the rich, chordally derived textures of some romantic composers, those of Mahler come from a true polyphonic attitude. Because there is so much that is important happening at the same time on different levels, it is possible to hear this music over and over again, always with fresh experience.

TRIO (PART B): Meas.

The Trio, in F major, establishes a different mood. Gone is the atmosphere of a folk bachannale. Instead, Mahler writes music of exquisite tenderness, a remembrance perhaps of Vienna, and of its elegant waltz tradition. There are two themes in the Trio. The first shows Mahler at his most genial:

EXAMPLE V-11

Note the glissandos in the violins above characteristic pizzicatos in the cellos. At measure three, a contermelody sounds in the violas and then is answered above by the solo oboe. The mood is sentimental, the orchestral sonority velvety; yet the close intertwining of melodic lines works to avoid any suggestion of the maudlin.

The key changes for Theme 3 (F major to G major), Again Mahler assigns it to the expressive violins: ·

EXAMPLE V-12

It is lyric as is Theme 2, but with more flow. A bumptious momentary reference to Part A interrupts, but, Theme 2 returns to reinstate the reflective mood of the Trio.

PART A: Meas.

When Part A returns it is shorter than before but remains lively to the end.

Peter Tchaikovsky
b. Kamsko Votinsk May 7, 1840
d. St. Petersburg Nov. 6, 1893

Characteristic Areas of Composition: 11 operas, 3 ballets, 6 oratorios and cantatas, other choral works, 6 symphonies, 11 overtures and tone poems, 3 piano concerti, 3 string quartets, 1 piano trio, 1 string sextet, 2 piano sonatas, numerous collections including The Seasons and Children's Album, over 100 songs.

Father, government inspector of mines.

1850 Family moves to St. Petersburg, sent to preparatory classes for the School of Jurisprudence. Joins choral class and continues piano lessons.
1855 Mother dies of cholera.
1859 First-class clerk in Ministry of Justice.
1861 Studies theory at Russian Musical Society.
1863 Enters Conservatory, studies with Zaremba, and Rubenstein.
1865 Leaves Conservatory. Setting of Schiller's Ode to Joy for solo voices, chorus, and orchestra as graduation piece.
1866 Joins Moscow Conservatory as professor of harmony. Symphony #1 "Winter Dreams", Festival Overture on the Danish National Hymn.
1868 Visits St. Petersburg, meets Balakirev and Rimsky-Korsakov. Symphonic poem Fate, first opera The Voyevode. Meets Desiree Artot, actress.
1869 Artot marries Mariano Padillo, spanish baritone in Warsaw. First version of Romeo and Juliet.
1872 Symphony #2.
1873 Tempest fantasy.
1875 Piano Concerto in Bb disapproved by Rubenstein, strong affect on Tchaikovsky. Symphony #3.
1876 The Seasons, Variations on a Rococo Theme, String Quartet #3, Francesca da Rimini Fantasy, Swan Lake. Close to a nervous collapse, summers at Vichy and Bayreuth festival.
1877 Marries Antonia Miliulova, leaves her nine weeks later, to Switzerland and Italy. Madame von Meck bestows annual allowance. Symphony #4.
1878 Eugene Onegin, Violin Concerto, Children's Album, resigns from Conservatory.
1880 Serenade for Strings, final revision of Romeo and Juliet, Capriccio Italien, 1812 Overture, Piano Concerto #2.
1881 Rubenstein dies.
1883 Opera Mazeppa.
1885 Manfred Symphony for Balakirev.
1888 Begins conducting in concert tour of Germany, France, and England. Symphony #5, Hamlet Overture.
1889 Tours Germany again, meets Brahms, to England. Sleeping Beauty.
1890 Opera Queen of Spades. To Italy, Sextet for Strings. Madame von Meck forced to discontinue annuity.
1891 Sister dies just before tour to USA, conducts in New York, Philadelphia, and Baltimore. Ballet Nutcracker, opera Iolanthe, incidental music to Hamlet, symphonic ballad The Voyevode.
1892 Honorary Ph.d. from Cambridge with Boito, Saint-Saëns, Bruch, and Grieg.
1893 Symphony #6, Piano Concerto #3 (one Movement). Drinks unboiled water during a cholera epidemic. Dies of cholera, two months before Madame von Meck.

The Symphonies:
    Symphony No. I, G minor, "Winter Daydreams", Op. 13, (1866)
    Symphony No. 2, C minor, Op. 17, (1872)

148

Symphony No. 3, D major, Op. 29, (1875)
Symphony No. 4, F minor, Op. 36, (1877)
"Manfred" Symphony, Op. 58 (1885)
Symphony No. 5, E minor, Op. 64, (1888)
Symphony No. 6, B minor "Pathetique" Op. 74, (1893)

Tchaikovsky wrote six true symphonies, of which the last three are the most important. Although he wrote the last symphonies in a four-movement plan and used the standard romantic orchestra, they nevertheless show considerable originality of form.

Listening Guide   Symphony No. 4

The 4th Symphony marks a turning point in the composer's style. It was the first to result from his long relationship with Nadezhda von Meck, a wealthy patron of the arts. By mutual consent they never met, but an extensive correspondence developed between composer and patron, much of which sheds light on Tchaikovsky's work. A famous letter to Mme. Meck about the 4th Symphony shows an emotional program typical of Tchaikovsky:

"The Introduction is the kernel, the quintessence, the chief thought of the whole symphony." (Opening, theme, sounded by horns and bassoons, Andante, F Minor, 3/4). "This is Fate, the fatal power which hinders one in the pursuit of happiness from gaining the goal, which jealously provides that peace and comfort do not prevail, that the sky is not free from clouds - a might that swings, like the sword of Damocles, constantly over the head, that poisons continually the soul. This might be overpowering and invincible. There is nothing to do but to submit and vainly complain." (Theme for strings, Moderato con anima, F minor, 9/8) "The feeling of despondency and despair grows ever stronger and more passionate. It is better to turn from the realities and to lull one's self in dreams." (Clarinet solo with accompaniment of strings.) "O Joy! What a fine sweet dream! A radiant being promising happiness, floats before me and beckons me. The importunate first theme of the allegro is now heard afar off, and now the soul is wholly enwrapped with dreams. There is no thought of gloom and cheerlessness. Happiness! Happiness! Happiness! No, they are only dreams, and Fate dispels them. The whole of life is only a constant alternation between dismal reality and flattering dreams of happiness. There is no port; you will be tossed hither and thither by the waves, until the sea swallows you. Such is the program, in substance, of the first movement."

"There is no determined feeling, no exact expression in the third movement. Here are capricious arabesques, vague figures which slip into the imagination when one has taken wine and is slightly intoxicated. The mood is now gay, now mournful. One thinks about nothing; one gives the fancy loose reins, and there is pleasure in drawings of marvelous lines. Suddenly rush into the imagination the picture of a drunken peasant and a gutter song. Military music is heard passing by in the distance. There are disconnected pictures, which come and go in the brain of the sleeper. They have nothing to do with reality; they are unintelligible, bizarre, out-at-elbows."

"Fourth movement. If you find no pleasure in yourself, look about you. Go to the people. See how well they know how to be jolly, how they surrender themselves to gaiety. The picture of a folk holiday. Scarcely have you forgotten yourself, scarcely have you had time to be absorbed in the happiness of others, before untiring Fate again announces its approach. The other children of men are not concerned with you. They neither see nor feel that you are lonely and sad. How they enjoy themselves, how happy they are! And will you maintain that everything in the world is sad and gloomy? There is still happiness, simple, naive happiness."

"This is all that I can tell you, my dear friend, about the symphony. Rejoice in the happiness of others - and you can still live. My words naturally are not sufficiently clear and exhaustive. It is the characteristic feature of instrumental music that it does not allow analysis."

There is insight to be gained from Tchaikovsky's words on the Fourth Symphony, but a study of its overall structure gives even more. Its form is cyclic. At the head of the slow introduction to the first movement comes a stentorian motive in the horns:

"this is Fate, the fatal power which hinders one in the pursuit of happiness. . ."

EXAMPLE V-13

At important points in the first movement proper, the "Fate" motive interrupts the already gloomy atmosphere. The motive does not appear in movements 2 and 3, but is given a most dramatic entrance in movement 4 (see below).

Sonata allegro form with slow introduction and coda is the pattern of movement 1.

EXAMPLE V-14

It sets a morose mood for the entire movement. It is a kind of syncopated slow waltz suggesting both weariness and pathos.

The second movement, a lyrical Andantino in B flat minor, gives little relief to the mood of despair established in the first movement.

"Here is that melancholy feeling which enwraps one when he sits at night alone in the house, exhausted by work;. . . "

Movement three, a scherzo in ternary form, is scored largely for pizzicato strings, producing a tone color unique to symphonies of that period. Part B features woodwinds and brass playing folk-like melodies and rhythmic patterns.

" . . . Suddenly rush into the imagination the picture of a drunken peasant and a gutter song. Military music is heard passing by in the distance."

Movement four, the finale, is almost entirely happy, requiring a virtuoso orchestra to negotiate its dazzling technical gymnastics.

" . . . Go to the people, See how well they know how to be jolly, how they surrender themselves to gaiety."

An authentic folk song "In the field there stands a birch tree", heard as the second theme, lends extra substance to the holiday mood.

EXAMPLE V-15

Near the movement's end the motive heard in the "Fate" introduction to the first movement brushes away the gay mood.

"Scarcely have you forgotten yourself, scarcely have you had time to be absorbed in the happiness of others, before untiring Fate again announces its approach."

Once the "Fate" idea has made its point, its terror gives way to soft, low groans, and gradually the festive mood returns, building to the end. A crescendo is heard, the tonic major key (F major) returns, and the entire symphony closes with a full, joyful sound.

Symphony No. 5

Tchaikovsky's Symphony No. 5, in E minor, is interesting because of its thorough use of cyclic form. A cyclic theme, Slavic in atmosphere and sharply different from the cyclic theme (above) of the 4th Symphony, is quietly presented by the clarinets;

EXAMPLE V-16

It does not again appear during the course of the first movement, but crops up twice in the slow movement; It is heard again within the coda of the waltz movement, and then dominates the entire finale.

Each time it appears in successive movements its physiognomy is altered to fit a new musical context.

For example, when the cyclic theme appears at the end of movement 3, it is recast in triple meter, played by bassoons, and otherwise modified so that it can be assimilated into the atmosphere of a symphonic waltz.

Symphony No. 6

With the Symphony No. 6, in B minor, the "Pathetique", the composer abandoned cyclic form. But the work is innovative in other ways. Particularly unusual is the way Tchaikovsky lays out his overall movement plan in terms of tempo. Rather than follow the usual tempo scheme heard in the romantic symphony -- fast, slow, fast, fast -- Tchaikovsky arranges his movements this way:

Movement 1 Adagio-Allegro non troppo (slow introduction leading into a moderately fast
          tempo)
Movement 2 Allegro con grazia (fast but graceful)
Movement 3 Allegro molto vivace (Fast and very lively)
Movement 4 Adagio lamentoso-Andante (Very slow and melancholy, then moderately slow)

The fiery third movement is a march-scherzo ending with the kind of declarative exultation one usually expects in the finale. It would be pre-climactic if it were not for the total "rightness" of the concluding 4th movement, Adagio. It is right in terms of the composer's personal life, and of his development as a late romantic composer of the symphony.

This intensely subjective movement is filled with a pathos that sometimes borders on the morose. It can be seen as a creative sublimation of the end- both of the composer's life and of an era. Tchaikovsky died four months after the completion of the "Pathetique", ending a life filled perhaps with more personal tragedy and pain than with triumph and fulfillment.

ANALYSIS AND COMMENTARY

Symphony No. 6, B minor, Op. 74, "Pathetique". Movement 2

Orchestra:

2 flutes, piccolo, 2 oboes, 2 clarinets, 2 bassoons; 4 horns, 2 trumpets, 3 trombones, tuba; timpani, bass drum, cymbals, tam-tam; strings. The orchestra here is ample, slightly larger than that in the Brahms 2nd and considerably larger than those of Mendelssohn's 4th and Schumann's 1st. Yet it is smaller than those of Mahler and Strauss at the waning of the romantic century. The writing for winds is superb.

General Characteristics:

This symphony is perhaps the finest work by Tchaikovsky. Of obvious originality is the charming second movement, a kind of waltz with five beats per measure. The third movement, a march-scherzo, achieves the ultimate in brilliance, verve and excitement and the finale, cast as an Adagio is saturated with sob and pathos.

MOVEMENT 2

Key: D major
Meter: quintuple
Tempo;   Allegro con grazia
Form: ternary with coda
Orchestra: Bass drum, cymbals, tam-tam-tacet

This gracious movement is one of the composer's most original creations. Its five-four meter was quite daring for its time (1893) although Brahms many years before had set his Variations on a Hungarian Theme for piano solo in alternating duple and triple measures.

But it is not the asymmetrical meter itself in this Allegro that is extraordinary. Rather, it is how the composer creates the atmosphere of the ballroom, by writing music that sounds like a waltz without really being in waltz time.

PART A: Meas. 1-56

Part A concerns itself entirely with materials taken from Theme I, first heard in the cellos:

EXAMPLE V-17

Once the cellos play Theme 1, it is repeated by the woodwinds above. All of this is then repeated exactly.

Next, the violins take up what at first seems like a new idea, but which turns out to be a

EXAMPLE V-18

153

modification of Theme 1. After this, listen carefully for bright pizzicato scales in the upper strings. This will signal the return of Theme 1 in the woodwinds. Next a crescendo builds as the brass join the woodwinds to develop Theme 1. Part A ends quietly in the tonic key, D major.

PART B: Meas. 57-95

The elegance and grace of Part A gives way in Part B to a brooding intensity tinged with Slavic melancholy. A new theme appears:

EXAMPLE V-19

Note the bass part: a single tone, "D" repeated over and over again. The technical term for this structural device is pedal point. It will stay until the very end of Part B, lending a hypnotic insistency to the dark atmosphere.

Note also the repetitions of tones within Theme 2 and the repetition of its phrases. This is a characteristic of Russian folk music which has seeped into the concert music of many Russian composers, especially that of the nationalist school of the late 18th century called "The Mighty Russian Five" Though Tchaikovsky was not part of that group (Balakirev, Borodin, Cui, Mussorgsky, Rimsky-Korsakov) much of his music, including portions of the Pathetique Symphony, reflects the folk music of the Russian people.

Towards the end of Part B listen for a fragment of Theme 1 alternating with a fragment from Theme 2. Tchaikovsky prepares you gradually for the return of Theme 1, complete in Part A.

PART A: Meas. 95-151

This is almost an exact repetition of Part A at the beginning. A slight change occurs; the violins join the cellos in Theme 1. Also there is no repetition of the first sixteen measures as

154

there was at the beginning of the movement.

CODA: Meas. 151-

The coda begins with a rising D major scale starting in the cellos and rising up through the violins. At the same time, the woodwinds head downward with the same scale in longer note values. Again the strings start up, but this time it is the brass that play the dropping scale passage.

As they are about to converge, the cellos twice play a fragment from Theme 2. This fragment is then heard passed from flute, to oboe, to clarinet, to bassoon. As the coda draws to a close, Theme 1 joins in and the movement ends with a soft tonic chord.

Antonin Dvorak
b. Muelhausen, Bohemia Sept. 8, 1841
Prague May 1, 1904

Characteristic Areas of Composition: 9 operas, 12 choral works with orchestra, 21 unaccompanied choral works, 9 symphonies, 4 concerti, 10 orchestral works (overtures and symphonic poems), over 30 chamber works, numerous piano solos and duets, plus songs.

Important Life Facts

Father Frantisek Dvorak, butcher and innkeeper

1841 Born eldest of eight children.
1849 Plays in father's band and sings in parish choir.
1853 Sent to Zlonice to learn German and music from Antonin Liehmann, schoolmaster, organist, and band leader.
1857 Enters the Prague Organ School, studies theory, organ and voice, plays violin in Orchestra of Society of St. Cecilia.
1859 Leaves Organ School, plays viola in orchestra of National Theatre at Prague under Smetana, also gives lessons.
1861 Opus 1, Quintet in A minor.
1865 The Bells of Zlonice Symphony.
1874 Organist at St. Ethelbert's Church. Symphony in Eb wins Austrian State Prize. Marries Anna Cermakova, contralto and former pupil.
1875 Chamber works Opus 77, 21, 22, 23. Symphony Opus 18, Opera, King and Collier.
1876 Moravian Duets. First child dies, Stabat Mater and Piano Concerto Opus 33.
1877 Brahms recommends him to Simrock, publishes Moravian Duets.
1878 First eight Slavonic Dances Opus 46. Nationalism now an important influence.
1883 Stabat Mater first performed in London.
1884 Dvorak goes to London and Worcester to conduct Stabat Mater, very successful.
1886 National oratorio St. Ludmilla. More visits to London.
1889 Symphony in G Opus 88.
1890 Tours Russia, Germany, and England. Receives honorary doctorate and is elected member of Czech Academy of Arts and Sciences.
1891 Honorary doctorate from Cambridge, Requiem, Overture Trilogy Opus 91, 92, 93. Appointed professor in composition and musical form at the Prague Conservatory.
1892 Mrs. Thurber, founder of National Conservatory of Music in New York City, invites Dvorak to become Director, and he accepts. Summer in Spellville, Iowa.
1893 Symphony E minor Opus 95, String Quartet F Opus 96, and Quintet Eb Opus 97.
1895 Returns to Prague Conservatory.
1898 Opera Devil and Kate.
1901 Appointed director of Conservatory, and member of Austria House of Lords.
1902 Opera Armida, a fiasco.
1904 Dies of apopleptic stroke, day of national mourning proclaimed for his funeral.

The Symphonies:

Symphony No. 1, C minor, Op. 3. Bells of Zlonice (1865)
Symphony No. 2, B flat major, Op. 4, (1865)
Symphony No. 3, E flat major, Op. 10, (1873)
Symphony No. 4, D minor, Op. 13, (1874)
Symphony No. 5, F major, Op. 76, (1875, rev. 1887) (Old No. 3)
Symphony No. 6, D major, Op. 60, (18 80) (Old No. 1)
Symphony No. 7, D minor, Op. 70, (1885) (Old No. 2)
Symphony No. 8, G major, Op. 88 (1889) (Old No. 4)
Symphony No. 9, E minor, Op. 95 "From the New World", (1893) (Old No. 5)

Dvorak, as far as is known, did not indulge in actual Bohemian or Slavonic folk music in his symphonies. But the spirit and essence of middle-European dances such as furiants, polkas, and dumkas abound in his nine symphonies. And though the Symphony No. 9 is called From the New World and does contain melodies influenced by American plantation songs, it is still Bohemian in essence. An American critic, writing of its first performance in New York said, "Dr. Dvorak can no more change his nationality than the leopard can change its spots."

LISTENING GUIDE

Symphony No. 8, in G major, Op. 88 (old No. 4)

The 8th Symphony is characteristic of Dvorak's overall compositional style. Its pastoral, lyric character reflects the simplicity and beauty of his land and its Slavonic people. But despite obvious ethnic references throughout this work, Dvorak's artistic debt to Brahms and the German symphonic tradition is evident at many points. For example, the first theme of the fourth movement played by the cellos (see below) bears a close resemblance to the first theme of the Allegro in the Finale of Brahms' Symphony No. 1.

The work is in traditional four-movement aggregate sonata form:

Movement 1 . . . Allegro con brio
Movement 2 . . . Adagio
Movement 3 . . . Allegretto grazioso
Movement 4 . . . Allegro ma non troppo

Movement 1

Movement 1 is a sonata allegro form, without introduction. Although the work is in G major as a whole, typically, Dvorak opens with a first theme in G minor played by cellos doubled by low winds:

EXAMPLE V-20

156

The use here of the natural G minor scale (Aolian mode) lends to this theme a distinct Slavonic sound, while its contour and the way it is orchestrated suggests the symphonic Brahms. Other themes are more clearly written in folk style:

EXAMPLE V-21

Movement 2

This profound Adagio in C minor shows Dvorak at his most thoughtful, influenced not only by Brahms but perhaps by Beethoven. Theme 1 resembles the first theme in the <u>Funeral March</u> of Beethoven's "<u>Eroica</u>" <u>Symphony</u> (see Example IV-6):

EXAMPLE V-22

Once the string choir has played this theme, the flute presents a new motive, then immediately gives way to clarinets with yet another motive:

EXAMPLE V-23

Note especially the material in the clarinets suggesting an exotic middle-European scale.

About half-way through the movement listen for soft, descending scales in the violins. Above these, in the flute and oboe, a new expansive theme (Theme 3) enters. Ultimately this theme will lead to a massive climax in the full orchestra resembling those in the music dramas of Wagner, another influence on Dvorak.

157

Movement 3

This piquant waltz in ternary form with coda, is divided tonally between tonic major and tonic minor. Part A is in G minor, while Part B and the coda are in G major. Thus the ambiguity of mode established in the first movement (major or minor?), continues to tantalize the ear.

There are two basic melodic ideas in this movement. Theme 1, which begins Part A suggests the gypsy violinist at a cabaret:

EXAMPLE V-24

Theme 2 in the solo oboe at the beginning of Part B, sounds more like a folk dance.

Movement 4

Movement four finally settles all doubt about mode; it is clearly in the tonic major . . . at the beginning, at the end, and through much of the middle. The form used is rondo, with introduction and coda:

Introduction . . . Bright, herald theme in trumpets.

Refrain 1 . . . Brahms-like theme in the cellos:

EXAMPLE V-25

Episode . . . Features new, sprightly theme in the solo flute, backed up by a gentle, broken-
               chord accompaniment in the strings.
Refrain 2 . . . Theme 1 in full orchestra. (Only last part of first refrain used)
Episode 2 . . . Long, developmental in style. Several new melodic ideas. Ends with a full-
               throated statement of the heraldic theme form the introduction.
Refrain 3 . . . Like that of the beginning, cello theme returns.
Coda . . . Brilliant. Based on Theme 1. Like a Czeck Furiant

Movement 4 contains much of interest. On the one hand, Dvorak again clearly bows to the German symphonic tradition with a theme such as that for the cellow (Example V-25). Also,

158

the strong development heard in portions of Episode 2 points toward Beethoven and Brahms.

On the other hand the music often sounds as if it wants to break out into pure folk dance, as in the coda and the second refrain. The fourth movement's mixture of seemingly divergent content . . . Slavonic nationalism and German symphonicism . . . sums up not only the entire 8th Symphony's ambivalent character, but also that of Dvorak's work in general. It was his, and other romantic nationalistic composers, role to achieve a synthesis of native with European "classical" traditions.

Jean (Johan) Sibelius
b. Tavastehus, Finland Dec. 8, 1865
d. Järvenpää (villa) Sept. 20, 1957

Characteristic Area of Composition: One unpublished opera, 16 choral works with orchestra, two choral works with organ, 39 unaccompanied choral works, 18 overtures and tone poems, 8 orchestral suites, 7 symphonies, 1 violin concerto plus 2 serenades for violin and orchestra, 3 string quartets, 2 piano trios and other chamber works, 11 works for violin and piano -- 3 for cello and piano, numerous piano works including a sonata and 16 Bagatelles, 2 works for organ, and 94 songs.

Father a doctor.

1885 Studies law at Helsinki University and then enters the Helsinki Conservatory as well as those at Berlin and Vienna.
1882 Piano Trio in A minor and Piano Quartet in E minor.
1888 Two Pieces for Violin and Piano listed as Opus 2.
1889 String Quartet Bb listed as Opus 4.
1891 Overtures in A minor and E.
1892 En Saga.
1893 Returns to Finland, Karelia, Swan of Tuonela.
1895 Cantata for the Coronation of Nicholas II.
1896 Opera The Maiden in the Tower. Teaches violin and theory at Helsinki.
1897 Life grant offered by state.
1898 Symphony #1 E minor
1901 Symphony #2 D.
1902 The Origin of Fire written for the opening of Finnish National Theatre.
1903 Valse Triste Op. 44.
1905 Incidental music to Pelleas et Melisande.
1906 Incidental music to Belshazzar's Feast. The Captive Queen, and Pohjola's Daughter.
1907 Symphony #3 C.
1909 Night-ride and Sunrise, tone poem. Voces Intimae string quartet.
1911 Symphony #4 A minor.
1912 Journeys to England.
1914 Visits USA, teaches at New England Conservatory in Boston. The Oceansides for combined Boston Symphony Orchestra and New York Philharmonic.
1915 Symphony #5.
1921 Visits England again. Suite Champetre.
1923 Symphony #6 D minor.
1924 Symphony #7 C.
1926 Tapiola Op. 112. Hints of a Symphony #8, but it never appears.
1929 Esquisses Op. 114, last composition.
1957 Dies of cerebral hemorrhage at his villa, buried in his garden.

The Symphonies:
    Symphony No. 1, E minor, Op. 39 (1898-99)
    Symphony No. 2, D major, Op. 43 (1901)

Symphony No. 3, C major, Op. 52 (1904-07)
Symphony No. 4, A minor, Op. 63 (1911)
Symphony No. 5, E flat major, Op. 82 (1914-15)
Symphony No. 6, D minor, Op. 104 (1923)
Symphony No. 7, C major, Op. 105 (1924)

The seven symphonies of Jean Sibelius, the Finnish composer, chronologically are very late: the first was done in 1899, the last in 1925. But the approach to form is Classical: logic, cohesiveness, and unity prevail. At the same time the inner materials of harmony, melody, and rhythm are thoroughly Romantic. Added to this is a strong feeling of nationalism brought about not so much by the use of true folk elements but by a kind of north-country sturdiness and a certain hardiness of texture. As the composer himself put it: "When we see those granite rocks we know why we are able to treat the orchestra as we do."

LISTENING GUIDE

Symphony No. 2, D Major, Op. 43

This symphony was written by Sibelius in 1902 during an extended visit to Italy. There is a pastoral quality in much of this work as there is in the 2nd Symphony of Brahms and the 8th Symphony by Dvorak.

This pastoral atmosphere perhaps reflects Sibelius's stay in sunny Mediterranean climes. Certainly the outer movements (1 and 4) project an expansive, relaxed feeling. But the geographical locale suggested in not that of Italy; it is that which Sibelius remembered in his homeland, Finland.

For several years Sibelius had written orchestral tone poems reflecting the folk lore of his native land. With the 2nd Symphony, an absolute work, he goes beyond specific literary reference. In it the composer achieves synthesis: an application of traditional sonata principles to a melodic, rhythmic, harmonic content abstracted from Finnish folk sources. As you hear this symphony you will experience a feeling of structural strength and logical progression, as strong as any since Beethoven. Yet themes, and overall orchestral color will turn your imagination to the northern terrain: the people in Finland and the poetry of their history.

The 2nd Symphony is divided into four movements, following a normal tempo plan:

Movement 1. Allegretto
Movement 2. Andante
Movement 3. Vivacissimo
Movement 4. Allegro moderato

The orchestra is modest for 1902; 2 flutes, 2 oboes, 2 clarinets, 2 bassoons; 4 horns, 3 trumpets, 3 trombones, tuba; timpani; and strings.

Movement 1

Movement 1 begins with soft, repeated chords in the strings. They continue their quiet pulsations while above, in the oboes and clarinets, a folk-like theme is heard:

EXAMPLE V-26

ALLEGRETTO

Later on another important theme is heard, again in the woodwinds, and again backed up by pulsating chords in the strings:

EXAMPLE V-27, Theme 2

Unlike Theme 1, this idea has no suggestion of the folk. Its shape is typical of Sibelius: a long, single tone intensifying through crescendo, finally dropping by a single skip. These contrasted first and second themes symbolize the polarity of content throughout the symphony. There is an interaction from theme to theme, and movement to movement -- between folk-like expression and the composer's more personal expression derived from his European symphonic heritage.

Sibelius chose sonata allegro form without slow introduction for this first movement. The form is very economical; nothing is wasted; every moment is filled with precisely enough sound and idea to complete the total pattern.

While Sibelius's ideas develop, in steady by inevitable progression, all is enveloped in unique orchestral color.

"Perhaps in no other way is it (Sibelius' style) more unique than in orchestral timbre. . . . Orchestral coloring is of a somewhat dark, somber cast, yet it is clear and bold. The low winds in choir are much in evidence giving the texture an organ-like solidity. And it is not only the bass and tenor winds that heavily anchor the total sound; soprano instruments such as the oboe and clarinet often are made to plunge to the lower limits of their range. In these lower registers they give out a plaintive, nostalgic sound suggestive of the dark forests and somber landscape of Finland."*

Movement 2

Nowhere in the symphony does the "somber cast" of orchestral sound more effective than at the beginning of the second movement, in D minor.

---

* Listen, A Guide to the Pleasures of Music, Nadeau and Tesson, Allyn and Bacon Inc., Boston 1971.

161

The movement begins with the low strings playing a steady, pizzicato bass line. There is a primieval loneliness to the sound recalling perhaps the sight of craggy rocks, mists, and vapors. As it turns out this pizzicato passage is a preparation for the entrance of Theme 1. Two bassoons an octave apart play a dark, chant-like theme of modal color. Although the remainder of this movement contains passionate outbursts of great intensity and much diversity of mood, it is the dark first theme that sets the mood for the whole.

Movement 3

Movement 3 is a scherzo following the pattern, ABAB. Two moods are present. The first, in Part A, is wild and impetuous. This motive moves through the orchestra at a furious pace.

EXAMPLE V-28

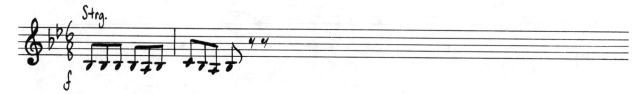

Above it, Theme 1 enters in the woodwinds:

EXAMPLE V-29

Throughout Part A, sudden dissonant stabs, unexpected modulations, climaxes and quick dynamic drops, show that Sibelius need not have been, nor was at all times a conservative romantic. In fact, for its time (1902), this portion of the scherzo anticipates a true twentieth-century musical temper.

The mood of the scherzo changes in Part B. Here again is Sibelius at his lyric best. A genial country atmosphere returns:

EXAMPLE V-30

Note the repeated tones intensifying to an interval drop in this theme. Compare to Theme 2 in movement 1.

There is no break between the scherzo and the finale. Instead, Sibelius writes a bridge which grows in volume leading directly into the finale.

162

<u>Movement 4</u>

The finale as is movement I , is in sonata allegro form. Theme 1 is ponderous and majestic.
It moves strongly but not quickly ahead propelled by a kind of grinding rhythmic pattern in the
trombones, tuba, and timpani:

EXAMPLE V-31

It is built up of four, seminal motives: the first in the strings, the next in the trumpets, the
following in the horns, and the last back in the strings.

After a brief episode in the violins, a crescendo builds and Theme 1 returns considerably
transformed. Only the first motive now is used. Richer harmonies, and full support in the
winds give it a feeling of spiritual fervor. The atmosphere gradually becomes quiet and the
lower string then play a scale-like, circling idea in eight-notes. This is a preparation and
background for Theme 2:

EXAMPLE V-32

Again Sibelius presents a theme forged from a short, simple motive, in the oboe and clarinet very
low in their ranges. The effect of the woodwinds sounding in their low registers over the circling
figure in the bass is uncanny. As he does so often Sibelius gives the impression of time/
motion held back and suspended. We are brought back to a primieval earth where the measure
of time is slow and still.

The development section is concerned chiefly with explorations of the first motive from Theme 1
(Example 31) and of a herald motive in the brass.

Ultimately, the three- note motive from Theme 1, repeated over and over again with crescendo,
leads to a resplendant statement of Theme 1, complete.

The finale's end is approached with the swirling scale idea from above gradually intensifying
to a huge climax. The herald motive is heard four times in the brass, another short crescendo,

and the Molto largamente section (coda) begins. The sonority is tremendous, all choirs full blown and rich. For this massive conclusion Sibelius has saved up a chorale-like theme in the brass:

EXAMPLE V-33

"In the cold my song was resting,
Long remained in darkness hidden,
I must draw the songs from Coldness,
From the Frost must I withdraw them."
From the Finnish epic, Kalevala.

OTHER SYMPHONISTS

There are several other important figures in the late Romantic period who were involved with the symphony. One of these, Cesar Franck, wrote a single Symphony in D minor which is distinguished for its high spiritual tone and its strong organic structure.

Cesar Franck (August Jean Gillaume Hulbert)
b. Liege, Belgium Dec. 10, 1822
d. Paris November 8, 1890

Characteristic Areas of Composition: 3 operas (none performed during his lifetime), 2 masses, 15 church motets, 4 oratorios, 5 symphonic poems, Variations Symphonique, 10 chamber works, numerous piano, organ, and harmonium works, 3 organ chorales, and 22 songs.

Important Life Facts

1833 Enrolled in Liege Conservatory with brother Joseph.
1837 Enrolled in Paris Conservatory.
1838 Grand Prix d'Honneur in pianoforte.
1840 First prize for fugue.
1841 Second prize for organ.
1842 Withdrawn from Conservatory by father for career as pianist, tours Belgium.
1845 Composes Ruth, favors composition over concerts.
1846 Breaks away from father.
1848 Marries Mlle. Desmousseaux, daughter of an actress, against his father's wishes. On
       the way to church in Paris Cesar tears trousers on a barricade erected by 1848 Revolutionaries.
1851 Organist at St. Jean-St. Francois au Marais.
1858 Organist and Choirmaster at St. Clotilde, position he will hold until death. Messe
       Solonnelle (includes Panis Angelicus).
1862 Six Pieces pour l'Orgue.
1872 Succeeds Benoist as organ professor at Conservatory.
1873 Redemption (first version).
1874 Final version of Redemption.
1878 Trois Pieces (Fantasie in A, Andante Cantabile, and Piece Heroique).
1879 Les Beatitudes, Piano Quintet in F minor.
1881 Rebecca
1882 Le Chasseur Maudit, tone poem.
1884 Franck festival sponsored by his students at Cirque d'Hiver. Les Djinns

1885 <u>Variations Symphonique</u> for piano and orchestra.
1886 <u>Sonata in A</u> for violin and piano.
1888 <u>Psyche</u>, tone poem. <u>Symphony in D minor.</u>
1889 First performance of <u>Symphony</u>, unsuccessful.
1890 Opera Giselle, <u>Trois Chorales pour l'Orgue</u>. Struck by omnibus while on way to student's house for lesson. Attack of pleurisy. Dies.

Franck finished his only symphony in 1888, two years before his death at the age of 68. In many ways it reflects his long experience as church organist in Paris. The harmonic scheme throughout is heavily chromatic. Harmonic progressions, where rich chords seemingly "slide" one to the other suggest the church organist's improvisation, fingers quietly searching for new sonorities. The orchestra texture is clearly influenced by the full sonority of the typical romantic pipe organ.

The work's steady use of chromatic harmony not only suggests organ improvisation but, more importantly, the influence of Wagnerian harmony. The Wagnerian influence is strongly corroborated by Franck's structural style. As does Wagner, Franck builds an entire work around a few carefully chosen leading motives (leit motif). The D minor Symphony's seminal motive is first heard in the Lento introduction to the first movement:

EXAMPLE V-34

It then is transformed to become Theme 1 in the following sonata allegro form, the structural pattern of the first movement.

EXAMPLE V-35

In movement 2, this leading motive again is transformed to become the basis of an elegiac theme in the english horn.

EXAMPLE V-36

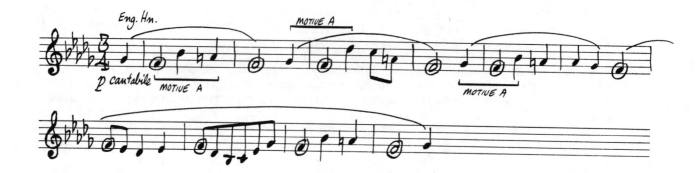

It enters again toward the end of the third, concluding movement. Thus the D minor Symphony is cyclic, its opening motive visiting each of the two succeeding movements. We are reminded of Debussy's wry comment on his own cyclic work, the Violin Sonata of 1917: "The main theme . . . is subjected to the most curious deformations and ultimately leaves the impression of an idea turning back upon itself, like a snake biting its own tail".

Of course, there are other important motives in the symphony. Each tends to project an aura of fervid sincerity tinged with mysticism.

Also, there is one curious technical point about many of Franck's themes. They have a tendency to turn back and resolve around a single note. Note the circled notes in the example V-37 below and in example V-36 above.

EXAMPLE V-37

Perhaps the emphasis on a single pitch is the composer's way of balancing the fluid chromaticism flowing around these melodic ideas.

Others

There are two fine program symphonies by Liszt based on works of Goethe and Dante. Written as they were in the 1850's, they are transitional, leading from the early Romantic symphonies of Berlioz to those of Mahler and Strauss.

Two symphonies by Richard Strauss, the Alpine Symphonie and the Domestic Symphony, are luxuriant and exorbitantly detailed in program.

166

Sergei Prokofiev

In France, the symphonic tradition continued to interest composers after Berlioz. Gounod, essentially an operatic composer, contributed charming specimens. Bizet, as a boy of 17, produced the slight but well-wrought Symphony in C Major. Later, D'Indy, Chausson, and Saint-Saens produced symphonies whose principal quality is one of lyricism and clarity of orchestration.

In Russia, Glazounov, Borodin, and Rimsky-Korsakov wrote symphonies saturated with color and passion. The Symphony No. 2 by Borodin is a staple of the repertory. Rachmaninoff's Symphony No. 2 is as familiar to concert audiences as the Borodin piece. Again, personal intensity, soaring lyricism, and pungent orchestral coloring are primary.

THE CONTEMPORARY SYMPHONY

The symphony has not figured as successfully as have other forms in the 20th century. Its very nature is perhaps bound inextricably with traditional tonality and a coherent system of modulation. It follows that with the near-dissolution of traditional harmony in this century, symphony as a major compositional concern declined. Symbolic of this decline is the fact that three of this century's most important composers, Debussy, Ravel, and Bartok, did not write symphonies.

The triumvirate of 12-tone composers--Schoenberg, Berg, and Webern--produced only two symphonies, both for reduced orchestra. Schoenberg's Chamber Symphony, Op. 9 (1906), scored for 15 solo instruments, was one of the last of his works in the tonal idiom. Webern's nontonal Symphony for Small Orchestra, Op. 21 (1928), is organized through the purest sort of serial technique.

For those contemporary composers who still choose to work within tonal systems, the symphony continues to offer challenge and opportunity for expression. Among the many modern masters who have contributed important works to the symphony repertory are: Shostakovitch, Prokofiev, Honegger, Nielsen, Roussel, Martinu, Vaughan Williams, Stravinsky, Hindemith, Copland, Ives, and Messiaen.

Sergei Prokofiev
b. Sontsovka, Russia April 23, 1891
d. Moscow March 4, 1953

Characteristic Areas of Composition: 8 operas, 7 ballets, 10 choral works, 7 symphonies, 6 suites, 5 piano concerti, 2 violin concerti, 11 chamber works, 8 piano sonatas, other works for piano, 36 songs.

1896 Writes first piano piece.
1897 Studies piano with mother and begins composition.
1900 Completes an opera.
1902 Orchestral suite scored "Desert Island".
1903 Enters St. Petersburg Conservatory, pupil of Rimsky-Korsakov and Tcherepnine.
1909 Awarded diploma with highest honors.
1911 Piano Concerto #1 Db draws wrath of faculty.
1914 Plays Piano Concerto #1 at graduation excercise and is nearly prevented from graduating. Scythian Suite.
1917 Concerto #1 for Violin and Orchestra. Classical symphony.
1918 Leaves Russia for world tour through Japan, Hawaii and USA. USA debut in New York. Composes opera Love for Three Oranges commissioned by Chicago Opera Company.
1920 Ballet The Buffoon.
1922 Moves to Paris.
1924 Symphony #2.
1927 Visits Russia for three months, opera The Gambler.

1928 Symphony #3.
1930 Symphony #4.
1932 Returns to Russia permanently, Piano Concerto #5.
1934 Lieutenant Kije.
1935 Concerto #2 for Violin and Orchestra, Romeo and Juliet ballet.
1939 Cantata Alexander Nevsky.
1942 Opera War and Peace.
1944 Symphony #5.
1948 Denounced by the Central Committee of Communist Party for "decadent formalism" and "cerebralism". Admits his music was wrong and ". . . the ways of the eradication of the formalist disease have also become clear."
1949 Symphony #6, and opera A Tale of a Real Man. Denounced again.
1950 Oratorio On Guard for Peace and suite Winter Bonfire, wins approval. Wins Stalin Prize.
1952 Symphony #7.
1953 Dies of cerebral hemorrhage, same day as Stalin.

The symphonies:
    Classical Symphony, D Major, Op. 25 (1916-17)
    Symphony No. 2, Op. 40 (1924)
    Symphony No. 3, Op. 44 (1928)
    Symphony No. 4, Op 47 (1924-30)
    Symphony No. 5, Op. 100 (1944)
    Symphony No. 6, E flat minor, Op. 111 (1949)
    Symphony No. 7, Op. 131 (1959)

The Russian Sergei Prokofiev has written seven symphonies. They represent a melding of purely Classical formal considerations with Romantic lyricism and native Russian color. Despite a considerable amount of dissonance and dislocated rhythms, his symphonies find ready response with audiences. The Soviet state has generally looked with favor on his music. Prokofiev's tonality is obvious and his unquestioned high lyricism may have convinced the state of the social utility of his music. Perhaps his best symphony is No. 5, written in 1944. It shows a simplicity that goes beyond the forced utilitarianism of certain works by his colleague, Shostakovitch. The overall feeling is grand and massive, the structure convincing, the line lyric and winning. The Classical Symphony, written much earlier (1917), is deliberately light and obviously meant to entertain general audiences. Harmonic and melodic content is very near that heard in the composer's Lieutenant Kije Suite and the children's fable, Peter and the Wolf.

Listening Guide: Sergei Prokofiev, "Classical" Symphony, Op. 25

Written only three years after Prokofiev graduated from the St. Petersburg Conservatory, this work is a particularly effective example of the twentieth-century neo-classic symphony. In form and style it follows patterns much used by Haydn and Mozart in the eighteenth-century. Its prevailing mood, one of hearty good humor, points expecially to Haydn. The work's instrumentation is exactly that of the typical late classical symphony: flutes, oboes, clarinets, bassoons, trumpets, horns, timpani in pairs; plus full strings. Yet the harmonic and melodic language is contemporary.

Movement 1 - Sonata Allegro Form, D Major

Listen first for this movement's traditional sonata allegro structure: exposition, development, recapitulation.

Exposition -- Meas. 1-85

There are two distinct and contrasted themes: Theme 1, skitters about in the strings.

EXAMPLE V-38 *

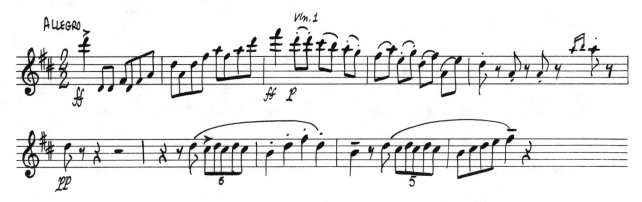

A transition built around a new, dance-like motive modulates to the dominant key for the second theme, A major.

Theme 2, is played mostly by the first violins with support from the basses playing pizzicato, the bassoons playing staccato.

EXAMPLE V-39 *

The exposition closes with rising broken chords in the strings and woodwinds. Then short downward scales in the strings lead to a strong dominant/tonic cadence, in the key of A major.

Development -- meas. 87-141

The short development section uses all of the melodic materials from the exposition, in the same order, but gives each new twists or shapes.

Theme 1 starts the development in the tonic minor key (D minor). Immediately, the dance-like motive from the transition   takes over, progressing through exotic unrelated keys. Next, theme 2 receives a canonic treatment: low strings imitated by upper strings. The whole section is very loud and exciting.

RECAPITULATION -- meas. 142-207

All the melodic ideas from the exposition return in the same order but with a different key scheme for the recapitulation. To hear this, use a recording or tape and skip back and forth from exposition to recapitulation comparing the key setting of each theme.

This is what you will hear:

Theme	Key in exposition	Key in recapitulation
1	D major (tonic)	C major
2	A major (dominant)	D major (tonic)
3	A major (dominant)	D major (tonic)

The overall key scheme is what one might expect in a Beethoven or Schubert sonata allegro form. This, with the regular rhythmic patterns and the classical instrumentation is why this is titled the "Classical Symphony".

Yet, this work also sounds modern. How is this done? In two ways: by chord progression, and by melodic range. Listen for the unusual chord progression in the immediate repetition of theme 1. With no warning or modulation, a D major chord (meas. 10) is followed by a C major chord (meas. 11). The sudden intrusion of this C major entrance completely undercuts the original tonic feeling (D major).

Another unusual chord progression occurs in the measures 5 - 10 of theme 2. Here the progression is:

EXAMPLE V-40

Both of the above examples show Prokofiev "twisting" traditional chord connections to achieve modern harmonic color.

Now listen for his use of unusual range. Glance again at Theme 2 (example 39), played by the first violins. Note how this theme skips from high to low and back again covering two octaves (16 notes) with each leap. Though large leaps do occur in music of the Classical period, they do not occur consistently. The composer's exaggeration of disjunct melodic motion in Theme 2 is what is modern. Thus the "Classical Symphony" looks backward in form, rhythmic pattern, overall key scheme, and instrumentation; but looks to its time for harmonic color and melodic shape.

Movement 2 - Ternary Form (ABA) A major

Part A -- (meas. 1-20) -- This part begins with a soft introduction so melodic that it could pass for a theme, except that the real first theme shortly enters (meas. 5) and dispels all doubt.

EXAMPLE V-41

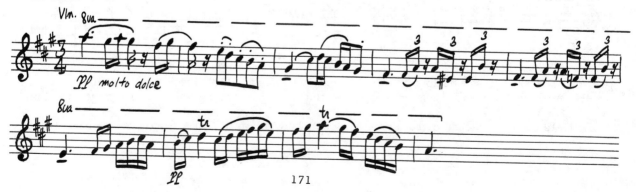

171

Note the unusually high register of Theme 1.

Theme 1 is neatly shaped and well dotted with graceful, ornamental tones, suggesting Haydn and Mozart.

Part B -- (meas. 20-41)

A steady, rising staccato idea in the bassoon and low strings begins Part B. After some colorful chord shifts (meas. 28-32) a climax is reached and we are prepared for the return of Part A.

Part A^1 (meas. 42-71)

Theme 1 comes back as expected in the same key and instrument, but now not alone. Accompanying it below are staccato scales, derived from Part B. Part B now combined with Theme 1 of Part A gives the movement great unity.

The movement's end comes with the initial 4-measure introduction now serving as a coda.

Movement 3 -- Gavotta, Ternary Form ABA^1, D major

This Gavotte in the dance style of the eighteenth century, is the shortest and simplest of the four movements. Its three-part structure is easy to hear and understand. Part A starts like this:

EXAMPLE V-42

Part B like this,

EXAMPLE V-43

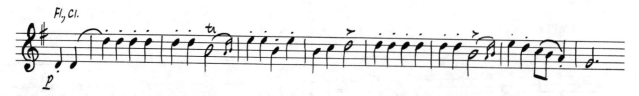

Part A^1 is exactly half as long as Part A simply because the initial repeats are omitted. A^1 is also a bit slower than A (meno mosso,), and flutes play the dance tune rather than the violins.

Listen to the dislocated chord progressions of the theme to Part A (meas. 2-4; meas. 10-13),

172

and also note the many melodic skips.

Movement 4, Finale, Sonata Allegro Form, D major

This Finale is similar to movement 1; both use sonata allegro form and both are very gay.

Exposition -- Meas. 1-90

As in movement 1 there are three themes:

Theme 1, firmly sets the tonic key, the first 8 measures all in D major. The theme's tones do

EXAMPLE V-44

little more than outline the three notes of the tonic chord -- D -- F sharp -- A. This is in keeping with many 18th century sonata themes that established the key early and solidly in the tonic. (See, for example, Haydn's Symphony No. 45, the "Farewell", 1st theme, 1st movement, p. 62).

A bright transition leads to theme 2, in the dominant (A major):

EXAMPLE V-45

Theme 3, graceful yet piquant, is played first by the flutes and then by violins. The exposition

EXAMPLE V-46

closes forcefully on the dominant (A major).

Development -- meas. 91-128

    The development is very brief and tight. It uses each of the three exposition themes, either whole or fragmented. For example, Theme 3 in full is heard by the clarinet, then shortened a bit, it is tossed about in canon from instrument to instrument.

Recapitulation -- meas. 129-224

    Themes 1, 2, 3 come back in proper classical order, in the proper tonic key, D major. But Prokofiev cannot resist one final jest -- theme 2 is now inverted, it is upside down:

EXAMPLE V-47

    As noted above Prokofiev's "Classical Symphony" was the work of his creative youth -- he was 24 and not long out of the St. Petersburg Conservatory. Obviously, he had learned lessons of traditional music well. The "Classical Symphony" as Haydn might have written it had he lived in our day is a model of economy, clarity balance and symmetry, qualities particular to 18th century music. Yet, as we have seen, much of the harmonic and melodic content is modern, giving the work a neo-classic aspect. In short, Prokofiev showed -- as others had done and would do again -- that certain structural procedures from the past still had their use if modified to include new content. Though essentially light and entertaining, the Classical Symphony is an example of a serious effort by many composers to revive the structural principles of 18th century music. Significant works of this type were written by Stravinsky, Octet (1923); Hindemith, Ludus Tonalis (1943); Bartok, Concerto For Orchestra (1943); and many others.

STRAVINSKY

    Igor Stravinsky, with roots deep in Russia, nevertheless has spent most of his creative life elsewhere and has thus been able to follow what his muse dictated, not what was politically expedient. And his muse constantly pointed in new directions. After a distinctly Russian nationalistic phase, typified by the great ballets, Firebird, Petrouchka, and the Rite of Spring, he entered a Neo-Classic period which challenged him until the Second World War. The two mature symphonies, the Symphony in C Major (1938-1940) and the Symphony in Three Movements (1945), are clearly Neo-classic in style.

    This latter symphony is scored for a typical late Romantic orchestra. The piano is very prominent in the outer movements, though the piece never suggests concerto. It was one of the composer's last works in the tonal idiom before his exploration of 12-tone technique. Though extremely thorny in its use of dissonance, it is yet tonal. It is unquestionably Neo-Classic in its use of form and melodic figuration. The fact that crescendos and diminuendos are few points in the direction of Baroque severity.

    Typical of the work's stylistic orientation is the opening idea of the second movement, presented in the strings (example 48). This figure, so like standard accompaniments in the Classical period, is suggestive of D Major. It uses only notes of the D Major scale. However, melodic elements around it (harp, low strings) produce interesting harmonic clashes.

Igor Stravinsky

EXAMPLE V-48 Stravinsky, <u>Symphony in Three Movements</u>, second movement *

One feature of the work is its resemblance in certain passages to earlier works by the composer, notably the Rite of Spring. Note the "primitive" ostinato quality of the bass figure in the first movement (example 49) as well as the interesting metric changes.

*Issued by permission of Belwin Mills Publishing Corporation, Melville, exclusive agent for Schott Music Corporation

EXAMPLE V-49

Over this ostinato is heard a syncopated figure in the upper strings and piano

HINDEMITH

The titles of the three symphonies by Paul Hindemith are: <u>Symphony, Mathis der Maler</u> (1934); <u>Symphony, E-flat Major</u> (1941); and <u>Symphony, Harmonie der Welt</u> (1951). They are tonal and patently Neo-Classic. Perhaps the first is the most expressive of the three. It is a reworking of the materials in the opera <u>Mathis der Maler</u>, itself based on the altarpiece at Colmar by the 16th-century painter Matthias Grunewald.

IVES

Charles Ives has recently been recognized as an original and potent force toward the creation of an indigenous American symphonic style. There were other voices at the turn of the century that cried for a truly American idiom, of course. The Czech composer, Dvorak, during his stay in the United States in the 1890's, called for young composers to turn from the powerful magnet of European art and look to the rich mine of American folk song and dance already at hand.

At Columbia University, Edward MacDowell championed the cause of American music with words such as these: "We have here in America been offered a pattern for an 'American' national musical costume by the Bohemian Dvorak . . . what we must arrive at is the youthful optimistic vitality and the undaunted tenacity of spirit that characterizes the American man. That is what I hope to see echoed in American music."

Both Dvorak and MacDowell had immediate effect. Arthur Farwell particularly harkened to the advice of Dvorak, founding the Wa-Wan Press, which was devoted to the publishing of scores based on folk music. Indian melodies and plantation songs were the basis of its offerings. Though charming, these pieces showed limited originality of form and harmony.

It was left to Ives to fuse the thoughts of both Dvorak and MacDowell. National songs, hymns, and folk melodies permeate his few works in a thoroughly natural manner. Ives, through the influence of his bandmaster father and an intimate acquaintance with the hymns of the people developed while serving as a church organist, gained a deep appreciation for the music of Everyman. At the same time, he showed the "undaunted tenacity of spirit" so desired by MacDowell. Despite an almost complete ignorance of his music by the musical world, he continued to develop creatively and to experiment constantly. All the while, he pursued a successful career in the field of insurance, stealing the time from his business interests for his composition. The great men of American letters, Emerson and Thoreau, were his idols.

There are four symphonies by Ives. Each is unique, leaving rich clues to be followed by later American composers. The third, called <u>The Camp Meeting</u>, though not revolutionary as are many of his works, is nevertheless fascinating. The harmony is homely; the structure and orchestration conservative. The three movements are subtitled, "Old Folks Gatherin'," "Children's Day," and "Communion." Thematic material is derived primarily from familiar American hymns. The melody to the third movement played by the horn (example 50) is taken from the hymn, "Just as I Am." And though the score is tame and traditional, the adventuresome spirit of Ives does break through

EXAMPLE V-50 Ives, <u>Symphony No. 3</u>, third movement

in the last two measures. Here Ives superimposes the sound of bells in a key somewhere near B Major over a simple cadence in B-flat Major.

Olivier Messiaen
b. Avignon Dec. 10, 1908

Characteristic Areas of Composition: 5 choral works including a <u>Mass for 8 Sopranos</u>, 11 orchestral works including <u>Turangalila Symphonie</u>, 4 chamber works, 11 piano solos, 11 organ solos, 9 songs.

<u>Important Life Facts</u>
    Father Pierre Messiaen, professor of literature.
    Mother Cecile Sauvage, poetess.

1916 Self-taught on piano, begins composition.
1919 Enters Paris Conservatory, studies with Gallon, Dupre, and Dukas.
1924 Wins second prize for harmony.
1926 Wins first prize for counterpoint and fugue.
1928 Wins first prize for accompaniment. Composes <u>Le Banquet celeste</u> for organ.
1929 Wins first prize for organ and improvization, also for history of music.
1930 Wins first prize for composition. Simple <u>Chant d'une ame</u> for orchestra. Also <u>Les Offrandes oubliees</u>.
1931 Appointed organist at Trinite in Paris. <u>Les Tombeau resplendissant</u> for orchestra.
1933 <u>L'Ascension</u> for organ.
1934 <u>L'Ascension</u> for orchestra.
1935 <u>La Nativite du Seigneur</u> for organ.
1936 Appointed professor at Ecole Normale and Schola Cantorum. <u>Les Corps Gladieux</u> for organ.
1941 Captured by Germans and held as prisoner of war. Composes <u>Quatuor pour la fin du temps</u> which is performed in prison camp.
1942 Released and repatriated. Appointed Professor of Harmony at Paris Conservatory.
1947 Appointed professor of Analysis, Aesthetics and Rhythm at Paris Conservatory.
1948 Composes <u>Turangalila-Symphonie</u>, commissioned by Serge Kussevitsky.
1949 Teaches master class in composition at Berkshire Music Center in Massachusetts. Turangalila premiered in Boston with Bernstein conducting.
1956 Creative period returns after eight years, again interested in musical use of bird songs. <u>Oiseaux Exotiques</u>.
1960 <u>Chronochromie</u> for large orchestra.

Turangalila-Symphonie

Turangalila is Messiaen's one symphony. Yet this massive work places the composer within a tradition- that of the French attitude towards creative art. This attitude leads the French composer generally to distrust the possibility that music transmits spiritual states, elevation of the soul, or kindred effects. Rather does he take the position that music ornaments the good life, an, as a corollary, that it refines the aural sense through the precise art of composition. As Martin Cooper put it in his book, French Music, ". . . to seek in French music primarily for a revelation of the composer's soul or for marks of the sublime is to look for something which the French consider a by-product."

Listening Guide: Turangalila Symphonie

The Turangalila Symphonie is a ten- movement work based on the Sanskrit words Turanga (time, movement, rhythm), and Lila (the play of life and death, love). Eight of the ten movements have program titles; two, the first and last, are simply labelled according to their position within the whole:

1. Introduction
2. Chant d'amour 1 (Song of Love 1)
3. Turangalila 1
4. Chant d'amour 2
5. Joie du sang des etoiles (Joy from the Blood of the Stars)
6. Jardin du sommeil d'amour (Garden of the Dream of Love)
7. Turangalila 2
8. Development de l'amour (The development of Love)
9. Turangalila 3
10. Final

Because it is a programmed work it descends from the French tradition in instrumental music. This includes the clavecinists of the late Baroque; Harold in Italy, and the Symphonie Fantastique by Berlioz; the tone poems of Saint Saens, Franck, and Dukas; and the impressionism of Debussy, Ravel and others.

Also clearly in the French tradition is Messiaen's search for new orchestral sonorities in Turangalila. The ear feasts on extraordinary tone color that goes beyond the original orchestral sonorities of Debussy and Ravel, of Stravinsky in the Paris ballets of 1910-13,and of Koechlin in his Bandar-log. Yet, this symphony could not have existed as it is without their influence.

Particularly interesting is the use of a new instrument, The Onde Martenot, which plays a leading role (along with the solo piano) throughout. The sound of the Onde Martenot is somewhat like that of the soprano voice, disembodied and refined. It lends a mystic quality appropriate to the expressive intentions of the work as they relate to Indian philosophy.

EXAMPLE V-51 *

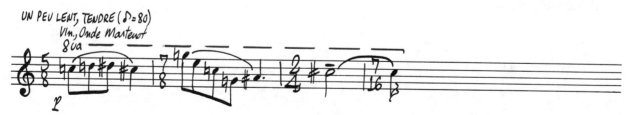

Messian scores intentionally to produce sonorities suggestive of the East. In a note on Turangalila Messiaen states: The three keyboard instrument, glockenspiel, celesta and

*
_____

Copyright, 1953, Durand et Cie. Used by permission of the publisher Elkan-Vogel, sole representative U.S.A.

vibraphone, have a special part similar to that of an East Indian gamelan as used in the islands of Sonde (Java and Bali)."

EXAMPLE V-52

In addition to the keyboard instruments playing the figure in example 52, the Onde reinforces the Eastern atmosphere with glissandi.

Influences other than from the East are also present. Messiaen has made a special study of bird song, and melodic materials derived from actual bird calls can be heard in many of his works. Movement six, Jardin du sommeil d'amour, finds a full exploration of possibilities of bird song-like melodic material. The solo piano (later joined by the woodwinds) plays intricate aviary sounds that are set as counterpoint to a broad, expressive melodic line in the full strings and Onde Martenot.

EXAMPLE V-53

The above characteristics - fresh orchestral sonorities and detailed imagery - relate essentially to Turangalila as a programmed work within the French tradition. But other characteristics link the work to a broader tradition, that of symphonic structure.

One important structural factor is its cyclic form. There are four cyclic themes that bind the symphony together. The first, in the low brass, massive and ponderous, has in Messiaen's words, "the terrifying brutality of old Mexican monuments."

EXAMPLE V-54

The third cyclic idea is the "theme of love", thoroughly tonal, and lyric. (See example 51 above).

Each of these cyclic themes enters at important points in the symphony, and joins other themes particular to individual movements. This was a common procedure in symphonies by romantic composers such as Berlioz, Franck, Tchaikovsky, Liszt, and Dvorak.

In addition to cyclic form, Messiaen introduces very important structural innovations in the area of rhythm. Messiaen designates the new rhythmic principle involved as "trois personnages rythmique" (three rhythmic actors). He assigns specific dramatic power to fixed patterns of duration. "The active personnage rythmique is the one whose durations increase; the submitting personnage rythmique is the one whose durations decrease; the immobile personnage rythmique is the one whose durations do not change."

Reduced to a simple formula, the principle behind Messiaen's rhythmic characters is as follows:

EXAMPLE V-55

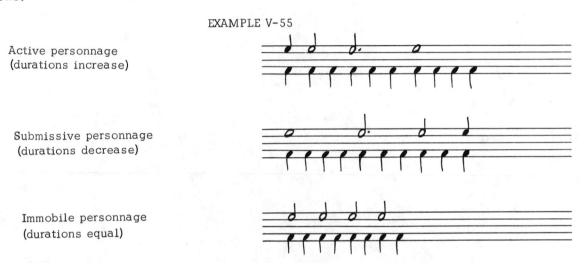

Active personnage
(durations increase)

Submissive personnage
(durations decrease)

Immobile personnage
(durations equal)

The use by Messiaen of rhythmic characters as well as the use of a rhythmic mode of seventeen durations in the ninth movement (Turangalila 3) forshadow the total rhythmic serialization in the music of younger composers such as Stockhausen and Boulez.

Messiaen's use of cyclic structure, fixed rhythmic patterns as structural units, and traditional forms such as the scherzo, solo cadenza, refrain with trio, etc., conclusively prove that he concerned himself with the principle of form as much as he did with imagery and experimental timbres. Turangalila comes out of its past, yet, because of its many innovations it is also of its time. Although the twentieth-century symphony has not been as successful as have certain other genres- opera, ballet, program music, for example -- it is not dead. Turangalila and other symphonies of this century point to interesting new directions for the future.

bassoon

double bass

serpent

cello

bass clarinet

recorder

viola d'amore

english horn

cor anglais

PART III
How to Listen to a Symphony

Chapter VI

HOW TO LISTEN TO A SYMPHONY

Listening to a symphony effectively can never be a casual experience. In the initial stages, concentration and consistency are absolutely necessary. Listening while reading a book or playing bridge is not a total loss, but very near it. Some of the music is bound to seep in, but the listener who wants to gain a new experience through the symphony never allows his attention to wander.

A symphony is in many ways more complex in structure than a play, essay, or novel. Its language is highly abstract: Instead of words with generally understood meanings, enigmatic groupings of pitches are used progressing in a flow of time. True, the individual word out of context can itself be vague. For example, the word <u>light</u> can signify many things. However, the words placed around it clarify and <u>specify a concrete experience</u>. We speak of a light load of hay, or a light class schedule, or a light rain, or a light literary style, or a light color.

Individual tones also gain meaning through context; but this meaning can <u>never be specified</u>. The tones

EXAMPLE   VI-1

e-d-c-e offer little or no meaning by themselves. Placed in melodic context (as in example 2), there is

EXAMPLE   VI-2

suggested a feeling, a mood, but again, nothing specific. The addition of the verbal label "Russian dance," indicated by its title "Trepak" (from the ballet <u>Nutcracker</u> by Tchaikovsky), adds a clarifying dimension. And if we actually see a Trepak danced to these tones, then they indeed point to a concrete situation.

However, these same four tones, even in melodic context can never define the specific or concrete. They might possibly have cropped up in a symphony by Dvorak or a string quartet by Borodin. The noted art and music editor Roy McMullen strongly emphasizes this when he writes: " . . . music by its very nature . . . is general in its effects rather than . . . specific."

The symphony as a form challenges many composers as no other. For Brahms it was a musical enterprise to be approached only with great care and patient industry. He did not produce his first symphony (Op. 68) until he had reached the age of 43, and then only after upwards of a dozen years of work. In it will be found the most complex of musical thoughts. To gain meaning from the symphonies of Brahms, where themes and motives are subjected to the most sophisticated transformations imaginable, is a formidable task. To the beginner, the music often seems like pure chaos. He looks for a "tune" and seldom hears one, though the most magical melodic and harmonic happenings may be right in front of his ears. To become aware of this musical magic, one must know how to listen and what to listen for.

To repeat: The first, most important thing to remember is that attention must be full. The wise listener plans ample time for his symphony exploration, either at live concerts or at home closeted with a phonograph or radio. Learning to listen to the symphony effectively should be considered as a serious study--with adequate time allotted for both intellectual and emotional growth.

Next, and extremely important, you should understand fully that listening once to a symphony is not enough. Repeated hearings are essential. There simply are too many things going on at the same time for the unpracticed ear to assimilate in one hearing. You should plan to live with a symphony: to listen over and over again until a meaningful pattern emerges. This is most easily done with recordings. Accordingly, you should plan to invest in recordings just as you would in good books. This can lead eventually to the building of a large record library, itself one of the great pleasures resulting from the serious study of music.

At first, plan on taking your symphonies in small doses. Care should also be taken to begin with the less complex and more lyric symphonies. Mozart and Haydn are perfect. Their symphonies are relatively short, simple in texture, and lyric. Slow movements from Romantic symphonies also make a good beginning.

Following is a listening sequence calculated to carry you along by gradual steps from general to particular musical experiences:

Taking only one movement at a time, simply listen all the way through, letting the sounds seep in. Though you are not listening for anything in particular, concentrate your full attention on the sounds heard. Listen in this way several times. Try to listen in a quiet room with as little distraction as possible. If your listening area is unavoidably noisy, consider investing in a fine set of earphones. These will not only shut out unwanted noise, but may upgrade considerably the quality of the sounds reproduced on your phonograph.

Sit back or lie down, dim the lights perhaps, relax completely and allow your imagination to be nudged and activated by the wash of tones.

The music may immediately suggest to you pictures, scenes, situations, things, moods, colors, smells, former experiences, people, or whatever. This is perfectly natural, even though the particular symphony heard may have been conceived by the composer strictly in abstract terms. It is the special attribute of music, precisely because of its nonconcrete nature, that it can represent anything or everything to any listener. You bring yourself to a symphony; at first you draw emotionally from it what you need. Later it may draw out from you facets of your emotional and intellectual self of which you were not aware.

Attention can now be directed to an important but easily perceived aspect of the symphony, instrumental color--the sound sensations that result from the individual timbres of the instruments and from their combination one with another.

You should try to identify instruments that are assigned solo parts. Know when one choir is featured, when all choirs are sounding together in the tutti sections, or when a section within a choir is prominent. Ask yourself: who has the melody? Does the resulting tone color involve only one timbre, or is it mixed? If the flute seems to have the tune, is there another instrument also playing it, perhaps in a lower range? How are the instrumental forces used in the climaxes? In the quiet sections? Which instruments are assigned accompaniment roles? Who plays the harmony or the counterpoint as background to the melody?

Let us listen for orchestral color in a most lyric movement, the second from the Symphony No. 5 by Tchaikovsky. Though the scope here is larger than in any slow movement in Haydn and Mozart, it is yet very lyric and easy to assimilate. As you first listen, one lovely melody captures your attention (example 3). It is immediately arresting in its high lyricism, and is heard no less than four times, each

EXAMPLE VI-3 Tchaikovsky, Symphony No. 5, Op. 64, second movement

time with different instrumental color. First the melody is taken up by the solo french horn; then, after a brief interlude, it returns in the sobbing warmth of the cellos. It is in the background for a considerable time while yet another theme is presented and developed. After a thundering climax in the brass, calm is regained and the pensive melody returns, but this time played by the first violins in the lowest reaches of their range. Soon afterwards it appears for the last time, higher than before and in the woodwind choir. Thus the lovely tune is introduced by a solo brass instrument, is carried forth by low strings, later re-appears in the low violins, and ultimately is spun out by the concerted woodwinds.

And, further, each time the theme appears, it is supported by different instrumental combinations. In the initial entry, the horn drifts lazily over a velvety cushion of string sound. When it is the turn of the cello section to play the melody, above are heard atmospheric murmurings in the horn, clarinet, and bassoon. These sympathetic wisps of tune in the background winds are the perfect foil for the rich sound of the cellos.

A magical moment of tone color occurs when the theme returns again. After some extraordinarily dramatic pauses punctuated by sharp chords, pizzicato (example 4), the strings continue in steady measure, still

EXAMPLE VI-4

pizzicato, while the first violins splinter off to take up the theme (example 5).

EXAMPLE VI-5

As the theme wends its way over the _pizzicato_ chords, intricate countermelodies enter, led by the oboe, adding a further contrast of color. Even if we fail to take into account the music's solid formal structure, the unique sounds in the orchestra make for enchanting listening. And this is true of every measure of the movement.

By now you will be familiar with the general sound of the music. Certain things will stay in the memory: You will anticipate melodies and textures automatically. It is now time to focus the ear and mind on the structural materials of the music. It is time to gain a perception of form: How the music holds together. You must feel how the music is unified and then how it achieves contrast and variety within this unity.

Most basic to unity and musical cohesiveness is repetition. Without any previous knowledge of the materials of music, you can easily become aware of repeated elements.

In listening for timbre, you have already heard a leading melodic line return three times. By listening for fresh, new orchestral coloration in this theme, you have indeed experienced the primary principle underlying musical form: unity and variety.

A movement (not including introductions) usually opens with the most important theme of the work. Separating themes, as we have seen, will be transitions, or bridge passages. These will tend to be more figurative and rhythmically active than the themes. They will have the feel of going somewhere, of leading to a musical event, usually another theme.

At this point, it is advisable that you stop the recording often at important moments, to repeat discovered themes and motives. Once the leading melodic ideas are firmly entrenched in your mind, allow your ear to trace their progress and evolution throughout the movement. Then listen carefully for their repetition and ask yourself: Which idea seems to be repeated most often? Do these ideas return exactly the same way each time? If they do not, how do they vary? Does the instrumentation vary while the melodic idea remains unchanged? Does the melodic idea come back with the same accompaniment?

Listen for key center throughout the movement. It is not important that you name a new key that is arrived at, but you should know when it arrives. What is the relationship of each theme to key? Does a theme sound different when it returns in a new key? Are there themes--or portions of themes--which return in a different mode: major to minor, or minor to major?

Be aware of the modulatory passages connecting different key centers. Does modulation occur more often in certain sections within the movement? In different movements? With different composers? In different periods? Do the lengths of modulatory passages vary?

You now can make use of the analyses found in Part 2 of this book. All the important themes of each movement of the included symphonies are found there as well as the basic form, key, and meter. Instrumentation of each important theme is also indicated. Such analyses will corroborate what your aural analysis has already discovered and will serve to fix in your mind important details.

At this point you will have pretty much pulled the music apart in the attempt to understand its color and structure. It will now be time to put the pieces back together again. You will find that you can follow the direction of the musical thought: that your ear will expect and then relish certain occurrences within the work. Now is the time to enjoy thoroughly and deeply the beauty of the sound and the structure. Background reading on the life of the composer, on his philosophy, on his artistic creed, on the feeling of the time or period he lived in, will greatly enhance your enjoyment of the music.

Once the entire symphony is assimilated, further pleasures await you. If you have heard the work on recordings alone, make an effort to hear it "live" at a fine performance. No mechanical reproduction can ever equal the beauty of sound and excitement found at a concert. You will find that once you lay the work aside, study other works, and then come back to it, the music will appear familiar but somehow newly exhilarating. Eventually you will become aware of the subtle differences among various conductors' interpretations. This gives great pleasure in itself.

And, finally, once you have truly felt and adequately understood a great work of symphonic art, it will lead to appreciation of other forms of music. This could lead in turn to a greater appreciation of other arts such as drama and painting; for all the arts are related, and in the core of their being, point to and amplify one another.

SYMPHONY NO. 6, OP. 68, BEETHOVEN, MOVEMENT I

Written in 1807-1808, the Pastorale is the only one of the nine Beethoven symphonies with a program. With the exception of the trio of birds at the close of the second movement, the music is more a deep evocation of Beethoven's feelings about the countryside and country people than a specific tone painting. Beethoven always responded warmly to wood, field, and stream:

"How fortunate . . . to have been able to go to the country so early this year. . . . I look forward to it with childish anticipation. How glad I shall be to wander about amidst shrubs, forests, trees, herbs and rocks! No man can love the country as I do. For it is forests, trees and rocks that provide men with the resonance they desire."*

ORCHESTRA

1 Piccolo
2 Flutes
2 Oboes
2 Clarinets
2 Bassoons

2 Horns
2 Trumpets
2 Trombones

2 Timpani

Violins
Violas
Violoncellos
Contrabasses
Piccolo, trumpets, trombones, timpani do not play in Movement I

* From a Beethoven letter.

189

FORMAL ANALYSIS

MOVEMENT 1--"AWAKENING OF HAPPY FEELINGS ON
ARRIVAL IN THE COUNTRY"

Key: F Major
Meter: Two-four
Tempo: Allegro ma non troppo
Form: Sonata-allegro

EXPOSITION (Meas. 1-138)

Movement 1 is cast in standard sonata-allegro form--the traditional structure for first movements of
symphonies at that time.

It has no introduction, but starts immediately with a folk-songlike theme (theme 1) in the violins over
a drone fifth in the violas and cellos (meas. 1).* Theme 1 begins in a very leisurely manner. After ten
repetitions of a little dance figure in the first violins (meas. 16), theme 1 is repeated in full orchestra.
A transition begins (meas. 53) with a triplet figure in the clarinets and bassoons, alternating with a figure
derived from theme 1. This leads to a bi-theme (theme 2, meas. 67). This bi-theme consists of an
arpeggiated figure combined with a folk-songlike countertheme, building in crescendo and leading directly
to theme 3.

Theme 3 consists of a rocking figure in the strings (meas. 93), answered by the woodwinds (meas. 97)
descending in thirds. Theme 4, the final thematic idea of the exposition, also features a combination of
two figures (meas. 115). The woodwinds sing a dipping motive centering around the interval of the fourth,
while the violins give out a jiggling three-note idea.

Each one of the four basic melodic ideas described above strongly suggests folk song and folk dance.
Each is very simple, marked by easily remembered rhythmic figures, and supported by straightforward,
transparent harmony. This simplicity of structural elements is just what is wanted for a "Country Symphony."

DEVELOPMENT (Meas. 139-278)

This section, using melodic elements derived entirely from theme 1, is remarkable for its simplicity.
Repeated melodic bits from theme 1 are frozen within single chords stretched over many measures. Note
measures 163-190--28 measures in all--in which a rhythmic fragment is repeated over and over again,
solidly encased within a D Major chord. To be sure, Beethoven scores beautifully and writes into the
music a long majestic crescendo followed by a diminuendo. Thus we are never bored, despite the simplicity.

The end of the development is punctuated by a particularly stunning harmonic effect. Beginning at
measure 263, the music swells until it reaches climactic proportions, poised on top of an insistent
dominant chord. This chord in its natural course would lead to a tonic F Major chord. But instead it
bursts unexpectedly into the subdominant (meas. 275) and then lazily falls back into theme 1 in the
expected key of F (meas. 279).

RECAPITULATION (Meas. 279-413)

Theme 1 returns as expected at the head of the recapitulation but is interrupted by a leisurely cadenza
*See actual score for measure reference. Measure numbers are found at upper left of each full score.

in the first violins. When theme 1 resumes its course in the second violins (meas. 289), it now finds itself accompanied by a new obbligato in the first violins which is derived from the figuration of the cadenza mentioned above.

The recapitulation, on the whole, is regular, with all four themes from the exposition arriving on time and in the expected sequence. Themes 2, 3, and 4 now join theme 1 in the home tonic, F Major. In the exposition these last three were heard in C Major, the key of the dominant.

CODA (Meas. 414-512)

This section is unexpectedly long, considering that the movement is not dramatic. Theme 1 is featured as theme 4 (meas. 428), now camouflaged in softening legato triplets. The solo clarinet entertains toward the close with a charming passage in buffo style (meas. 476).

1) HOW TO FOLLOW A SCORE

Acquaint yourself with basic data of the Pastorale. Before listening to the recording, examine the score throughout. Look for all non-notational signs and words pertaining to the performance of the music. You will find directions and signs for tempo, dynamics, articulations, repeats, instrumental forces, and so on. If you do not already know what these mean, look them up in a music dictionary or a comprehensive music appreciation text. Write on the score the translations of terms that you are not already familiar with. Many of these terms will be found in the Glossary of this book.

It is especially important that you understand the tempo indication at the beginning of each movement. This will appear immediately above the first measure. It will tell you how fast your eye will have to move from note to note or measure to measure.

Find the time signature. It immediately follows the clef sign at the beginning of the first measure. The upper number will give you the number of counts (beats) in each measure. If the upper number is either 6, 9, or 12, and the tempo is moderate or fast, divide by three. The resulting number will indicate the actual number of counts in each measure. If the sign is **C** , count four; if it is **₵** , count two.

2)

Now listen to the recording without looking at the score. Get the feeling of the pulse rate. Tap your hand each pulse at the correct tempo. Listen very carefully for fluctuations of tempo (rubato) when, for purposes of phrasing and interpretation, the tempo will sometimes slacken or move ahead temporarily.

As you tap each pulse at the correct tempo, count to yourself the number of beats indicated by the time signature. If you listen carefully you will feel that much of the time one of the pulses receives more stress than the others. This is usually the first count. Count "one" beginning with each stressed pulse and follow through for each measure while you tap.

3)

Return to the score. This time listen while you follow. Find the staff for the first violins on each page. Again count the correct number of beats for each measure at the correct tempo. But now, each time that you say "one," place your finger below and immediately to the right of each successive bar line of the first violin part. Continue to the end. Do this several times. Soon you will be able to dispense with counting as you follow the music. Choose another staff for another instrument and repeat the above process. You need not be able to identify pitches or durational note values.

Once you have acquired the ability to keep your place in the <u>Pastorale</u>, you will have found the means toward considerable enjoyment and understanding. You may now examine the music in depth for structure, melodic contour, timbre, rhythmic figures, and so on. You will have a solid sense of the <u>harmonic depth</u> of music as well as its <u>melodic direction</u>.

Terminology and Symbols Used in the Following Annotated Score

A) <u>Terminology for Formal Analysis</u>

1) Sections and transitions: full term above score.
   Example: EXPOSITION

2) Themes: boxed abbreviation with arabic numeral.
   Example: | Th 3 |

3) Key: Below Score
   Example: G minor (supertonic)

B) <u>Arrow-line System</u>

1) Long, continuous arrow-line: basic melodic line.
   Example: ⟩————————————————

2) Angled arrow-line at beginning of staff: continuation of basic melodic line(s).
   Example: ↘

3) Short arrow-line: basic melodic line doubled.
   Example: ⟩——

SECHSTE SYMPHONIE
(Pastorale)
von
L. van BEETHOVEN.

Serie 1. No 6.

Dem Fürsten von Lobkowitz und dem Grafen Rasoumoffsky gewidmet.

Op. 68.

Erwachen heiterer Empfindungen bei der Ankunft auf dem Lande.
EXPOSITION *(Awakening of Happy Feeling on Arrival in the Country)*
Allegro ma non troppo.

Transition

195

198

from Th 1

143

BΦ Major (subdominant)

165

175

186

from Th I

G Major

E Major

218

228

203

A Major

250

D Major

G minor (supertonic)

258

from Th I

Dominant
preparation

RECAPITULATION

270

from m.16

Th I

(V)
Regression

IV

F Major (tonic)

205

209

from Th 4

from Th 4

F Major
(tonic)

213

Appendices

A GLOSSARY OF INSTRUMENTAL FORMS

The composer's symbol making process is difficult to explain, but the composition itself can be analysed in terms of its structural units. The relationship of these units to the whole is what is called musical form. The forms to be discussed should be considered only as rough approximations of the living composition. However, since imagination as well as intelligence are required to feel and understand music a basic knowledge of its forms is indispensable.

AGGREGATE FORMS

Aggregate forms are multiple structures consisting of any of several possible smaller single-member forms. There are two basic types of aggregate forms: aggregate sonata form, and aggregate suite form.

Sonata Form

Aggregate sonata form, originating in the Baroque but not fully developed until the Classical period, consists of a cohesive, closely knit grouping of single-member forms called movements. There are usually four movements, but sometimes there are more, sometimes less. Each single - member movement is different and contrasts vividly with the others: yet, the composer somehow manages to forge them all into an organic whole. Organic unity is provided primarily by key and tonal relationships among the movements, but other unifying forces apply such as cyclic form and/or a program.

Compositions in Aggregate Sonata Form

1-Symphony: aggregate sonata for full orchestra.
2-Concerto: aggregate sonata for full orchestra with soloist(s)
3-Chamber music such as duo, trio, quartet, etc., for various instrumental combinations.
4-Solo sonata: for solo instrument such as piano, organ, harp, or violin.

Suite Form

Like the sonata, the suite originated in the Baroque period. It became fully developed in the late Baroque and has challenged the composer to this day. In one impor tant way it resembles the aggregate sonata: its individual members offer striking contrast to each other. But there the similarity ends. The total number of members in the suite is quite indeterminate, whereas the sonata normally shows four members. Also, the formal structure of each member of the suite tends to be simple, while the structure of the sonata movement is often densely intellectual, and extensive in duration. Because of this, the suite makes for less challenging listening than does the sonata. In its evolution through the centuries, side by side with its companion form the sonata, the suite generally provided a lighter, more entertaining vehicle for the composer's creative efforts.

Compositions in Aggregate Suite Form

1-Dance Suite: a grouping of dances in contrasted tempo, meter, and style.
2-Opera Suite: a grouping of operatic excerpts such as dances, intermezzos, overture or prelude, instrumental arrangements of arias, choruses, etc.

3-Ballet Suite: a grouping of dances from a ballet.
4-Suite of Incidental Music: a grouping of music originally meant to accompany a play.

Other Aggregate Groupings

In addition to the two basic types of forms seen above, there are important grouped forms that do not fall neatly into either the sonata or suite pattern.

TheDivertimento, also called Serenade, Cassation, Notturno, is a grouping of light, entertaining music. Sometimes it is organized like the sonata, sometimes like the suite.

Groupings of character pieces such as those from Brahms' "Fantasien, Op. 16", (three capriccios, and four intermezzos), and Schumann's "Faschingschwank aus Wien," Op. 26, (Allegro, Romanze, Scherzino, Intermezzo, Finale), are also variants of the two basic types.

Collections

Collections of pieces all of one type into "books" are quite common. Typical are the Forty-Eight Preludes and Fugues from the Well Tempered Clavier (in two books), and the two and three-part Inventions by J.S. Bach; the Etudes by Chopin; and the Preludes by Rachmaninoff, all for keyboard. Here overall design is not to the point. Selections from these collections grouped into attractive "packages" often are seen on the recital program.

Single Member Forms

While there are only two basic aggregate forms in instrumental music, there are several single-member forms. These individual forms are often grouped within aggregate forms, but just as often stand singly. For example, ternary form as used in the dance titled minuet, is commonly found in both the aggregate sonata (third movement) and in the aggregate suite. Yet they are sometimes collected together with other minuets (Mozart, 19 Minuets, K. 103, for orchestra); or appear as single items, (Ravel, "Menuet antique").

Sonata Allegro

A rigorously intellectual structure built on the principle of development. Divided into sections designated as:

1-exposition-presentation of themes
2-development-development of these themes using techniques such as fragmentation, modulation, sequence, augmentation, diminution, contrapuntal combination, etc.
3-recapitulation-return of original themes in same order as before.

Often added to these basic sections are a slow introduction leading directly into the exposition, and a coda following directly from the recapitulation.

Suggested listening:

In a grouping-Beethoven, Symphony No. 2, Op. 36, 1st movement.
Independent-Brahms, "Tragic Overture", Op. 81.

Rondo

A circular pattern where the main theme (refrain) returns at least twice. Separating the appearances of the refrain are contrasted sections called episodes. The typical small rondo shows the following plan: Refrain-Episode 1-Refrain-Episode 2-Refrain-(Coda).

Suggested listening:

In a grouping: Mendelssohn, <u>Violin Concerto</u>, Op. 64, last movement
Independent - Beethoven, "Fur Elise."

Theme and variations

An open-end pattern involving a complete melodic statement (theme) followed in direct succession by a minimum of two variants. Each variation contrasts with the one before. In earlier periods the kinship of variation to theme is easily seen, but, beginning with Beethoven, the relationship becomes more subtle and less obvious.

Suggested listening:

In a grouping-Shubert, "<u>Trout</u>" <u>Quintet</u>, Op. 114, movement 4
Independent-Schoenberg, <u>Variations for Orchestra</u>, Op. 31

Fugue

A contrapuntal structure, in two or more voices (melodic parts) featuring the techniques of imitation and transformation. The subject (theme) enters in one voice-line. It then is transferred to another voice while the first voice continues with new melodic ideas. The process continues until all voices have carried the subject. Transformation techniques often used: augmentation, diminution, sequence, fragmentation, retrograde, inversion, etc.

Suggested listening:

In a grouping: Franck, <u>Prelude, Chorale et Fugue for Piano</u>.
Independent - Beethoven, <u>Grosse Fuge</u>, Op. 133.

Other contrapuntal structures where, as in the fugue, the vertical relationship of voices are as important as horizontal succession of units:

1-Invention-(two or three voices) features imitation and inversion of voices.
2-Canon-(two or more voices) features strict imitation
3-Chorale prelude-(two or more voices) consists of a setting of a Lutheran hymn (chorale).
  Often, but not always for organ.

Part Forms

Simpler structures whose inner units are called parts. The most common are: binary part form (AB), and ternary part form (ABA)

Suggested listening:

Ternary in a grouping-Mozart, "Musical Joke," K. 522, 2nd movement
Ternary independent-Debussy, "Prelude a L'Apres-midi d'un Faune"

Binary in a grouping-Haydn, <u>Sonata in D major</u>, 2nd movement
Binary, independent-Gibbons, <u>Pavan</u>, "Lord of Salisbury"

COMPOSITIONS USING SINGLE MEMBER FORM

1-Dances (minuet, gavotte, waltz, polonaise, etc.,): often use simple part-forms but also
  extended forms resembling the rondo.
2-Scherzo: cast in ternary part form. Evolved from the minuet.
3-Prelude: tends to be free in pattern, but sometimes clearly in a part-form.

4-Concert overture: tends toward sonata allegro form.

5-Passacaglia, Chaconne: uses theme with variations form. Theme is short, as is each of the variations. Contrapuntal in texture.

6-Fantasie: often in free form. Resembles an improvisation.

7-Rhapsody: uses any of several possible single member forms, but just as often as free in structure.

8-Tone poem: Extensive programmatic work often in sonata-allegro form.

9-Character Piece (Impromptu, Intermezzo, Song Without Words, Album Leaves. Ballade, etc.) tends toward ternary part form. Most often for piano.

Glossary of Technical Terms

Accent (dynamic): a tone played louder than those before or after.

Adagio: in slow, calm tempo.

Aeolian scale: a diatonic, seven-note mode consisting of five major and two minor seconds.
 Ex.: a-b-c-d-e-f-g

Agitato: agitated.

Allegro: in quick tempo

Andante: in moderately slow tempo.

Animato: animated.

Antiphony: a musical idea in dialogue from one orchestral choir to another.

Appassionato: passionately.

Arpeggio: chords whose individual tones are played successively, not simultaneously.

Articulation: how tones are played relative to clarity, or to legato/staccato.

Assai: very.

Asymmetrical: meters with five or more beats, whose measures are not divisible into even sub-grouping   Ex.: 5/8, 7/4, 11/2

Attacca: play the next movement without a break in sound.

Augmented (interval): a perfect or major interval increased in size by one semitone.

Augmented sixth chord: a dissonant four-note chord whose characteristic interval (the augmented sixth) usually resolves to an octave.

Bass: the lowest tone or melodic part in a musical texture.

Broken chord: (See Arpeggio)

Buffo: comic.

Cadence (harmonic): a short succession of chords either holding back or terminating the flow of music.

Cadenza: improvisation-like portion of a work, often of a brilliant character and sometimes rhythmically free.

Canon: strict imitation between two or more melodic parts.

Cantabile: songlike.

Cantilena: a lyric melody.

Chaconne: a contrapuntal structure consisting of variations on a subject often heard initially in the bass line.

Chorale (form): an early hymn of the Protestant Church.

Chord: three or more tones sounding simultaneously.

Chromatic: characterized by the interval of the minor second.

Compound (meter): any meter whose beats are divisible into three even units. Ex.: 6/2, 9/8, 15/16

Con anima: with animation.

Con brio: with brilliance.

Concert master: the principal first violinist of a concert orchestra.

Con fuoco: with fire.

Con moto: with motion.

Con spirito: with spirit.

Continuo: a bass line played by low strings and keyboard; the figures accompanying certain bass notes indicate the chords to be realized by the keyboard player.

Counterpoint: applied polyphony (See Polyphony).

Counterstatement: a second presentation of a theme (usually the first) in the exposition section of a sonata-allegro form.

Crescendo: increasing gradually in volume.

Dance suite: an aggregate structure consisting of an indeterminate number of varied instrumental dances.

D. C. (Da Capo): sign indicating that the initial part of a musical pattern is to be repeated.

Diaphony: a two-part polyphonic texture.

Diatonic (scale): characterized by a combination of five whole steps and two half steps. The distance between half steps is always either two or three whole steps in succession.

Diminuendo: gradually becoming softer.

Diminution: the consistent and equal shortening of the duration of each tone in a melodic line.

Disjunct (melodic contour): characterized by skips (intervals of a third or more).

Dissonance: two or more notes sounding together, creating tension and, in traditional music, requiring resolution.

Dominant (harmony): chord built on the fifth degree of the major or minor scale.

Dominant pedal: (See Pedal)

Double stop: two notes played simultaneously on an instrument of the violin family.

Drone fifth: the interval of the fifth sounding as a pedal point, usually in the bass register.

Duple meter: two beats per measure.

Dynamics: pertaining to volume of tone.

Episode: a subsidiary contrasted section of a rondo structure, usually following the principal section called the refrain. Also used to define similar sections in fugal structures.

Fantasia: fantasy-like, free structure.

Fermata: hold the tone at will.

Forte: loud.

Fortissimo: very loud.

Fragmentation: the breaking up of a theme into its constituent motives.

Fugato: a short fugal section from a predominantly homophonic composition.

Grace note: an ornamental note appended to a tone of a melody.

Grazioso: graceful

Gregorian chant: liturgical melody of the early Catholic Church.

Half cadence: a progression of chords ending with a dominant harmony, and thus giving the effect of incompleteness.

Harmonic minor scale: a chromatic alteration of the natural minor scale, the seventh degree being raised a half step.

Homophony: a texture where one predominant melodic part is supported closely by subsidiary harmonic elements.

Imitation: one melodic part imitating another.

Improvisation: the spontaneous performance/composition of a work by its composer or composers.

Interval: the pitch distance between two tones.

Inversion (melodic): the inverse of a given melodic contour, achieved by reversing the direction of each melodic interval.

Janizary music: featuring cymbals, triangle, and bass drum.

Key: the letter designation of a tonal center which can either be major or minor. Ex.: E-flat Major, C-sharp Major, A Major, B minor

Largo: broad, slow.

Leading tone: the tone a minor second below the tonic, functioning as the seventh degree of a diatonic scale.

Legato: connected articulation.

Lied: a song with German text often of high poetical quality.

Lieder cycle: a group of lieder organized around one pervasive idea or literary theme.

Maestoso: majestic.

Measure: the distance from one bar line to that following.

Mediant: the third degree of any diatonic scale.

Meter: rhythmic impacts usually accented at regular, predictable time intervals, thus establishing groupings of strong and weak pulses.

Metronome: any of several devices or mechanisms used to establish precise tempos, as indicated by a number on the score page. M.M. ♩-120 means that the metronome is to be set at 120. Each quarter note in the measure will be equivalent to the time span from one "tick" of the metronome to the next.

223

Minor (diatonic mode): originated with the Aeolian mode; later designated 12 possible minor keys, each with its own key signature. Also called minor scale. Melodic and harmonic minor scales refer to chromatic intervallic adjustments of the sixth and seventh degrees.

Mode: a system of successive single tones which can be represented by various diatonic scale patterns designated as Ionian, Lydian, Aeolian, etc.

Moderato: moderate.

Modulation: the process of passing from one tonal center (key) to another.

Molto: much.

Monothematic: a composition built around only one theme or subject.

Motive: a short, plastic melodic idea.

Neapolitan (sixth) chord: a major triad built on the scale degree a minor second above the tonic. Usually seen in first inversion.

Neo-Classicism: a style of 20th-century composition which derives certain structural elements from 18th-century Classical music, such as rhythmic pattern, formal pattern, articulation, and melodic contour.

Non troppo: not too much.

Obbligato: a subsidiary melodic line set against another primary melodic line.

Octave: an interval consisting of two notes whose vibrations are at the ratio of 2 to 1.

Off-beat: that fraction of a beat occurring between regular metric pulses.

Orchestral texture: the aural effect of various combinations of instruments in an orchestra.

Ostinato: a short melodic or rhythmic figure that is repeated steadily throughout all or a significant portion of a composition.

Overture: an instrumental form often prefacing an extensive vocal composition.

Parallel (major/minor): keys of contrasted mode on the same tonic note. Ex.: C Major/C minor

Patetico: of a pathetic character

Pedal, dominant: the continuous sounding of the fifth scale degree of any major or minor key, often while contrasted melodic and harmonic elements are sounding.

Phrase: four measures   Often ends with either a half or full cadence.

Pianissimo (pp): very soft.

Piano (p): soft

Piu mosso: at a faster tempo.

Pizzicato: strings of the violin family of instruments being plucked with the finger rather than stroked with the bow.

Poco: little

Polychord: a complex chord that consists of two or more chords originally of separate and independent character.

Polyphony: the combining of two or more independent melodic parts.

Progression (harmonic): a series of chords.

Quadruple (meter): four beats per measure indicated by a time signature whose upper number is always 4.

Quintuple (meter): 5 beats per measure indicated by a time signature whose upper number is always 5.

Range: all the tones possible from the lowest to the highest notes that can be produced by a voice or instrument.

Relative (major/minor): two keys with identical key signatures separated by the interval of a minor third. A minor key a minor third below a major key; a major key a minor third above a minor key. Ex.: D minor/F Major; B-flat minor/ D-flat Major

Retransition: a transition leading back to an important, previously heard section or theme in a composition.

Rhythm: anything dealing with the duration of musical sound.

Rhythmic pattern: a grouping of varied durational values often used as a basic structural element in a composition.

Root: the lowest tone of any chord when it is in fundamental position.

Saltarello: a quick Italian dance featuring the division of each beat into triplets.

Sempre: always.

Sequence: the successive repetition of a melodic pattern beginning on different scale steps, each of which is related by a fixed interval.

Serial technique: a technique of organization in atonal music in which an arbitrary melodic ordering of all 12 tones of the chromatic scale is used as the basis for the entire harmonic, contrapuntal, and thematic structure.

Seventh chord: a triad with an interval of a third added above. Ex.: g-b-d-f.

Six-five chord: an inverted seventh chord with the third in the bass.

Sonata: an aggregate (sometimes single-member) structure for any of various single or combined instruments.

Sonata da chiesa: a Baroque structure for strings with continuo, usually consisting of four movements following the tempo order: slow-fast-slow-fast.

Song form: a ternary form often symbolized by the letters ABA.

Sostenuto: sustained.

Staccato: detached articulation.

Steigerung: a climax approached through the accumulating tension of several subsidiary climaxes.

Step (interval): a major or minor second, up or down.

String quartet: a performance medium consisting of two violins, one viola, and one cello.

Subdominant: the fourth degree of the major or minor diatonic scale.

Symphonic poem: an orchestral composition suggesting a program usually taken from a well-known literary work.

Syncopation: accents on expected weak beats, off-beats, or rests instead of tones at expected expected strong beats.

Tacet: silent. Indicated in an instrumental part when that part is not heard for a significant span of time.

Tempo: the pace of the beats.

Ternary: a three-part form.

Tetrachord: either the first four or last four adjacent steps of the major scale.

Texture (compositional): the prevalent vertical relationship of tones, which is either polyphonic or homophonic.

Theme: a melodic structure often basic to an extensive composition.

Tied note: a note whose durational value is added to that of the same tone immediately preceding.

Timbre: the tone color of an instrument.

Tonality: the gravitation of several tones around and towards one primary tone called the tonic.

Tonic: the central tone in a tonal system of musical organization.

Tonic six-four chord: the inversion of triad where its fifth is in the bass.

Triad: a chord consisting of three tones separated by the interval of the third.

Transition: a fluid passage linking important themes, usually in an exposition section of a sonata-allegro form.

Tremolo: the quick repetition of the same tone on bowed string instruments.

Trill: the alternating (usually quick) of tones a step apart.

Triple meter: beats grouped in three's with a metric accent every third beat. The upper number of time signature is always 3.

Triplet: the division of a durational unit into three equal subdivisions.

Twelve-tone technique: (See Serial technique)

Unison: a sounding of the same tone by two or more voices or instrumental parts.

Variation: any alteration or transformation of a previous musical idea in a composition: identity with change.

Vivace: lively.

BIBLIOGRAPHY

GENERAL REFERENCE

Affelder, Paul. How to Build a Record Library. N. Y.: E. P. Dutton, 1947.

Apel, Willi, The Harvard Dictionary of Music, Second edition, Cambridge, Mass., Belknap/ Harvard, 1969.

Austin, William, A., Music in the 20th Century, N. Y. Norton, 1966.

Borge, Victore, My Favorite Intermissions. Garden City: Doubleday, 1971.

Brown, Calvin, Music and Literature, A Comparison of the Arts. Athens, Ga.: University of Ga. Press, 1948.

Ewen, David, Listen to the Mocking Words. N. Y.: Arco, 1945.
Ewen, David, The World of Twentieth Century Music. Englewood Cliffs, N. J.: Prentice Hall, 1968.
Gillis, Don, The Unfinished Symphony Conductor. Austin: Pemberton Press, 1967.

Graf, Max, Modern Music: Composers and Music of Our Time. N. Y.: Philosophical Library, 1946.

Groves' Dictionary of Music and Musicians. edited by Eric Blom, New York: St. Martin's Press, 1955.

Hindemith, Paul, A Composer's World, Horizons, and Limitations. Cambridge, Mass.: Harvard University, 1952.

Huxley, Aldous, On Art and Artists. N. Y.: Harper, 1960.

Lesure, Francois, Music and Art in Society. University Park: Penn. State University Press, 1968.

Mencken, Henry Louis, H. L. Mencken on Music. N. Y.: Knopf, 1961.

Nadeau and Tesson, Listen: a Guide to the Pleasures of Music, Boston, Allyn and Bacon, 1971,

O'Connell, Charles, The Victor Book of Overtures, Tone Poems; and Other Orchestral Works. N. Y.: Simon, 1950.

Seaman, Julian, Great Orchestral Music, A Treasury of Program Notes. N. Y.: Rinehart, 1950.

Sessions, Roger, The Musical Experience of Composer, Performer, Listener. N. Y.: Atheneum, 1950.

Siegmeister, Elie, The Music Lover's Handbook. New York: Morrow, 1943.

N. Slonimsky, ed., Baker's Dictionary of Music, Cambridge, Mass. Harvard University Press.

Taylor, Deems, Music to My Ears. N.Y.: Simon & Shuster, 1949.

Taylor, Deems, Of Men and Music, N.Y.: Simon & Shuster, 1937.

Taylor, Deems, The Well Tempered Listener. N.Y.: Simon & Schuster, 1940.

Thompson and Slonimsky, International Encyclopedia of Music and Musicians, N.Y.: Dodd and Mead, 1953.

MUSIC HISTORY

Einstein, Alfred, Music of the Romantic Era. New York: Norton, 1947.

Einstein, Alfred, A Short History of Music. New York: Random House Vintage, 1937.

Grout, Donald Jay, A History of Western Music. New York: St. Martin's Press, 1955.

Krehbiel, Henry, Music and Manners in the Classical Period. N. Y.: Scribner, 1898.

Lang, Paul Henry, Music in Western Civilization, N. Y., Norton, 1941.

Longyear, Rey, Nineteenth Century Romanticism in Music. Englewood Cliffs: Prentice Hall, 1969.

Pincherle, Marc, An Illustrated History of Music, N. Y., Reynald   Co. 1959.

Sachs, Curt, World History of Dance, N. Y. The Norton Library, 1963.

Ulrich and Pisk, A History of Music and Musical Style, N. Y. Harcourt, Brace, and World, 1963.

MUSICAL FORM

Berry, Wallace, <u>Form in Music</u>. Englewood Cliffs, N. J.: Prentice-Hall, 1966.

Erickson, Robert, <u>The Structure of Music</u>. N. Y.: Noonday Press, 1955.

Green, Douglass Marshall, <u>Form in Tonal Music</u>. N. Y.: Holt, Rinehart & Winston, 1965.

LaRue, Jan, <u>Guidelines for Style Analysis</u>. N. Y.: Norton, 1970.

Leichtentritt, Hugo, <u>Musical Form</u>, Cambridge, Mass. Harvard U. Press, 1951.

Tovey, Sir Donald Francis, <u>Essays in Musical Analysis</u>, 7 Vols., London, Oxford University Press, 1935.

Winold, Allen, <u>Elements of Musical Understanding</u>. Englewood Cliffs, N. J. Prentice Hall, 1966.

PERFORMANCE AND MEDIA

Baines, Anthony, Musical Instruments Through the Ages. Baltimore: Penguin, 1961.

Bekker, Paul, The Orchestra. New York: Norton, 1936.

Carse, Adam, The History of Orchestration. New York: Dover, 1964.

Cooper, Martin, The Concise Encyclopedia of Music & Musicians. N. Y.: Hawthorn, 1958.

Dickson, Harry Ellis, Gentlemen, More Dolce, Please. Boston: Beacon Press, 1969.

Dorian, Frederick, The History of Music in Performance. N. Y.: Norton, 1942.

Howe, Mark, The Tale of Tanglewood. New York: Vanguard, 1946.

Lang, Paul Henry, A Pictorial History of Music. Norton, 1960.

Mueller, John Henry, Trends in Musical Taste. Bloomington, Ind.: Indiana University, 1942.
Marsh, Robert, Toscanini and the Art of Orchestral Performance. Philadelphia: Lippincott, 1956.
Sachs, Curt, History of Musical Instruments, N. Y. Norton, 1940.

Stoddard, Hope, From These Come Music: Instruments of the Band and Orchestra. New York: Crowell, 1957.

Swoboda, Henry, The American Symphony Orchestra. New York: Basic Books, 1967.

Braunstein, Joseph, Musica Aeterna, Program Notes, 1961-67. N. Y., Musica Aeterna, 1968.

Cuyler, Louise, The Symphony. New York, Harcourt Brace Jovanovich, Inc. 1973.

Doernberg, Erwin, The Life and Symphonies of Anton Bruckner. New York: Dover, 1960.

Downes, Edward, Adventures in Symphonic Music. New York: Farrar, 1944.

Ewen, David, The Complete Book of Classical Music. Englewood Cliffs, N.J.: Prentice Hall, 1965.

Ferguson, Donald M., Masterworks of the Orchestral Repertoire. Minneapolis Minnesota Paperbacks, 1954.

Goetschius, Percy, Masters of the Symphony. New York: C. H. Ditson, 1919.

Grove, Sir George, Beethoven and His Nine Symphonies. London: Novello, 1903.

Hill, Ralph, The Symphony. London: Pelican, 1952.

Hopkins, Antony, Talking About Symphonies. Belmont, Calif.: Wadsworth, 1961.

Landon, H. C., Haydn Symphonies. London, BBC Music Guides, 1966.

Moore, Gail Vincent, The Symphony and the Symphonic Poem. Ann Arbor, Mich.: Ulrich, 1966.

O'Connell, Charles, The Victor Book of the Symphony. New York: Simon & Schuster, 1948, second revision.

Saint-Fox, Georges, The Symphonies of Mozart. New York: Knopf, 1949.

Simpson, Robert, The Symphony. 2 Vols. Baltimore: Penguin Books, 1966.

Spaeth, Sigmund, Great Symphonies, How to Recognize and Remember Them. Garden City: Garden City, 1936.

Tovey, Sir Donald, Essays in Musical Analysis, Vol. I., Symphony. London: Oxford University Press, 1935.

Ulrich, Homer, Symphonic Music. N. Y. Columbia, 1962.

SCORE ANTHOLOGIES

Hoffmann-Erbrecht, Lothar, The Symphony. (Kolben Translation) New York: Leeds, 1967.

Kamien, Roger, The Norton Scores: An Anthology for Listening. N. Y.: Norton, 1968.

Lang, Paul Henry, ed., The Symphony, 1800-1900, New York, A Norton Music Anthology.

Nadeau and Tesson, Scores and Sketches: an Anthology for the Listener, Reading, Mass., Addison and Wesley, 1971.

Weir, Albert, The Symphonies of Brahms and Tchaikovsky. New York: Bonanza, 1935.

Weir, Albert, The Symphonies of Haydn, Schubert, and Mozart. New York: Harcourt Brace, 1936.

Weir, Albert, Symphonies in Score, New York: Bonanza, 1937.

DISCOGRAPHY

Composer	Symphony	Disc Number
Arriaga, Juan (1806-1826)	Symphony in D	MHS 578
Bach, C. P. E. (1714-1788)	Symphony in D	VOX DL 463
	Symphony in Bm	VOX DL 463
Barber, Samuel (1910-)	Symphony #1	Mercury 90420
	Symphony #2	Everest 3282
Beethoven, Ludwig (1770-1827)	Symphony #1	RCA Victor LCS-6096
	Symphony #2	Angel S-35509
	Symphony #3	Angel S-36461
	Symphony #4	Heliodor 2548704
	Symphony #5	Heliodor 2548704
	Symphony #6	London STS-15064
	Symphony #7	RCA Victor LSC-6096
	Symphony #8	DGG 139015
	Symphony #9	RCA Victor LSC-6096
Berlioz, Hector (1803-1869)	Harold in Italy	RCA Victor LSC-2228
	Romeo and Juliette	RCA Victor VICS-6042
	Symphonie Fantastique	Columbia MS-7278
	Symphonie Funebre & Triomphale	Phillips 802913
Bizet, Georges (1838-1875)	Symphony in C	London 6208
Borodin, Alexander (1833-1887)	Symphony in #2	Seraphim S-60106
Brahms, Johannes (1833-1897)	Symphony #1	Pickwick S-4004
	Symphony #2	DGG 2530125
	Symphony #3	Columbia MS 6685
	Symphony #4	Angel S 36040
Bruch, Max (1838-1920)	Symphony #2	Louisville S-703
Bruckner, Anton (1824-1896)	Symphony #0	Phillips 802724
	Symphony #1	London 6706
	Symphony #2	Urania 5243
	Symphony #3	Columbia MS 6897
	Symphony #4	Angel S-36245
	Symphony #5	Angel S-3709
	Symphony #6	Angel S-36271
	Symphony #7	Angel S-3626
	Symphony #8	Columbia M2-30070
	Symphony #9	Dgg 139011
Cannabich, Christian (1731-1798)	Symphony #5	Mace S-9069
Carter, Elliot (1908-)	Symphony #1	Louisville 611
Chausson, Ernest (1855-1899)	Symphony in Bb	Louisville 6540
Chavez, Carlos (1899-)	Sinfonia India	Columbia MS-6541
Cherubini, Luigi (1790-1842)	Symphony in D	RCA LSC-3088
Clementi, Muzio (1752-1832)	Symphony in D	Mace S-9051
Copland, Aaron (1900-)	Dance Symphony	Columbia MS-7223
	Symphony for Organ and Orchestra	Columbia MS-7058
	Short Symphony	Columbia MS-7223
	Symphony #3	Everest 3018
Cowell, Henry	Sinfonietta	Louisville S-681
	Symphony #5	Desto S-6406

Composer	Symphony	Disc Number
	Symphony #16	CR1-179
Creston, Paul (1906-)	Symphony #2	Westminister 9708
Dello Joio, Norman (1913-)	Triumph of St. Joan	Columbia CML-4615
Diamond, David (1915-)	Symphony #4	CSP CMS-6089
Dittersdorf, Karl Ditters (1739-1799)	Metamorphoses	Turnabout 34274
	Symphony in A Minor	Lyr 726
Dvorak, Antonin (1844-1904)	Symphony #1	London 6523
	Symphony #2	London 6524
	Symphony #3	London 6525
	Symphony #4	London 6526
	Symphony #5	London 6527
	Symphony #6	RCA LSC-3017
	Symphony #7	Col D35-814
	Symphony #8	Col D35-814
	Symphony #9	Col D35-814
Elgar, Edward (1857-1934)	Symphony #1	Seraphim S-60068
	Symphony #2	Seraphim S-6033
Fasch, Johann (1688-1758)	Symphony in G	Nonesuch 71123
Franck, Cesar (1822-1890)	Symphony in D	RCA LSC-2514
Glinka, Mikhail (1804-1857)	Overture-Symphony on Russian Themes	Monitor S-2080
Gossec, Francois (1734-1829)	Sinfonia Concertante	MHS CC-1
Goldmark, Karl (1830-1915)	Rustic Wedding	Vanguard 2142
Gould, Morton (1913-)	Symphony #4 for Band	Mark 21360
Hanson, Howard (1896-)	Symphony #2	Mercury 90162
Harris, Roy (1898-)	Symphony #3	Col MS-6303
	Symphony #5	Louisville S-655
Hartmann, Karl (1905-1963)	Symphony #4	DGG 139359
	Symphony #8	DGG 139359
Haydn, Franz Joseph (1732-1809)	Complete edition available through Musical Heritage Society, also in process of completion by London.	
Henze, Hans (1926-)	5 Symphonies	DGG 2707024
Hindemith, Paul (1895-1963)	Mathis der Maler	Angel S-35949
	Symphonia Serena	Angel S-35491
	Symphony for Band	Seraphim S-60005
	Symphony in Eb	Everest 3008
Holzbauer, Ignaz (1711-1783)	Symphonies	Mace S-9069
Honegger, Arthur	Symphony #2	London 25320
	Symphony #3	London 6616
	Symphony #4	London 6616
Hovhaness, Alan (1911-)	Symphony #4	Cornell 2
	Symphony #7	Mace S-9099
	Symphony #11	Posiedon 1001
	Symphony #14	Mace S-9099
	Symphony #15	Louisville S-662
	Symphony #17	Mark 1112
	Symphony #20	Mark 1112
D'Indy, Vincent (1851-1931)	Symphony on a French Mountain Air	RCA VICS-1060
Ives, Charles (1874-1954)	Holidays	Col MS-7147
	Symphony #1	RCA LSC-2893
	Symphony #2	Col MS-6889

Composer	Symphony	Disc Number
Ives, Charles, cont.	Symphony #3	Col MS-6843
	Symphony #4	Col MS-6775
Janacek, Leos (1854-1923)	Sinfonietta	Col MS-6815
Khatchaturian, Aram (1903-)	Symphony #3	RCA LSC-3067
Khrennickov, Tikhon (1913-)	Symphony #1	Monitor S-2077
Lalo, Edouard (1823-1892)	Symphonie Espagnole	Col MS-7003
Liszt, Franz (1811-1886)	Dante	Urania 57103
	Faust	Everest 3294
Mahler, Gustav (1860-1911)	Symphony #1	Odyssey 32 160286
	Symphony #2	Col M2S-601
	Symphony #3	RCA LSC-7046
	Symphony #4	Angel S-35829
	Symphony #5	Angel S-3760
	Symphony #6	Angel S-3725
	Symphony #7	Col M2S-739
	Symphony #8	Col M2S-751
	Das Lied von der Erde	London 26005
	Symphony #9	Angel S-3652
	Symphony #10	Col M2S-735
Martin, Frank (1890-)	Petite Symphonie Concertante	Dec. DL 9774
Martinu, Bohuslav (1890-1959)	Symphony #5	Louisville S-663
Mendelsohn, Felix (1809-1847)	Symphony #1	Col MS-7391
	Symphony #2	Phillips PHS-2-904
	Symphony #3	Vox 511310
	Symphony #4	DGG 138684
	Symphony #5	DGG 138684
	String Symphonies #9, 10, 12	Argosy 5467
Mennin, Peter (1923-)	Symphony #5	Mercury 90379
Messiaen, Olivier (1908-)	Turangalila	RCA LSC-7051
Miaskovsky, Nicolai (1881-1950)	Symphony #21	RCA LSC-3022
Milhaud, Darius (1892-)	Symphony #3	Westminster 17101
	Symphony #4	Turnabout 34154
	Symphony #6	Candide 31008
	Symphony #8	MHS 1089
Monn, Georg (1717-1750)	Symphony in Eb	MHS 856
Mozart, Wolfgang (1756-1791)	Symphony #24	DGG SKL-2721013
	Symphony #25	Angel S-35407
	Symphony #26	DGG 139159
	Symphony #27	Argosy ZRG-653
	Symphony #28	RCA VICS-1630
	Symphony #29	Angel S-36329
	Symphony #30	Nonesuch 71055
	Symphony #31	Angel S-36216
	Symphony #32	DGG 138112
	Symphony #33	Angel S-36329
	Symphony #34	Angel S-36216
	Symphony #35	RCA VICS-1630
	Symphony #36	Angel S-36770
	Symphony #38	Angel S-36129
	Symphony #39	Angel S-36129
	Symphony #40	Angel S-36772
	Symphony #41	Angel S-36772

Composer	Symphony	Disc Number
Nielsen, Carl (1865-1931)	Symphony #1	RCA LSC-2961
	Symphony #2	Turnabout 34049
	Symphony #3	Col MS-6769
	Symphony #4	Col M-30293
	Symphony #5	Col MS-6414
	Symphony #6	Col MS-6882
Persichetti,Vincent (1915-)	Symphony for Band	Coro S-1247
Piston, Walter (1894-)	Symphony #2	DGG 2530103
	Symphony #5	Louisville S-653
Prokofiev, Sergei (1891-1953)	Classical	London 6679
	Symphony #2	Everest 3214
	Symphony #3	London 6679
	Symphony #4	Melodia-Angel S-40040
	Symphony #5	RCA LSC-2707
	Symphony #6	RCA LSC-2834
	Symphony #7	Everest 3214
Rimsky Korsakov, Nikolai (1844-1908)	Symphony #1	Melodia-Angel S-40094
Riegger, Wallingford (1885-1961)	Symphony #4	Louisville S-646
Rosetti, Francesco (1746-1792)	Symphony in C	Mace S-9021
Roussel, Albert (1869-1937)	Symphony #3	London STS-15025
	Symphony #4	London STS-15025
Saint-Saëns, Camille (1835-1921)	Symphony #3	RCA LSC-2341
Sammartini, Giovanni (1701-1775)	Symphonies	Nonesuch 71162
Schoenberg, Arnold (1874-1951)	Chamber Symphony #1	Westminster 17086'
	Chamber Symphony #2	Angel S-36480
Schubert, Franz (1797-1828)	Symphony #1	Nonesuch 71230
	Symphony #2	Nonesuch 71230
	Symphony #3	Command S-11017
	Symphony #4	London STS-15095
	Symphony #5	London STS-15095
	Symphony #6	London 6453
	Symphony #8	RCA LSC-3132
	Symphony #9	DGG 138877
Schubert, Franz (1707-1828)	Symphony #3	Col MS-7442
Schuman, William (1910-)	Symphony #1	RCA VICS-1436
Schumann, Robert C. (1810-1856)	Symphony #2	Angel S-36606
	Symphony #3	London 6582
	Symphony #4	London 6582
	Symphony #3	S-40098
Scriabin, Alexander (1872-1915)	Symphony #3	RCA LSC-3095
Sessions, Roger (1896-)	Symphony #1	Col MS-6124
Shostakovitch, Dmitri (1906-)	Symphony #5	Melodia-Angel S-400004
	Symphony #7	Melodia-Angel S-4107
Sibelius, Jean (1865-1957)	Symphony #1	Angel S-36489
	Symphony #2	Angel S-36425
	Symphony #3	London 6591
	Symphony #4	DGG 138974
	Symphony #5	DGG 138973
	Symphony #6	DGG 139032
	Symphony #7	DGG 139032
Smetana, Bedrich (1824-1884)	Festive Symphony	Cross, 22160142
Stamitz, Johann (1717-1757)	Symphony in A	Nonesuch 71076
Strauss, Richard (1864-1949)	Alpensinfonie	RCA LSC-2923
	Symphonia Domestica	RCA VICS-1104

Composer	Symphony	Disc Number
Stravinsky, Igor (1883-1971)	Symphony of Winds	London 6225
	Symphony in Eb	Col MS-6989
	Symphony of Psalms	Col MS-6548
	Symphony in C	Col MS-6548
	Symphony in 3 Movements	Col MS-6331
Tchaikovsky, Peter (1840-1893)	Symphony #1	DGG 2530078
	Symphony #2	London STS-15120
	Symphony #3	London 6428
	Symphony #4	London 6429
	Symphony #5	London 6376
	Symphony #6	RCA LSC-2683
	Symphony #7	Col MS-6349
	Manfred	RCA VICS-1315
Thompson, Virgil (1896-)	Symphony on a Hymn Tune	Mercury 90429
Vaughan Williams, Ralph (1872-1958)	Symphony #1	Angel S-3739
	Symphony #2	Angel S-36478
	Symphony #7	Angel S-36763
Wagenseil, Georg (1715-1777)	Symphony	MHS-856
Walton, William (1902-)	Symphony #1	RCA LSC-2927
Weber, Carl Maria (1786-1826)	Symphony #1	Music Guild S-813
Webern, Anton (1883-1945)	Opus 21	Col KL 5020
Weill, Kurt (1900-1950)	Berliner	Angel S-36506

INDEX

240